Published by
California Chamber of Commerce
P.O. Box 1736
Sacramento, CA 95812-1736

1-57997-620-4

5   4   3   2   1

The information compiled in this handbook is being provided by CalChamber as a service to the business community. Although every effort has been made to ensure the accuracy and completeness of this information, CalChamber and the contributors and reviewers of this publication cannot be responsible for any errors and omissions, nor any agency's interpretations, applications and changes of regulations described herein.

This publication is designed to provide accurate and authoritative information in a highly summarized manner with regard to the subject matter covered. It is sold with the understanding that the publisher and others associated with this publication are not engaged in rendering legal, technical or other professional services. If legal and other expert assistance is required, the services of competent professionals should be sought.

This publication is available from:

CalChamber
P.O. Box 1736
Sacramento, CA 95812-1736
(800) 331-8877
store.calchamber.com

Table of Contents

Chapter 3

Chapter 4

Chapter 5

Chapter 6

Chapter 7

Chapter 8

Chapter 9

What's New for 2017?

This preface lists additions and changes to the *2017 HR Quick Guide for California Employers*, detailed in chapter order.

Getting Started With This Book

- New notice requirements for hair salons/nail salons. See "Notice Requirements for Hair Salons/Nail Salons" on page 9.

Hiring Employees

- New notice requirement for victims of domestic violence, sexual assault and stalking (employers with 25 or more employees). See "Fill Out or Provide These Forms on the Employee's First Day of Work" on page 31.

- A new law puts limits on California employers' inquiring into juvenile criminal history. See Juvenile Criminal History in "California Law" on page 35.

- The federal government approved a revised *Form I-9*. See "Completing the *Form I-9*" on page 43.

- A new law makes "document abuse" unlawful in California. See ""Document Abuse" and Completing the *Form I-9*" on page 47.

- A new law affects choice of litigation related to employment agreements. See "Written Contracts" on page 58.

Leaves of Absence

- New notice requirement related to victims of domestic violence, sexual assault and stalking. See "Notice Requirements" on page 115.

Providing Benefits

- A new law will make changes to the amount of paid family leave benefits an employee can receive, effective January 1, 2018. See "Duration and Timing of the Benefits" on page 135.

- Changes were made to the seven-day waiting period for State Disability Insurance benefits. See "Eligibility Requirements" on page 137.

Paying Employees

- A court decision affirmed the requirement to provide "suitable seating" to employees. See "Wage Order Provisions" on page 160.

- A new law prohibits paying employees differently based on race or ethnicity. See "Wages and Salaries" on page 164.

- The minimum salary threshold for the administrative, executive and professional exemptions is set for 2017. See "Executive, Administrative and Professional Exemptions" on page 165.

- New 2017 minimum hourly rate, minimum monthly salary and minimum annual salary set for the computer professional exemption. See "Computer Professional Exemption" on page 167.

- New hourly minimum wage for the licensed physicians or surgeons exemption set for 2017. See "Licensed Physicians and Surgeons" on page 168.

- California's minimum wage increased in 2017. See "California Minimum Wage" on page 169.

- A court ruling affirmed the general rule as to the timing of rest breaks. See "Rest Break Requirements" on page 177.

- A new law creates overtime pay requirements for agricultural employees. See "Overtime and Agricultural Employees" on page 187.

- A new law affects the minimum earnings test for private school teachers to be classified as exempt. See "Overtime for Private Elementary or Secondary School Teachers" on page 188.

- A new law affects pay rules for temporary service employees. See "Temporary Service Employees" on page 191.

- A new law affects how hours are tracked and logged on itemized wage statements. See "Itemized Wage Statement" on page 194.

- New information on the 2017 wage base limit for Social Security tax deductions. See "Social Security (FICA)" on page 197.

- New information on the 2017 SDI withholding rate and taxable wage limit. See "State Disability Insurance (SDI) Tax" on page 198.

Ensuring Workplace Safety

- A new law changed the rules on smoking in the workplace. See "Smoking In the Workplace" on page 217.

- In 2016, California joined several other states in legalizing recreational use of marijuana by adults. See "Proposition 64 and Workplace Policies" on page 217.

- New standards for hospitals' injury and illness prevention plans. See "Injury and Illness Prevention Program" on page 218.

- The U.S. Occupational Safety and Health Administration issued a final rule relating to the tracking and reporting of workplace injuries. See "Reporting and Recording Work-Related Injuries and Illnesses" on page 239.

Preventing Discrimination

- A new law affects how single-user toilet facilities are identified. See "Transgender Employees in the Workplace" on page 262.

- Two new laws affect California's Fair Pay Act. See "Pay and Gender" on page 262.

Preventing Harassment

- New requirement relating to providing a discrimination, harassment and retaliation prevention policy to employees. See "Establish a Policy" on page 286.

- New requirement relating to translating a discrimination, harassment and retaliation prevention policy in a multilingual workplace. See "Policies In a Multilingual Workforce" on page 287.

- New requirements for documentation and recordkeeping related to mandatory harassment-prevention training. See "Documentation and Recordkeeping Requirements" on page 291.

- New requirement on recordkeeping related to mandatory harassment-prevention training webinars. See "Types of Training" on page 291.

Chapter 1

About This Book

This book is designed to make it easy for you to quickly find the information you need.

Formatting

Use these formatting conventions to identify important information:

Table 1. *HR Quick Guide* **Formatting**

Bold	Emphasizes important terms
Italics	Identifies forms and checklists
❗	Identifies information you should pay close attention to
TIP	Identifies definitions of terms and helpful advice
New 2017	Identifies new laws, regulations and court decisions for 2017

Does This Employment Law Apply to Me?

Use the chart on the next two pages to determine if a particular employment law applies to your company. Some laws apply to all employers. Other laws apply only to employers with a certain number of employees (two or more, four or more, and so on).

For more information about each law, see the Index, which refers you to material throughout this book.

Law/Requirement	All	2 or more	4 or more	5 or more	15 or more	16 or more	20 or more	25 or more	50 or more	75 or more	100 or more
Affirmative Action									✓	✓	✓
Alcohol and Drug Rehabilitation								✓	✓	✓	✓
Americans with Disabilities Act (ADA)					✓	✓	✓	✓	✓	✓	✓
Cal-COBRA (2–19 employees only) (*pg. 4)		✓	✓								
Child Labor	✓										
Civil Air Patrol Leave						✓	✓	✓	✓	✓	✓
COBRA (health insurance continuation)							✓	✓	✓	✓	✓
Crime Victims' Leave	✓										
Disability Insurance	✓										
Discrimination and Foreign Workers			✓	✓	✓	✓	✓	✓	✓	✓	✓
Discrimination Laws (State)				✓	✓	✓	✓	✓	✓	✓	✓
Discrimination Laws (Federal)					✓	✓	✓	✓	✓	✓	✓
Domestic Violence, Sexual Assault and Stalking Victims' Leave: Legal Proceedings/Reasonable Accommodation	✓										
Domestic Violence, Sexual Assault and Stalking Victims' Leave: Medical Treatment								✓	✓	✓	✓
Employee Safety	✓										
Equal Employment Opportunity (EEO) Reporting (**pg. 4)											✓
Fair Employment and Housing Act (FEHA)	✓										
Family and Medical Leave (FMLA and CFRA)									✓	✓	✓
Illiteracy Accommodation								✓	✓	✓	✓
Immigration Reform and Control Act (IRCA)	✓										

Law/Requirement	All	2 or more	4 or more	5 or more	15 or more	16 or more	20 or more	25 or more	50 or more	75 or more	100 or more
Independent Contractors	✓										
Injury and Illness Prevention Program (IIPP)	✓	✓	✓	✓	✓	✓	✓	✓	✓	✓	✓
Jury Duty Time Off	✓										
Mandatory Paid Sick Leave	✓										
Mandatory Supervisor Sexual Harassment Training									✓	✓	✓
Military Leave (USERRA)	✓										
Military Spouse Leave								✓	✓	✓	✓
New Employee Reporting	✓										
Organ and Bone Marrow Donor's Leave					✓	✓	✓	✓	✓	✓	✓
Paid Family Leave (PFL)	✓										
Pay and Scheduling	✓										
Posters and Notices	✓										
Pregnancy Disability Laws				✓	✓	✓	✓	✓	✓	✓	✓
Privacy	✓										
School Activities Leave (***pg. 4)								✓	✓	✓	✓
School Appearance Leave	✓										
Smoking in the Workplace	✓										
Unemployment Insurance (UI)	✓										
Volunteer Civil Service Leave	✓										
Volunteer Civil Service Training Leave									✓	✓	✓
WARN Act (plant closings)										✓	✓
Workers' Compensation	✓										

Cal-COBRA, EEO Reporting, School Activities Leave

*Cal-COBRA covers employers with 2-19 employees who offer health insurance benefits to employees. Cal-COBRA covers employers with 20 or more employees when the employee loses COBRA coverage, if the COBRA coverage was for less than 36 months.

.**EEO reporting also applies to employers covered by Title VII who have fewer than 100 employees if the organization is owned or affiliated with another organization or there is centralized ownership, control or management (such as central control of personnel policies and labor relations) so that the group legally constitutes a single enterprise, and the entire enterprise employs a total of 100 or more employees.

***A covered employer must employ 25 or more employees working at the same location.

Required Posters and Revisions

The information in the following charts is current as of this book's publication date.

Table 2. Required Posters

Federal Law			
Title	**Who Must Post?**	**Source**	**Version/Date**
Employee Polygraph Protection Act	All employers	U.S. Department of Labor	WH1462 Rev 07/16 WH1462 SPA Rev 07/16
Equal Employment Opportunity is the Law	All employers	Equal Employment Opportunity Commission	EEOC-P/E-1 Revised 11/09 Includes GINA
Federal Family and Medical Leave Act Poster	Employers of 50 or more employees and all "public agencies"	U.S. Department of Labor	WH1420 Rev 04/16
Federal Family and Medical Leave Act Poster - Spanish	Employers of 50 or more employees and all "public agencies"	U.S. Department of Labor	WH1420 SPA Rev 04/16
Federal Minimum Wage	All employers must post the federal and state minimum wage notices	U.S. Department of Labor	WH1088 Rev 07/16 WH1088 SPA Rev 07/16
Your Rights Under USERRA (Veterans Benefits)	All employers	U.S. Department of Labor	Publication Date — October 2008

California Law			
Title	**Who Must Post?**	**Source**	**Version/Date**
California Minimum Wage	All employers must post the state and federal minimum wage notices	Industrial Welfare Commission	MW-2017
California Wage Orders	All employers must post the industry-specific Wage Order for their business	Department of Industrial Relations	There are 17 Wage Orders that bear a revision date of 07-2014
Discrimination and Harassment in Employment are Prohibited by Law	All employers	Department of Fair Employment and Housing	DFEH-162 (Dec. 2014) DFEH-162s (Dec. 2014)
Emergency Phone Numbers	All employers	Department of Industrial Relations/Division of Occupational Safety & Health	S-500 March 1990

California Law			
Title	**Who Must Post?**	**Source**	**Version/Date**
Family Care and Medical Leave (CFRA Leave) and Pregnancy Disability Leave	All employers with 50 or more employees and all public employers. Covered employers must provide notice to employees of the right to request CFRA leave in a conspicuous place where employees tend to congregate. The employer may include both pregnancy disability leave and CFRA leave in one notice. Any employer whose workforce at any facility or establishment contains 10 percent or more of persons who speak a language other than English as their primary language must translate the notice into the language or languages spoken by this group or these groups of employees	Department of Fair Employment and Housing	DFEH-100-21 (07/15) DFEH-100-21s (07/15)
Healthy Workplaces/ Healthy Families Act of 2014 Paid Sick Leave Poster	All employers. This poster advises employees of their sick leave rights under the law	Division of Labor Standards Enforcement	11/2014
Notice to Employees - Injuries Caused by Work	All employers	Division of Workers' Compensation	DWC 7 (1/1/2016)

California Law			
Title	**Who Must Post?**	**Source**	**Version/Date**
Notice to Employees - UI, SDI, PFL	All employers. EDD posting DE 1857D gives employees notice of their rights under the Unemployment Insurance program. It's intended for use by employers not subject to SDI/PFL. CalChamber includes the DE 1857A because it contains not only the UI information, but the SDI/PFL information as well	Employment Development Department	DE 1857A Rev. 42 (11/13) DE 1857A/S Rev. 42 (11/13)
Pay Day Notice	All employers	Department of Industrial Relations	DLSE 8 (Rev 06/02)
Safety and Health Protection on the Job (Cal/OSHA)	All employers	Department of Industrial Relations/Division of Occupational Safety & Health	No version number January 2016
Time Off for Voting	All employers Must be posted for 10 days preceding statewide election	California Secretary of State	No version number (No date)
Whistle-blower Protections	All employers	Department of Industrial Relations	CalChamber created (1/1/2016)
Your Rights and Obligations as a Pregnant Employee	All employers with 5- 49 employees. Covered employers must provide notice to employees of the right to request pregnancy disability leave. The notice must be posted in a conspicuous place where employees tend to congregate	Department of Fair Employment and Housing	DFEH-100-20 (04/16) DFEH-100-20s (04/16)

Required Local Employment Posters

Employers should be aware of posting requirements relating to local minimum wage ordinances or other local employment laws, which may vary by city and county. Employers should check with their local governments to determine whether any specific ordinances apply, or consult with legal counsel. For more information, see "Local Minimum Wage Ordinances" in Chapter 5, page 170 and "Local Ordinances" in Chapter 3, page 100.

Notice Requirements for Hair Salons/Nail Salons

 AB 2437 requires any establishment that is licensed by the Board of Barbering and Cosmetology (BBC) (e.g., hair salons, nail salons, estheticians, etc.) to post a notice regarding workplace rights and wage-and-hour laws.

The requirement takes effect **July 1, 2017**. The Labor Commissioner must create the model notice by **June 1, 2017**. The BBC is required to inspect for compliance with the posting requirement; failure to post the notice will result in a fine.

 In addition, AB 2025 requires the BBC to provide every licensure applicant with basic labor law education as part of the health and safety curriculum provided at BBC schools. This law is also effective **July 1, 2017**.

Log 300 and *300A* Notices

Some employers must comply with Cal/OSHA's *Log 300* recordkeeping requirements.

 CalChamber members can use the ***Log 300 Wizard*** in HRCalifornia's Forms & Tools section to determine whether they are required to record workplace injuries and illnesses.

If you are **not** exempt from these requirements, download and post the *Log 300* notices. Note: the *Log 300A* is not a year-round poster — it must be posted in February, March and April.

Table 3. Posters Required With Special Circumstances

Title	Who Must Post?	Source	Version/Date
Log of Work-Related Injuries and Illnesses (Log 300)	High hazard employers of 10 or more employees	Department of Industrial Relations/ Division of Occupational Safety & Health	Form 300 (Rev. 7/2007)
Summary of Work-Related Injuries and Illnesses (Log 300A)	High hazard employers of 10 or more employees	Department of Industrial Relations/ Division of Occupational Safety & Health	Form 300A (Rev. 7/2007)

Other Required Posting Information

Unique posters and notices may be required depending on certain circumstances, such as the use of heavy equipment or forklifts in the workplace, the use of chemicals in the workplace and whether your business works on government contracts.

Human Trafficking Disclosure Notice

State law requires some retail sellers and manufacturers doing business in California to post on their website a link to the company's efforts to eradicate slavery and human trafficking from its direct supply chain.

Human Trafficking Public Posting Requirements

Under state law, specified businesses are required to post an 8.5 inch x 11 inch notice that contains information about organizations that provide services to eliminate slavery and human trafficking.

Businesses that are required to post this notice include:

- On-sale general public premises licensees under the Alcoholic Beverage Control Act of the Business and Professions Code

- Adult- or sexually-oriented business (as defined in subdivision (a) of Section 318.5 of the Penal Code)

- Primary airports

- Intercity passenger rail or light rail stations

- Bus stations

- Truck stops (privately owned and operated facilities that provide food, fuel, shower or other sanitary facilities, and lawful overnight truck parking

- Emergency rooms within general acute care hospitals

- Urgent care centers

- Farm labor contractors

- Privately operated job recruitment centers

- Roadside rest areas

- Businesses or establishments that offer massage or bodywork services for compensation

The notice must be posted near the public entrance or another conspicuous location where the public and employees may view the notice. The notice must be written in a 16-point font and must be in English, Spanish and one other language that is the most widely spoken language in the county where the business is located and for which translation is mandated by the federal Voting Rights Act.

The notice must state the following:

If you or someone you know is being forced to engage in any activity and cannot leave-whether it is commercial sex, housework, farm work, construction, factory, retail, or restaurant work, or any other activity — call the National Human Trafficking Resource Center at 1-888-373-7888 or the California Coalition to Abolish Slavery and Trafficking (CAST) at 1-888-KEY-2FRE (EDOM) or 1-888-539-2373 to access help and services.

Victims of slavery and human trafficking are protected under United States and California law. The hotlines are:

- Available 24 hours per day, seven days per week

- Toll-free

- Operated by nonprofit, nongovernmental organizations

- Anonymous and confidential

- Accessible in more than 160 languages

- Able to provide help, referral to services, training and general information

The California Department of Justice is responsible for developing a model notice and making it available for download on its website.

Failure to comply with the notice posting may result in a civil penalty of $500 to $1,000 per offense.

Online Forms

Throughout this book, you'll find references to many forms and checklists. Because regulations can change throughout the year, accessing your forms online ensures that you will always have the most current version of each form.

Be sure to check *https://www.calchamber.com/customer-service/Pages/Forms-Downloads.aspx* occasionally for updates to forms and descriptions of important midyear regulatory changes.

To download the forms mentioned in this book:

1. Open a web browser and go to *https://www.calchamber.com/customer-service/Pages/Forms-Downloads.aspx*.

2. Click *HR Quick Guide for California Employers* in the 2017 Product Forms list.

3. Open your copy of the *HR Quick Guide for California Employers* to the inside front or back cover to find the forms access code.

4. Enter the forms access code (exactly as it appears) into the input field and click "Submit."

5. On the *2017 HR Quick Guide for California Employers* page, click "All ESB2017 Forms" to download the .zip folder containing all of the available forms. To download a specific form, use the "Find by Name" feature to locate the form by its name.

Working With the ESB2017.zip Folder

Double-click the ESB2017.zip folder when the download is complete. A window will open automatically in your computer's File Explorer. Click "Extract All" to extract the forms from the .zip folder, then choose the folder on your computer to which to extract the forms. The forms will be stored in that folder.

CalChamber Resources

CalChamber produces books, websites, newsletters and online products to help employers comply with California's complex employment laws. For more information on CalChamber products, visit **store.calchamber.com**.

Below is a brief sample of our products:

- **HRCalifornia.com** is a comprehensive website designed to help California human resources supervisors deal with everyday issues. It's intuitive to navigate, great for powerful searches and contains dozens of user-friendly, time-saving features. It's included with CalChamber membership.

- **2017 California Labor Law Digest**

- **Employee Handbook Creator** (English or Spanish policies)

- **2017 Required Notices Kit** (English or Spanish), includes the **California and Federal Labor Law Poster**

- **California Employer Update** newsletter

- **HRCalifornia Extra** is a free electronic newsletter that gives you employment law updates every two weeks. Register at **www.calchamber.com/enewsletters**

- **HRWatchdog** is CalChamber's employment law blog

Chapter 2

Hiring Employees

Recruiting and hiring a new employee is a difficult process that involves significant legal risks. If employers don't handle the hiring process properly, they can open themselves to allegations of discriminatory hiring practices.

Continually review your policies, procedures and practices to make sure you follow the overall hiring process. If your policy states that you open all new positions to existing employees before looking outside the company and you fail to do so, you could open yourself up to an employee complaint and even legal action against you.

If you determine that your current process is satisfactory, be sure to reassess it frequently.

This chapter will provide answers to questions about:

- Lawful hiring and recruiting practices
- Credit and background checks for applicants
- Independent contractors
- Required and recommended forms
- Other hiring related issues

Hiring Process

You give yourself the best opportunity to create a smooth hiring experience and avoid litigation over your hiring practices if you establish and follow a sound hiring process.

A sound hiring process helps you:

- Find the best candidate for the open position.

- Meet extensive requirements for documentation associated with a new hire.

- Avoid violating complex discrimination laws.

- Avoid creating oral or written employment contracts that can create the potential for litigation.

Your hiring procedures should address important steps, such as creating job descriptions, conducting interviews, making the hiring decision and properly training new employees.

Sticking to an established process can help you comply with legal requirements throughout hiring a new employee. Use the *Pre-Hire Checklist* and the *Hiring Checklist*, described in Table 4 on page 62, to organize the steps you will follow to recruit, interview and hire new employees.

This section will help you:

1. "Define Job Requirements" on page 17.

2. "Create Job Descriptions" on page 17.

3. "Determine Which Type of Worker to Hire" on page 19.

4. "Properly Classify Workers" on page 21.

5. "Recruit For the Position" on page 22.

6. "Evaluate Potential Candidates" on page 24.

7. "Conduct Background Checks" on page 28.

8. "Make the Hiring Decision" on page 29.

9. "Complete the Appropriate Paperwork" on page 31.

10. "Welcome New Employees" on page 32.

Define Job Requirements

It's vital that you start the hiring process with up-to-date information about the job requirements. To do that, you need to understand and identify the job to be performed. If you don't have this information, the recruiter or manager wastes time and money in the recruiting process. Worse, the selected applicant may be ill-equipped for the job, require extended training and/or have a greater likelihood of failure.

If you're filling an existing position, locate the existing job description and make sure that it's accurate. If you're creating a new position, write a new job description that clearly outlines the job's "essential functions."

 Essential functions are the fundamental job requirements of the position or the reason the job exists. For guidance on documenting the job's essential functions in the job requirements, please see "What Should I Know About Essential Functions?" in Chapter 7, page 274.

Make sure that the job description does not use any language that might create an employment contract. For more information, see "Employment Contracts" on page 58.

Create Job Descriptions

No specific state or federal law requires you to create job descriptions, or specifies what they should contain or how they should be formatted. But it's a best practice that every position in your organization have a job description.

The requirements listed in the job description must support the essential functions and serve as the primary criteria for selecting/rejecting candidates. Remember that under the Americans with Disabilities Act (ADA) and California's Fair Employment and Housing Act (FEHA), you can't refuse to hire a qualified candidate with a disability who meets the requirements and whose disability can be reasonably accommodated.

Job descriptions clearly set forth job duties and expectations by:

- Clarifying the job's role and the expectations for the person performing the job.

- Taking the uncertainty out of differentiating between the expectations and requirements of various jobs.

- Minimizing employee discontent associated with pay differentials between jobs.

- Guiding initial training and helping management and employees agree on the expected outcomes of that training.

- Supporting the performance evaluation process.

- Supporting the proper classification of the employee as exempt or nonexempt.

Consider including these key elements in your job descriptions:

- **Job title:** Preparing the job description may guide you to selecting an appropriate job title. If you add a new function to an existing job, the new job title may match a previous job, but designate the job at a higher level, such as "Clerk II" or "Senior Mechanic."

- **Summary:** This should be a one- or two-paragraph summary of the job's essential functions and reporting relationships.

- **Essential functions:** This component serves as the heart of the job description. To identify a job's essential functions, first identify the job's purpose and the importance of actual job activities to achieve this purpose. For more information, see "What Should I Know About Essential Functions?" in Chapter 7, page 274.

  When evaluating the importance of a job's functions, consider the following questions:

  – How frequently is the function performed?

  – Does the job exist to perform this function?

  – Who else is available to perform this function?

  – What level of expertise or skill is required to perform this function?

  – What is the experience of previous or current employees in this job?

  – What is the amount of time spent performing this function?

  – What are the consequences of failing to perform this function?

  – What is stated in the job description and employment advertisements?

- **Physical requirements:** It's important to identify the job's essential physical requirements. Describe this component in terms of the physical activity and degree of strength, flexibility and agility required, and the frequency and duration of the effort that must be exerted.

- **Knowledge, skills and experience:** List all knowledge, skills and experience necessary to perform the job. You may wish to divide these components into requirements and preferences. Certain attributes may be absolutely required for a particular job. Other attributes may be desirable but not necessary.

- **Reporting relationships:** Each job occupies an important place in the organization, and it's important that the employee and others in contact with him/her thoroughly understand that place. The job description should identify the position's place in the organization's chain of command, including the position(s) to which it reports and the position(s) reporting to it.

- **Financial responsibility:** If the position includes responsibility for a profit or cost center, some companies prefer to quantify the extent of that responsibility. This aids the recruiter in evaluating the candidate's previous level of responsibility and clearly defines the expectations for the candidate or employee.

- **Compensation category:** The information gathered for the job description aids in determining whether the position is likely to be exempt or nonexempt. This decision should be confirmed by further analysis using the information provided in Chapter 5, "Paying Employees."

Determine Which Type of Worker to Hire

The next task in the hiring process is to figure out what kind of help you need and determine what type of employee will meet that need:

- Do you need a full-time employee?

- Do you need a part-time employee?

- Would an independent contractor or a temporary employee better suit your needs?

Full-Time Employees

A full-time employee works the number of hours that you designate as "full time." You can define "full time" as 40 hours or more per week, 32 hours or more per week or any other number of hours. You should define the number of hours that constitute full-time employment in your employee handbook or other policy document.

Part-Time Employees

A part-time employee works less than the number of hours that you designate as full time. You should define the number of hours that constitute part-time employment in your employee handbook or other policy document. Part-time employees may or may not receive the same level of benefits as full-time employees.

Regular Employees

A regular employee is someone who is not employed on a temporary or casual basis. Regular employees may be either full-time or part-time employees, depending on the number of hours they work.

Temporary Employees

Temporary employees are hired for specific assignments of limited duration. They may work full time or part time, but the length of their employment is usually specified. You should reserve the right to extend the duration of temporary employment without implying such employees' rights to benefits during the extension.

Benefits established by law, such as Workers' Compensation, State Disability Insurance and Unemployment Insurance, generally apply to temporary employees who otherwise qualify.

Independent Contractors

An independent contractor is not an employee. In general, an independent contractor works for another entity under a verbal or written contract, usually for a specific length of time.

The independent contractor is responsible for only his/her own work, and is generally responsible for his/her own schedule. The independent contractor must also be responsible for how the work is completed.

 Calling a worker an "independent contractor" does not make him/her an independent contractor in the legal sense. Mislabeling a worker as an independent contractor creates potential liability for employment taxes and penalties.

For a complete discussion of this employment relationship and the penalties associated with misclassifying a worker, see "Independent Contractors" on page 53.

Contingent Workers

These employees include the nearly one-quarter of this country's workers who are part time, temporary or seasonal, secured through temporary agencies, or under employee leasing arrangements. Contingent workers may be treated differently than permanent workers under some California and federal labor laws.

Employers may be held accountable for wage-and-hour violations when they use staffing agencies or other labor contractors to supply workers. If a labor contractor fails to pay its workers properly or fails to provide workers' compensation coverage for those employees, the "client employer" can be held legally responsible and liable.

 Contact legal counsel to determine how you can limit your exposure to liability for a labor contractor's wage-and-hour violations or failure to secure workers' compensation coverage.

Casual Employees (On Call, Per Diem, Irregular)

Casual workers perform intermittent service on an as-needed basis. For example, a retail establishment might have an employee who floats between departments as needed, or a preschool might bring in an additional teacher for a week to make sure state teacher/child ratios are met during attendance peaks, but the teacher isn't on staff all the time.

Interns

Employers should proceed carefully when deciding to use unpaid interns. Many employers believe interns are "unpaid" workers. The law does not define interns that way. Not all interns are unpaid, and interns may be considered employees in the eyes of the law.

California's Division of Labor Standards Enforcement (DLSE) applies the six-factor test used by the U.S. Department of Labor (DOL) to evaluate an employer's classification of a worker as an unpaid "intern."

 Employers shouldn't treat internships lightly. Always use caution when adding individuals to your workforce who are seeking training or "internship programs." Always consult with employment law counsel or an experienced HR professional when using interns.

Properly Classify Workers

Certain employees are exempt from wage and hour requirements. Because it is highly litigated, understanding the distinction between exempt and nonexempt employees is critical.

For a complete discussion of determining whether an employee is exempt or nonexempt, see "Exempt and Nonexempt Employees" on page 51.

Always assume employees are nonexempt unless they clearly meet the job duties of an exempt position and meet the applicable minimum salary requirement. For more information, see "Exempt Employees" in Chapter 5, page 164.

If you are not experienced in determining exempt and nonexempt status or if you are unsure about the status of a particular position, ask your employment law counsel to review your determination.

Exempt Employees

An exempt employee is not subject to any of the laws pertaining to overtime and meal and rest periods.

Generally, exempt employees are your key personnel, such as executive, administrative or professional employees, who possess management and decision-making responsibilities. Other exempt employee types include some inside and outside salespeople.

Nonexempt Employees

All other employees generally fall under the nonexempt category. A nonexempt employee is subject to all Wage Order rules and federal and state wage-and-hour laws.

You must:

- Pay nonexempt employees overtime for working more than eight hours in one day or more than 40 in one workweek;

- Provide required meal and rest breaks to nonexempt employees; and

- Track and record all hours worked by nonexempt employees and also the hourly rate of pay associated with each hour worked.

Recruit For the Position

Avoid even the appearance of the intent to discriminate by advertising in general interest venues or in a wide range of special interest venues, rather than recruiting from one source that does not yield a diversity of applicants.

You can use a variety of methods to let potential candidates know about the position:

- Advertising in magazines, newspapers or trade publications

- Posting job announcements on the Internet

- Recruiting in person at trade shows and job fairs

- Sending a job request to a staffing agency, California's Employment Development Department or schools

Make sure the language you use in your recruiting efforts doesn't:

- Imply a secure employment contract, which overrides employment "at-will." At-will is a legal concept, created by California law, that assures both employer and employee that either party can terminate the relationship at any time, for any reason or for no reason. Although California is an at-will state, courts have ruled that various factors, including employment advertisements and applications, can create an implied employment contract. For more information, see "Employment Contracts" on page 58.

  – Avoid advertisements that seem to guarantee future employment by using language such as "secure position," "looking for candidates willing to make a long-term commitment to the company," or "looking for someone who can grow with the company."

  – Make sure that recruiters know they don't have the authority to promise job security to applicants.

- Violate state and federal discrimination laws that prohibit limiting or excluding someone from employment because they have, or you think they have, certain characteristics. See "Discrimination" in Chapter 7, page 257, for a more complete definition. Make sure to avoid words and phrases that single out characteristics that could belong to a protected class.

Bona Fide Occupational Qualifications in Hiring

A "bona fide occupational qualification" (BFOQ) is a characteristic that employers are allowed to consider when making hiring decisions, even though, in other contexts, these characteristics would be considered discriminatory. For example, a religious school can require that teachers be members of the school's religion.

A BFOQ based on a protected class is extremely rare. Consult legal counsel before ever listing a protected class, such as sex or religion, as a job requirement.

California law outlaws discrimination based on gender or gender identity, making the use of sex as a BFOQ even rarer. State law defines "gender" as a person's "identity, appearance or behavior, whether or not that identity, appearance or behavior is different from that traditionally associated with the person's sex at birth." So advertising for a male model for a men's clothing photo shoot may no longer qualify as a BFOQ. For more information, see "Gender" in Chapter 7, page 261.

Evaluate Potential Candidates

Thoroughly examining potential candidates gives you the best chance of finding an employee who matches what your company wants. This person should have the necessary skills to do the job, but you should also find out about his/her work style, history and employment-related interests. Consider all this information to make sure the employment relationship will be a good fit for both of you.

Review Résumés

Applicants submit résumés that provide helpful information about their personal education, skills, past work experience and accomplishments. A résumé is the candidate's marketing tool, and should be treated as such. It does not contain all of the information you should gather about a potential candidate. But it can give you a way to preview the person before beginning the application process.

You are not required to keep unsolicited résumés. You can send them back to the applicant along with a note explaining that no openings currently exist for the position sought, or keep the unsolicited résumés to use as a pool of potential employees.

Review Applications

The questions you ask in your employment application also supply information about applicants. A good employment application should gather a broad range of standardized information to help you evaluate all applicants more equally.

Employers should use extreme caution about using job applications that contain a check box asking applicants about their criminal history. For more information, see "Criminal Background Checks" on page 34.

An employment application should request the applicant to provide information about his/her:

- Availability
- Experience and skills, including related military experience
- Licensing and/or certification
- Employment history
- Specialized knowledge or training, such as proficiency in a language other than English (if necessary for the job)

Compare the information in an applicant's résumé to the information the applicant supplied when completing your employment application to make sure that the information matches. For more guidance on correct note-taking techniques, see "Taking Notes" on page 27.

TIP To reduce the possibility of liability for discrimination, compare your own application with the provided sample *Employment Application – Short Form* and review your application using the *Guide for Pre-Employment Inquiries*, both described in Table 4 on page 62.

Employers should use caution with provisions and disclaimers for applications used in multiple states.

Job applicants might not notice certain provisions in "one-size-fits-all" applications, and applicants in California might answer questions that California law prohibits employers from asking. This could create potential liability for employers.

You should include the following "damage-control" provisions in the application and require the applicant to separately initial each provision:

- An *authorization to check all references* listed by the applicant. Since you may be liable for "negligent hiring" if you fail to check an applicant's references, this provision will help protect you from a claim that you invaded the applicant's privacy by checking his/her references without permission. It's also easier to gain information from former employers if they know that their former employee authorized disclosure to you.

This release can't protect you against claims of intentional misconduct or employment discrimination if you ask about protected information like the employee's medical history.

- *A statement that all answers given by the applicant are true*, and any omissions or false information are grounds for rejecting the application or for termination. Courts allow employers to use an applicant's placement of false information on a job application as evidence in wrongful termination lawsuits, even if the employer did not discover the information was false until after the employee was terminated.

- A statement that *employment is at-will*. This helps applicants understand that employment is at-will. State that for any contrary representations to be binding, they must be in writing.

Screen Candidates with a Phone Interview

A phone interview presents an informal way to screen a potential employee before interviewing the applicant in person. A phone interview gives you a chance to talk over points of the résumé or employment application and get more details on anything you want to know about the applicant.

As in all conversations, be careful not to create an implied contract or to open yourself to a discrimination charge. You might consider developing a script for the person conducting the phone interview:

- Use the *Guide for Pre-Employment Inquiries*, described in Table 4 on page 62, to make sure your script doesn't contain any illegal questions.

- See the *Employment Interview Checklist* described in Table 4 on page 62, for a series of questions you can ask. You can find these forms in your online formspack, described in detail in "Online Forms" on page 12.

For tips on steering clear of implied contracts, see "Employment Contracts" on page 58.

Interview Candidates

Interviewing candidates is your opportunity to learn more about your applicants and to determine which applicant is best for you, based on the candidates':

- Skills

- Suitability for the position

- Work style

- Employment-related interests

 You will probably only select a small fraction of the candidates for interviews and/or background checks.

Be careful of questions that can put you at risk for a discrimination lawsuit. In general, don't ask questions about:

- Marital status or children

- Age

- Disabilities

- Hobbies and outside activities that might indicate race, religion, age, etc.

The *Guide for Pre-Employment Inquiries*, described in Table 4 on page 62, can guide you in asking appropriate questions.

Also be careful of statements that can establish employment contracts or violate your policies. Read "Employment Contracts" on page 58 and the *Employment Interview Checklist*, described in Table 4 on page 62, for more information.

Taking Notes

It is usually necessary to take notes during interviews so you can review the notes later when making a final decision. However, it is important to ensure that you record interview information in a manner that will not cause you problems in court. Take brief, clear and legible notes that pertain only to the candidate's answers. Don't use abbreviations or a coded rating system that could be misinterpreted at a later date.

Keep objective records of why an applicant was or was not hired to avoid any inference of discriminatory motives. Consider these examples:

- Alarm installer
  - Do note: "Did not possess experience with necessary equipment."
  - Do **not** note: "Not impressed with his attitude."
- Retail store
  - Do note: "Did not have enough customer service experience."
  - Do **not** note: "Was not right for the job."

In addition, be sure that your interview notes evaluate criteria actually necessary to perform the job. For instance, when interviewing for a telemarketer, your notes should:

- Reflect **impartial items**, such as "Good interpersonal skills; types 75 WPM."
- Not reflect **personal observations**, such as "Did not like the way he talked."

Interview Tips

When conducting your interviews, consider these pointers:

- Create a script of questions to ask each applicant, using "Employment Contracts" on page 58 and the *Employment Interview Checklist*, described in Table 4 on page 62. Make sure other interviewing managers understand the guidelines for interviewing.

- Invite candidates to visit your office for the interview. This is their chance to learn more about your company and work environment and to meet potential co-workers. Additionally, it's a professional way to receive applicants and allows you to select a quiet place for talking with the candidate without distractions.

- It's up to you to decide whether to interview all applicants, maybe throughout a workweek, or to interview candidates one-by-one until you fill the position.

- Interviews generally last between 30 and 60 minutes, depending on the job requirements and the candidate's experience. Tell the candidate at the beginning how long the interview will last, and allow time to answer any of his/her questions.

- You may take notes during the interview, but you must exercise caution in how you phrase your written comments because the notes could be used in a legal claim.

Conduct Background Checks

Before selecting a new employee, it's advisable to check the applicant's references and/or background to evaluate the candidate's job-related abilities.

As part of a background check, you might examine each candidate's:

- Criminal background

- Credit history and/or investigative consumer reports

- References

- Educational background

- Drug/alcohol screening results (post-offer)

- Physical health (post-offer)

Federal and California laws place restrictions on employers' use of criminal background checks in the hiring process. Make sure you know the limitations on asking for applicants' criminal background information. For a complete discussion, see "Background Checks and Testing" on page 34.

 Improperly researching an applicant's background may expose you to legal liability in the form of a lawsuit alleging that you invaded the applicant's privacy. This includes investigating an applicant's online activities in various social media websites, such as Facebook or Twitter. For more information, please see "Checking Online Activities" on page 42.

The law does not specifically require you to check an applicant's references and background, but researching an applicant's background can provide you with valuable information and can make costly litigation far less likely. A court could hold you liable for negligent hiring if you don't perform a background check and the employee commits an offense that you could have predicted if you made a reasonable effort to research that person. A reasonable effort, even if former employers don't cooperate, can protect you from negligent hiring claims.

 It's considered negligent to hire someone whose documented past presents an unreasonable risk of harm to others; specifically, to co-workers and customers.

For example, if an employee with a record of violent behavior assaults someone in your office, the victim of the assault may bring a negligent hiring suit against you, alleging that you should have known about the employee's violent past and not hired the person.

 You may wish to do some of this research post-offer on the lead candidate only and make your offer contingent upon satisfactory results.

Records related to a credit check must be kept separate from the employee's regular personnel file. It's a best practice to keep these records confidential.

Make the Hiring Decision

Once you've reviewed résumés and applications and screened and interviewed candidates, it's time to make your hiring decision. Make all hiring decisions carefully. To prevent claims of unfair hiring practices:

- Be sure you have valid reasons for making the hiring decision, based on the person's:

  - Qualifications

  - Experience

  - Skills

  - Knowledge

  - Education

- Document the reasons why one person was selected over other candidates.

- Review documents from hiring supervisors to ensure decisions were based on valid reasons, and that no applicant was rejected for a discriminatory reason.

Make the Offer

Once you select a candidate, send an employment offer letter to him/her. The offer letter clarifies the terms of employment, such as:

- The start date

- "At-will" employment status

- Exempt or nonexempt status (see "Exempt and Nonexempt Employees" on page 51)

- Wage or salary: If the employee will be exempt, phrase the pay rate in terms of dollars weekly, biweekly or monthly. If the employee will be nonexempt, phrase the pay rate in terms of dollars per hour.

- Whether the offer depends on the applicant passing a medical exam, drug test, or reference or background check. For more information, see "Medical Exams and Inquiries" on page 41.

 If you send an offer letter, be sure that the salary for an exempt employee meets the minimum salary requirements for an employee to be exempt. See "Exempt Employees" in Chapter 5, page 164.

You are not required to send the successful candidate an offer letter, but many employees won't want to leave their current jobs until they have something in writing confirming the new job.

 Be careful that you don't create an employment contract in your letter, overriding employment at-will status. See "Employment Contracts" on page 58. To see a sample letter that contains no contractual language, read the *Employment Letter*, described in Table 4 on page 62.

How Do I Handle Unsuccessful Applicants?

Although you are not required to do so, you might consider sending a letter to all applicants not hired letting them know that they are no longer under consideration for the position. This is a courtesy to the applicants that pursued employment with your company. You can send a standard letter to all unsuccessful applicants. To see a sample letter, read the *Letter to Applicants Not Hired*, described in Table 4 on page 62.

Complete the Appropriate Paperwork

The paperwork involved with hiring a new employee is extensive. You can use the *Hiring Checklist* to help keep track of which forms/notifications you provided to your new employee and subsequently processed. This checklist is described in Table 4 on page 62.

Use the following forms throughout the hiring process:

- Employment applications (see "Review Applications" on page 24)

- Forms for checking background (see "Background Checks and Testing" on page 34)

- Forms for special types of workers:

  - Minors: see "Hiring Minors" on page 56 for more information

  - Independent contractors: see "Independent Contractors" on page 53

Fill Out or Provide These Forms on the Employee's First Day of Work

- Information and pamphlets about employee rights and benefits, such as:

  - *Sexual Harassment Hurts Everyone* pamphlet (available in the ***2017 Required Notices Kit*** at ***store.calchamber.com***)

  - *Your Rights to Workers' Compensation Benefits and How to Obtain Them* pamphlet (see "Workers' Compensation" on page 139)

  - *Paid Family Leave* pamphlet (see "Paid Family Leave Benefits" in Chapter 4, page 132)

  - *Disability Insurance Provisions* pamphlet (see "Required and Optional Benefits" in Chapter 4, page 131)

  - *New Health Insurance Marketplace Coverage Options and Your Health Coverage* (required if an employer is covered by the Fair Labor Standards Act. There are separate forms for employers who do/do not offer a health plan.)

  - COBRA and Cal-COBRA rights notifications (if you offer health benefits)

  - *Notice of Victims' Rights - Domestic Violence, Sexual Assault and Stalking* (for employers with 25 or more employees, beginning **July 1, 2017**)

- Safety information, such as:

  - *Emergency Information* form

  - *Initial Safety Training Certificate* (see Table 16 in Chapter 6, page 249)

- Government forms, such as:

  - *W-4 - Employee's Withholding Allowance Certificate*

  - *DE4 - California Employee's Withholding Certificate*

  - *Form I-9 - Employment Eligibility Verification*

  - The required written wage information (if the new employee is a nonexempt employee). Use the *Wage and Employment Notice to Employees (Labor Code section 2810.5)* form.

    - Employers must use the *Wage and Employment Notice*, which contains information regarding the mandatory paid sick leave law (Healthy Workplaces, Healthy Families Act of 2014). You can find this notice in Table 4 on page 62. For more information on this form, see "Notifying Employees About Paydays" in Chapter 5, page 192.

  - *New Employees Report - Form DE34*

- An employee handbook

- A copy of the company's Injury and Illness Prevention Program (IIPP) (see "Injury and Illness Prevention Program" in Chapter 6, page 218)

You can find these forms in your online formspack, described in detail in "Online Forms" on page 12. CalChamber's **Required Notices Kit** includes pamphlets on Unemployment Insurance, State Disability Insurance, Paid Family Leave, Sexual Harassment Prevention and Workers' Compensation.

Welcome New Employees

A new employee's first day of work is the ideal point in the employment relationship to make sure that he/she understands your policies and work rules; is informed of his/her legal rights and obligations; and receives the necessary training to do the job safely and efficiently.

Document all training and orientation. Proper records can help protect you from lawsuits. Use the *Employee Orientation Checklist*, described in Table 4 on page 62, and keep it in the employee's personnel file.

You might be tempted to designate the first few weeks or months of work as a "probationary" period, but this could be understood as a promise that, when the probationary period is over, the employee will have permanent status.

⟞ *CalChamber®*

Employee Orientation

Verify that the employee:

- Tours the building/facilities and learns the exits' locations

- Meets managers and other employees

- Understands information on company processes and resources

- Gets a chance to ask questions about anything he/she doesn't completely understand

Employee Training

You must provide all of your employees with the necessary knowledge and training to complete their tasks safely. If an employee gets hurt because you did not take the time to make sure that he/she understood how to operate a machine properly, you will be liable. See "Safety Training" in Chapter 6, page 237.

 Remember, time spent on orientation and training must be paid.

If you employ 50 or more people, you must provide at least two hours of sexual harassment prevention training to all supervisory employees every two years. All new supervisory employees must receive training within six months of assuming supervisory positions, either as a new hire or through a promotion. For more information, see "Provide Training" in Chapter 8, page 288.

Verifying Social Security Numbers

Though not required by law for most employers, you may choose to verify the Social Security number (SSN) of newly hired employees. The Social Security Number Verification Service (SSNVS) allows registered users (employers and certain third-party submitters) to verify employees' names and SSNs against Social Security Administration (SSA) records.

This service can only be used for wage reporting purposes. With SSNVS, you may:

- Verify up to 10 names and SSNs online and receive immediate results. You may use the SSNVS website an unlimited number of times per session.

- Upload electronic files of up to 250,000 names and SSNs and usually receive results the next government business day.

Employers can register to use the free SSNVS through the SSA's Business Services Online website at **www.ssa.gov/employer/ssnv.htm**.

The use of the SSNVS should be implemented and utilized in a nondiscriminatory manner. Employers should specify, through policy, what classifications of employees will be submitted to the SSNVS system. The SSA emphasizes that such verifications can only occur after an employee has been hired and that the use of SSNVS is applied to employees consistently.

Background Checks and Testing

Poor selection practices could potentially lead to claims of negligent hiring. You must exercise reasonable care in determining a candidate's fitness for employment and continued employment.

Reference checks are a part of good selection practices. Other types of background checks or pre-employment testing may also be necessary, depending on the position involved.

Criminal Background Checks

Conducting criminal background checks as part of the recruiting and hiring process has attracted a lot of attention over the past few years. The concern is that employers might discriminate against applicants because of their criminal history by choosing not to hire them.

Federal Guidance

Employers commonly ask on employment applications whether an applicant has a criminal background, using a box asking if the applicant has ever been convicted of a crime.

The Equal Employment Opportunity Commission's (EEOC) *Enforcement Guidance on the Consideration of Arrest and Conviction Records in Employment Decisions* discusses how an employer's use of an individual's criminal history in making employment decisions could violate prohibitions against employment discrimination.

The EEOC did not categorically ban the use of the criminal history check box, but the guidance recommends that "employers not ask about convictions on job applications and that, if and when they make such inquiries, the inquires be limited to convictions for which exclusion would be job related for the position in question and consistent with business necessity."

Under the guidance, an employer must demonstrate that any criminal history screening practice is job-related and consistent with business necessity. The guidance provides that a policy or practice that excludes everyone with a criminal record from employment will not be considered job-related and consistent with business necessity.

The rationale for not asking on the initial application form is that the employer is more likely to objectively assess the relevance of the conviction if it becomes known once the employer has already learned of the applicant's qualifications and experience.

EEOC guidance is not a federal law or regulation. It demonstrates the EEOC's position on a particular issue and shows what the agency will look for when deciding to investigate an employment practice and whether to file charges.

California Law

Most employers should not use a standard job application form that results in automatic disqualification. Instead, employers should ask about criminal history only when they can demonstrate that it is relevant to a specific job.

Include the optional request for criminal history information only when consistent with business necessity and limit inquiries to those that are truly job-related.

Under state law, you can't ask job applicants to disclose information about:

- Arrests or detentions not resulting in conviction

- Information concerning a referral to or participation in a criminal diversion program (a criminal diversion program is a work or education program as part of probation)

- Convictions for most marijuana possession offenses more than two years old

- Convictions that were judicially dismissed or ordered sealed pursuant to law

You are also prohibited from considering any such prohibited criminal information in determining any condition of employment, including decisions related to hiring, promoting, training or termination.

 Employers who must conduct criminal background checks to comply with various state laws should consult legal counsel.

Exceptions

There are some exceptions under California law. For example, state law requires the Department of Justice (DOJ) to send conviction and pending arrest information to the employer and the applicant if he/she is applying for a license, employment or volunteer position with supervisory or disciplinary power over vulnerable persons under his/her care. This includes the care of minors, the elderly or the mentally impaired.

The request for records must include the applicant's fingerprints. The DOJ accepts only electronically submitted fingerprints.

 If your organization employs or uses volunteers who care for minors, the elderly or the mentally impaired, consult legal counsel about criminal background checks.

Juvenile Criminal History

 AB 1843 prohibits employers from inquiring into an applicant's juvenile convictions or using such convictions as a factor in determining any condition of employment.

Specifically, the legislation prohibits employers from inquiring into any "adjudication" made by the juvenile court, including crimes listed under Welfare and Institutions Code Section 707(b) (e.g., murder, arson, rape, kidnapping, discharge of a firearm). "Adjudication" is a final determination by a court as to whether the juvenile committed the crime of which he or she is accused.

For health care facilities, AB 1843 allows employers to inquire into juvenile adjudications for felony or misdemeanor sexual offenses or drug possessions within the prior five years.

Businesses That Serve Minors

If you hire an applicant convicted of any of the crimes listed below, you must notify the parents of any minor who will be supervised or disciplined by the employee or volunteer. You must provide the notice at least 10 days prior to the day that the employee or volunteer begins his/her new duties or tasks.

Violations that must be reported include:

- Assault with intent to commit mayhem, rape, sodomy or oral copulation
- Unlawful sexual intercourse with a minor
- Rape

- Bodily harm to a child

- Cruel or inhuman corporal punishment to a child

- Corporal injury to another

A business that provides services to minors must provide a written notice to the parent or guardian of the minor receiving those services which addresses the business's policies relating to employee criminal background checks. Specified licensed child day cares and medical facilities/hospitals are excluded.

If criminal background checks are performed, the notice must state whether the checks include state and federal criminal history information and the nature of the offenses the business looks to identify. The written notice may include a posting on the business's website.

A "business that provides services to minors" is one that meets both of the following requirements:

1. A primary purpose of providing an extracurricular service or program of instruction, including academic tutors for minors; and

2. Has adult employees with supervisory or disciplinary power over a child or children.

Credit Checks

Employers may not use a consumer credit report for employment purposes unless the position of the applicant or employee will be:

1. A managerial position (as defined in the executive exemption of Wage Order 4)

2. A position in the state Department of Justice

3. That of a sworn peace officer or other law enforcement position

4. A position for which the information in the report is required by law to be disclosed or obtained

5. A position that involves regular access (for any purpose other than routine solicitation and processing of credit card applications in a retail establishment) to all of the following types of information of any one person:

   - Bank or credit card account information

- Social Security number

- Date of birth

- A position in which the person is, or would be, any of the following:

  - A named signatory on the bank or credit card account of the employer

  - Authorized to transfer money on behalf of the employer

  - Authorized to enter into financial contracts on behalf of the employer

6. A position that involves access to confidential or proprietary information

7. A position that involves regular access to cash totaling $10,000 or more of the employer, a customer or client, during the workday

If one of the exceptions applies and you are able to obtain and use the report, there are still restrictions on how you go about obtaining the report. The federal Fair Credit Reporting Act (FCRA) places additional restrictions on your ability to use credit reports for employment purposes.

If information from a credit report is used for employment purposes, you must complete the following actions:

1. Written disclosure — Make a clear and conspicuous written disclosure to the applicant before the report is obtained, in a document consisting solely of the disclosure, that a consumer report can be obtained. The notice must:

- Tell the person that a report will be used

- Identify the specific basis allowing use of the report (which exception applies)

- Inform the person of the report's source

- Contain a box that the person can check off if he/she wishes to receive a copy of the report

- Obtain prior written authorization from the applicant. You can use the *Notice and Authorization to Obtain Consumer Credit Report*, described in Table 4 on page 62

2. Provide a separate notice — give the applicant a copy of the *Fair Credit Reporting Act - Summary of Your Rights* when you tell the applicant of your intent to obtain a report.

3. Certification to a consumer credit reporting agency (CRA) — provide the agency with written certification that you made the disclosure and obtained authorization and that the information will not be used in violation of any federal or state law. You must also certify that if you take any adverse action based on the credit report, you will provide a copy of the report and a summary of the FCRA rights to the person. You can use the *Certification to Consumer Credit Reporting Agency*, described in Table 4 on page 62.

4. Employee/applicant request — if the employee or applicant requests a report, the employer must request that a copy be provided to the employee at the time the employer requests the report from the CRA. The report must be at no charge to the employee, and must be given at the same time as the employer's report.

If the information on the consumer credit report leads you to take adverse action against the applicant, you must give the applicant written notice of the following:

- Name, address and toll-free telephone number of the agency that provided the report

- A statement that the agency didn't make the adverse decision and can't explain why the decision was made

- A statement of the applicant's right to obtain a free copy of his/her files from the reporting agency (if requested within 60 days)

- A statement of the applicant's right to dispute directly with the consumer reporting agency the accuracy of any information provided by the agency

- A statement to the applicant that the decision to take adverse action was based in whole or part upon the information obtained in the consumer credit report

- A copy of the *Fair Credit Reporting Act - Summary of Your Rights*, described in Table 4 on page 62

Use the *Pre-Adverse Action Disclosure* and the *Adverse Action Notice*, described in Table 4 on page 62, when preparing the notice.

The credit-check process requires many mandatory forms, which you can find in your online formspack (described in detail in "Online Forms" on page 12).

Investigative Consumer Reports

These reports help you discover information about an applicant's character, general reputation, personal characteristics and mode of living. The information is typically obtained through personal interviews. If you intend to obtain such a report, you are required to provide:

1. Written disclosure — tell the applicant, in writing, that an investigative consumer report may be obtained. The disclosure must describe the applicant's

right to request additional disclosures of the nature and scope of the investigation, and must include a summary of consumer rights.

2. Certification to the consumer reporting agency — provide the agency with written certification that you made proper disclosure to the applicant.

3. Additional requested disclosure — if the applicant requests it, you must fully disclose the nature and scope of the requested investigation.

The FCRA prohibits consumer reporting agencies from providing consumer reports that contain medical information for employment purposes or in conjunction with credit or insurance transactions, without the specific prior consent of the applicant.

It's prudent to limit the scope of these investigations to specifically job-related information, because investigative reports that aren't job-related may violate federal and state civil rights laws if they create an unequal impact on minority applicants. See "Discrimination" in Chapter 7, page 257 for details.

Investigative consumer reports must include the Internet address of the investigative consumer reporting agency. If the agency has no Internet address, the report must include the telephone number of the agency.

Drug Testing

In general, the law doesn't require drug testing. If you wish to require drug testing for applicants, you should follow these guidelines:

- Be consistent. Decide whether drug testing is required for all positions or just those with potential safety concerns.

- Determine what levels of what substances will be considered "passing" levels.

- Obtain the applicant's signed authorization.

- Use an independent testing facility.

Certain transportation employees must pass drug tests, and certain companies with state or federal contracts must maintain drug-free workplace programs. See "Where Do I Go For More Information?" on page 74 for helpful resources.

 Be aware that the law limits drug testing on employees. If you want to perform any drug testing, it needs to happen in the application phase after a job offer is made. If you make your offer contingent on successfully passing a drug test, be sure to note this in the employment offer letter. The offer should be contingent on passing the exam. If an applicant refuses to take a drug test, you can refuse to hire the applicant.

Medical Exams and Inquiries

Employers may not conduct physical examinations prior to making an offer of employment.

The position may require job-related physical fitness, such as being able to lift a certain amount of weight. You may test only for necessary physical qualifications, and only after you have made an offer of employment. You may not test for an individual's HIV status.

An employer may withdraw an offer of employment based on the results of an examination only if the applicant is unable to perform the essential duties of the job with or without reasonable accommodation.

Disability discrimination laws restrict your right to require medical exams or to ask applicants and employees about disabilities. Untimely or unnecessary inquiries about health issues or disabilities put you in a vulnerable position if you later take adverse action against the applicant or employee.

Reference Checks

Though you are not required to check your future employee's references, doing so can protect you from liability. See "Conduct Background Checks" on page 28.

When contacting your applicant's listed references, stick to questions that directly relate to job performance to avoid liability for invasion of privacy. You may need written permission from the applicant to obtain salary information.

Education Checks

This is not required, but verifying an applicant's transcript and a university's accreditation can save headaches later.

Checking Online Activities

Employers are prohibited from requiring or requesting applicants to disclose information regarding their personal social media accounts as part of the hiring process. These same prohibitions also apply if you are interviewing to promote a current employee to an open position.

Specifically, employers are prohibited from requiring or requesting an applicant to:

- Disclose a user name or password for the purpose of accessing the applicant's/employee's personal social media

- Access personal social media in the presence of the employer

- Divulge any personal social media

Social media accounts can include Facebook, LinkedIn or Twitter accounts, as well as personal email accounts. Social media accounts are defined by this law as "an electronic service or account, or electronic content, including, but not limited to, videos, still photographs, blogs, video blogs, podcasts, instant and text messages, email, online services or account, or Web site profiles or locations."

Employers can't retaliate against, discipline, discharge or threaten to discharge an applicant for not complying with an employer's request or demand to reveal personal social media information in violation of this law.

Exceptions

Once an applicant becomes an employee, employers may require an employee to access, log in, or divulge personal social media in two instances:

- State law allows an employer to request an employee to divulge personal social media that is reasonably believed to be relevant to an investigation of employee misconduct or an investigation of an employee's violation of applicable laws and regulations. Social media obtained during the course of such investigation must be used solely for purposes of the investigation or related proceedings.

- State law allows an employer to require or request an employee to disclose a user name or password for purposes of accessing an employer-issued electronic device.

Verify the Employee's Authorization to Work

The Immigration Reform and Control Act (IRCA) of 1986 imposes compliance obligations and responsibilities on every employer regardless of size.

You must verify that an individual you hire is either a U.S. citizen or is authorized to be employed in the United States. You may not knowingly hire, contract for labor, recruit, retain or refer for a fee for employment an individual unauthorized to work in the United States.

Penalties for Not Complying With Worker Authorization Requirements

You may face the following penalties and fines for failing to comply with worker authorization requirements:

- Failing to properly complete, retain and/or make the forms available for inspection carries a fine ranging from $216 to $2,156 per violation.

- Knowingly hiring or continuing to employ workers who are not authorized carries civil penalties ranging from $589 to $21,563 per violation, depending on whether it is a first or subsequent offense.

- Engaging in unfair immigration-related employment practices carries a penalty of $445 to $17,816 per violation, depending on whether it's a first or subsequent offense.

- Document abuse (requiring employees to carry more or different documentation than the law requires) carries a minimum fine of $178 to $1,783 per violation.

- Document fraud can carry penalties from $376 to $7,512 per document, depending on the type of fraud and whether it's a first or subsequent offense.

- Engaging in a pattern or practice of knowingly hiring or continuing to employ unauthorized workers carries criminal penalties as high as $3,000 per unauthorized worker and/or six months of imprisonment.

Completing the *Form I-9*

You must verify that every new hire is either a U.S. citizen or authorized to work in the United States within three business days after the employee's first day of work for pay. You must use the *Form I-9 Employment Eligibility Verification* to do so.

Make sure that you use the most recent version of the *Form I-9* because the federal government regularly updates the form. Check the revision date, which is located in the lower left-hand corner of the form.

 In November 2016, the federal government approved a revised *Form I-9 Employment Eligibility Verification*. By **January 22, 2017**, employers must use only the new version of the *Form I-9*, dated 11/14/2016 N. Until then, employers can continue to use the version dated 03/08/2013 N or the new version.

Visit the I-9 Central website at ***https://www.uscis.gov/node/41488*** and subscribe to GovDelivery at ***https://public.govdelivery.com/accounts/USDHSCIS/subscriber/new*** to ensure you receive the latest news on the revised *Form I-9*.

TIP U.S. Citizenship and Immigration Services (USCIS) publishes the *Handbook for Employers, Instructions for Completing the Form I-9 (M-274)* for employers to consult for additional information on completing the *Form I-9*.

The *Form I-9* is made up of three sections.

Employee Completes Section 1

An employee may complete Section 1 of the *Form I-9* any time between accepting a job offer and the end of his/her first day of work for pay.

The employee must be allowed to choose which document(s) he/she wants to present from the lists of acceptable documents to verify his/her identity and employment authorization when completing the *Form I-9*:

- "List A" documents show identity and employment authorization.

- "List B" documents show identity only.

- "List C" documents show employment authorization only.

All documents used by the employee for *Form I-9* verification must be unexpired.

 A person may use one document from "List A" to verify his/her identity and employment authorization, or a person may use one item from "List B" *and* one item from "List C."

Example: A person who presents a California driver's license to establish identity must also present a valid document that establishes his/her right to work in the United States.

 You may not require more or different identity and work authorization documents than specified by the USCIS on the *Form I-9*, and you may not specify which documents an employee must provide. For more information, see ""Document Abuse" and Completing the *Form I-9*" on page 47.

The employee is not obliged to provide his/her Social Security number in Section 1 of the *Form I-9* unless he/she is employed by an employer who participates in the E-Verify program. For more information on this program, see "E-Verify" on page 49.

Employer Completes Section 2

You must fill out Section 2 and examine evidence of identity and employment eligibility within three business days of the employee's first day of work for pay.

If you hire a person for fewer than three business days, both sections 1 and 2 of the *Form I-9* must be fully completed by the end of the employee's first day of work for pay.

An employer may designate an authorized representative, including personnel officers, foremen, agents or notaries public, to fill out a *Form I-9* on behalf of the company. If you designate someone else to fill out a *Form I-9* on your behalf, he/she must carry out all responsibilities for completing and signing Section 2 of the *Form I-9*. The employer is still liable for any violations in connection with the verification process.

You must examine one document from "List A" OR a combination of one from "List B" and one from "List C." You must examine the original document(s) the employee presents and then fully complete Section 2 of the *Form I-9*. Follow the specific instructions in Section 2 of the form.

The *Form I-9* lists the acceptable documents. The USCIS provides photographic examples of List A, B and C documents on its website, at ***www.uscis.gov***.

Do not file the *Form I-9* with U.S. Immigrations and Customs Enforcement (ICE) or USCIS. You must keep the *Form I-9* for either three years after the date of hire or one year after employment is terminated, whichever is later. You must make the form available for inspection or audit within three days after receiving a request from authorized U.S. government officials (e.g., ICE, U.S. Department of Labor). It's recommended that *Form I-9*s are kept together in a file separate from individual personnel files for easier access.

The Spanish version of *Form I-9* may be filled out by employers and employees in Puerto Rico ONLY. Spanish-speaking employers and employees in the 50 states and other U.S. territories may print this for their reference, but may only complete the form in English to meet employment eligibility verification requirements.

For a non-citizen, make sure you re-verify expiring work authorization documents before the expiration date noted in Section 1 of the *Form I-9*. For more information about hiring non-U.S. citizens, see "What Should I Know About Employing Non-U.S. Citizens?" on page 51.

Receipts

In lieu of a "List A," "List B" or "List C" document, an employee may need to present an acceptable receipt, valid for a short period of time, for completing Section 2 or Section 3 (re-verification) of the *Form I-9*.

Employers cannot accept a receipt for the application for an initial or renewal employment authorization but can accept a receipt for the application for replacement of a lost, stolen or damaged employment authorization document. Employers cannot accept receipts if employment will last less than three days.

Only three types of receipts are acceptable:

1. A receipt showing that the employee applied to replace a document that was lost, stolen or damaged. The employee must present the actual document within 90 days from the date of hire.

2. The arrival portion of Form I-94/I-94A with a temporary I-551 stamp and a photograph of the individual. The employee must present the actual Permanent Resident Card (Form I-551) by the expiration date of the temporary I-551 stamp, or, if there is no expiration date, within one year from the date of issue.

3. The departure portion of Form I-94/I-94A with a refugee admission stamp. The employee must present an unexpired Employment Authorization Document (Form I-766) or a combination of a List B document and an unrestricted Social Security card within 90 days.

When the employee provides an acceptable receipt, the employer should:

1. Record the document title in Section 2 under the sections titled "List A," "List B" or "List C," as applicable.

2. Write the word "receipt" and its document number in the "Document Number" field. Record the last day that the receipt is valid in the "Expiration Date" field.

By the end of receipt validity period, the employer should:

1. Cross out the word "receipt" and any accompanying document number and expiration date.

2. Record the number and other required document information from the actual document presented.

3. Initial and date the change.

Electronic Form I-9

Employers may complete, sign, scan and store the *Form I-9* electronically, providing that certain requirements are satisfied:

- The *Form I-9* must be completed within three business days (not calendar).

- Paper, electronic systems or a combination of both is permissible.

- Employers may change electronic storage systems provided that performance requirements contained in the regulations are satisfied.

- An audit trail must be maintained when the *Form I-9* is created, completed, updated, modified, altered or corrected. However, such is not required each time the document is electronically viewed.

- Employers may provide confirmation that the *Form I-9* was completed, but are not required to unless requested by the employee.

Employers may choose between paper and electronic systems, but should apply consistent policies and procedures to all employees to avoid claims of discrimination. Providing an electronic version does not eliminate the employer's obligation to examine documentation provided by the employee prior to completing the *Form I-9*.

 Whether the *Form I-9* gets filled out manually or electronically, an employer representative must still physically examine required identification and work eligibility documentation.

"Document Abuse" and Completing the *Form I-9*

"Document abuse" is one form of discrimination that can occur during the I-9 process. Document abuse occurs "when employers treat individuals differently on the basis of national origin or citizenship status in the *Form I-9* process," according to the USCIS.

Employers can't specify which document(s) they will accept for verification, as long as they are on the list of acceptable documents included on the *Form I-9*. Instead, employees may choose which document(s) they wish to present from the lists of acceptable documents.

Limiting the types of documents an employee can present can be an unfair immigration-related employment practice in violation of the anti-discrimination provision of the Immigration and Nationality Act (INA), according to USCIS. The INA prohibits discrimination during the I-9 process and it is enforced by the DOJ.

 New 2017 SB 1001 makes this type of conduct unlawful under state law as well. The legislation gives the Labor Commissioner power to enforce the law and specifies a penalty of up to $10,000 as well as the ability to issue orders to stop further violations. This new state law may provide an easier remedy than federal law for workers who believe they have had their rights violated.

 The INA's document abuse prohibitions cover employers with four or more employees.

The USCIS considers four broad categories of conduct as document abuse:

1. Improperly requesting that an employee produce more documents than the *Form I-9* requires to establish the employee's identity and employment authorization;

2. Improperly requesting that employees present a particular document, such as a "green card," to establish identity and/or employment authorization;

3. Improperly rejecting documents that reasonably appear to be genuine and to relate to the employee presenting them; and

4. Improperly treating groups of applicants differently when completing the *Form I-9*, such as requiring certain groups of employees who look or sound "foreign" to present particular documents the employer does not require other employees to present.

California Driver's License

The California Department of Motor Vehicles (DMV) issues an original driver's license (known as an AB 60 driver's license) to an undocumented person who is unable to submit satisfactory proof that his/her presence in the United States is authorized under federal law if he/she:

- Meets all other qualifications for holding a license

- Provides satisfactory proof to the DMV of his/her identity and California residency

You may not discriminate against an individual because he/she holds or presents a license issued under AB 60. The California Vehicle Code and the Government Code provide that it is a violation of the state's Fair Employment and Housing Act (FEHA) for an employer to discriminate against an individual because he/she holds or presents an AB 60 driver's license.

You may not require applicants or employees to hold or present a driver's license unless:

- Holding a driver's license is required by law for a particular job; or

- You have a legitimate business reason for requiring drivers' licenses and you apply the reason uniformly.

In fact, it will be considered national origin discrimination under FEHA. For more information see "Immigrant Status" in Chapter 7, page 264.

For employers who hire commercial drivers, AB 60 states that its provisions do not authorize an individual to apply for, or be issued, a commercial driver's license without submitting his/her Social Security number with his/her application.

What If the Documents I'm Shown Aren't Valid?

You aren't liable for accepting documents that appear reasonably authentic, unless you know or have reason to know that the documents are false. You may not refuse to honor documents that appear valid on their face.

E-Verify

E-Verify is an Internet-based system operated by the Department of Homeland Security (DHS) and the Social Security Administration that allows employers to electronically verify the employment eligibility of newly hired employees.

Federal contractors and subcontractors are required to use the E-Verify system to verify eligibility of employees to work in the United States.

Some important points regarding E-Verify include:

- Federal contractors and subcontractors must enroll in E-Verify if and when awarded a federal contract or subcontract that requires participation in E-Verify as a term of the contract.

- California employers' participation in E-Verify is voluntary (unless you are a federal contractor or subcontractor).

- E-Verify must be used for new hires only. It can't be used to verify the employment eligibility of current employees.

- E-Verify must be used for all new hires regardless of national origin or citizenship status. It may not be used selectively.

- E-Verify must be used only after hire and after completion of the *Form I-9*. Employers may not pre-screen applicants through E-Verify.

- The program is currently free to employers.

Employers who use the E-Verify system to determine employment eligibility must display the English and Spanish notices supplied by the DHS in a prominent place clearly visible to prospective employees. The notices, "E-Verify Participation Poster" and "E-Verify Right to Work Poster," can be found on the DHS website.

The online formspack associated with the **HR Quick Guide for California Employers** also contains the forms, in English and Spanish versions.

To find out more or to sign up for E-Verify, visit the DHS' website at **www.dhs.gov/e-verify**.

Unless required by federal law, employers cannot be required to use E-Verify as a condition of receiving a government contract, applying for or maintaining a business license, or as a penalty for violating licensing or other similar laws. "Employers" does not include the state, a city, county, city and county or special district.

Unlawful Use of E-Verify

California employers may not use E-Verify to check the employment authorization status of an existing employee or an applicant who has not received an employment offer, unless the employers are required to do so by federal law or by a condition of receiving federal funds.

Employers who use the E-Verify system for applicants after an offer of employment has been made must provide the affected employee with any notification issued by the Social Security Administration or the U.S. Department of Homeland Security that contains information specific to the employee's E-Verify case or to any tentative non-confirmation notice.

 Employers who use E-Verify unlawfully are liable for a $10,000 penalty, per violation.

What Should I Know About Employing Non-U.S. Citizens?

If an employee has valid documents of his/her employment eligibility, you may not discriminate against the employee on the basis of:

- National origin

- Citizenship status

- Future expiration date of verifying documents

Employers are prohibited from engaging in "unfair immigration-related practices" when an employee asserts protected rights under the Labor Code. For more information, see "Immigrant Status" in Chapter 7, page 264.

In addition, you may not adopt an "English-only" policy in your workplace.

 An **English-only policy** prohibits the use of other languages in the workplace. It's illegal in California unless certain conditions are met, including business necessity and employee notice.

Exempt and Nonexempt Employees

Federal and state laws exempt certain employees from wage-and-hour requirements, especially overtime pay and meal- and rest-break requirements. If you have a problem distinguishing between exempt and nonexempt employees in your company, you are not alone. Some of the largest multimillion-dollar awards of back pay by the courts stem from employers' misclassification of nonexempt employees as exempt from overtime.

Nonexempt Employees

Nonexempt employees are subject to the laws pertaining to overtime, meal periods and rest periods. Nonexempt employees:

- Earn overtime pay (see "Overtime" in Chapter 5, page 190)

- Receive payment of at least minimum wage (see "California Minimum Wage" in Chapter 5, page 169)

- Must take meal and rest periods (see "Meal and Rest Periods" in Chapter 5, page 176)

Don't pay nonexempt employees a salary. This doesn't make them exempt. You must track and document all hours worked by nonexempt employees and the hourly rate of pay for each hour worked. See Chapter 5, "Paying Employees," for more information.

Exempt Employees

Federal and state laws exempt certain employees from wage and hour requirements, especially overtime pay and meal- and rest-break requirements. Whether you can classify an employee as exempt depends on the employee's duties and responsibilities, and how the employee is paid.

For California employees to be exempt, they must generally meet strict job-duties tests particular to each exemption and be paid a minimum salary.

Exempt employees typically hold managerial-level positions and assume responsibility for getting their job duties done regardless of the time it takes to complete their duties. However, employers need to be wary of creating situations in which "managers" also perform nonexempt duties.

> **Example:** A manager supervises other employees but simultaneously performs routine tasks, such as stocking shelves, cashiering or bagging groceries.

In such a scenario, the manager is not primarily engaged in performing exempt work if more than half of his/her time is spent performing nonexempt tasks. This employee should be classified as a nonexempt employee. If the employer misclassified the "manager" in this scenario as exempt, the employer could face a lawsuit and might have to pay substantial penalties to the employee.

Employment laws create five major types of exempt positions:

- Administrative
- Executive/managerial
- Professional
- Computer professional
- Outside salesperson/commissioned inside salesperson

Use the *Exempt Analysis Worksheets* (described in Table 4 on page 62) to help you decide how to classify your employee and whether your employee meets the applicable duties and salary tests. You can find these in your online formspack, described in detail in "Online Forms" in Chapter 1, page 12.

For more information on classifying exempt employees, see "Exempt Employees" in Chapter 5, page 164.

Independent Contractors

Many employers choose to hire independent contractors instead of direct employees. California labor law defines an independent contractor as "any person who renders service for a specified recompense for a specified result, under the control of his principal as to the result of his work only and not as to the means by which such result is accomplished."

An independent contractor works for another entity under a verbal or written contract, usually for a specific length of time. The independent contractor is responsible for only his/her own work, and is generally responsible for his/her own schedule. The independent contractor must also be responsible for how the work is completed.

Engaging an independent contractor can offer significant advantages over hiring an employee. In an independent contractor relationship, employers don't have to:

- Provide certain benefits, such as workers' compensation and unemployment insurance

- Meet overtime and minimum wage obligations

- Withhold income taxes from payments for services

However, use caution when classifying a worker as an independent contractor. Simply labeling a worker as an independent contractor does not mean the worker is truly an independent contractor in the eyes of the law. Courts and government agencies use many factors to determine whether a worker is an independent contractor and not an employee.

Misclassifying a worker as an independent contractor, rather than an employee, creates potential liability for employment taxes and penalties, and liability for failure to fulfill the many legal obligations owed to an employee, such as wage and hour requirements.

California law prohibits any person or employer from willfully misclassifying an individual as an independent contractor:

- The civil penalty for violation of this law ranges from $5,000 to $25,000 for each violation.

- Other remedies include requiring the employer to display on its website or in the workplace a notice of the serious violation of misclassifying an independent contractor; a statement that the employer has changed its business practices in order to comply with the law; and information on how to contact the Labor and Workforce Development Agency to report misclassification.

- The notice must be posted for one year, and signed by an officer of the employer.

- These civil penalties are in addition to any fines or taxes owed to the IRS and the EDD. Misclassification can result in denial of workers' compensation coverage, penalties for failure to provide workers' compensation, and payment of workers' compensation premiums from the date of hire of the independent contractor(s).

The law also prohibits employers from charging a misclassified independent contractor for goods, materials, space, rental, services, government licenses, repairs, equipment maintenance or fines that arise from the individual's employment, if the charges would have violated the law if the person had been an employee.

How Do I Properly Classify the Individual as an Independent Contractor?

No set definition of the term "independent contractor" applies for all purposes. In general, an independent contractor works for another entity under a verbal or written contract, usually for a specific length of time. The independent contractor is responsible for only his/her own work, and is generally responsible for his/her own schedule. The independent contractor must also be responsible for how the work is completed.

Independent Contractor Tests

Various state and federal agencies use their own tests to determine whether an individual meets the criteria to be classified as an independent contractor.

California courts and administrative agencies generally apply common-law principles to determine independent contractor status. One of the key factors is whether the worker has the right to direct and control the manner and means of performing the work. But the right to control is just one factor government agencies and courts use to assess an independent contractor classification.

Agencies and courts also use California Common Law and the "Balancing" tests to assess whether a worker is properly classified. The tests measure a variety of factors, including whether:

- The employer:

  - Has the right to terminate the contract

  - Pays by job, not by time

- Both parties believe they are creating an independent contractor relationship
- The worker:
  - Engages in a distinct occupational business
  - Possesses significant skills or education required for the particular occupation
  - Supplies the instruments and tools for performing the work
  - Performs services over a short or specified period of time
  - Has opportunity for profit or loss, depending upon his/her own managerial skills
  - Employs additional help at his/her own expense
- The work:
  - Usually occurs under the employer's general direction
  - Is performed by a specialist, without employer supervision
  - Is not part of the employer's regular business

You can also use the *Employment Determination Guide - Form DE38* to help you determine if the worker is an independent contractor. This form is described in Table 4 on page 62.

 Consult legal counsel to ensure proper classification.

Forms Related to Independent Contractors

Each independent contractor you hire needs to sign a contract, approved by your legal counsel, that includes the scope of work and the terms of the agreement.

You must also report independent contractors to the EDD's New Employee Registry within 20 days of the start-of-work date. Use the *Independent Contractors Report - DE542*, described in Table 4 on page 62, and in your online formspack, described in detail in "Online Forms" on page 12.

 Be careful in making your decision. It isn't enough that the two parties agree to an independent contractor relationship. You can classify an individual as an independent contractor only if the individual meets the requirements. Each case is unique, and the penalties for making a mistake can be costly. We recommend you consult legal counsel to help you determine an individual's status.

Hiring Minors

When you employ a minor, you must comply with child labor laws designed to help young people acquire work experience and income while safeguarding their scholastic advancement and physical well-being. You can use the *Employing Minors Checklist* as a guide, described in Table 4 on page 62.

 A **minor** is any person under the age of 18 required to attend school, or any person under the age of six.

To employ a minor, you must have a work permit on file year-round, even when school is not in session. You must have the permit on file the day the minor begins work. You can get the permit from the minor's local school district office, even if the student attends a charter school.

This applies to any minor, even:

- High-school dropouts

- Emancipated minors (those minors who declare independence from their parents for tax purposes), although they can apply for a work permit without their parent's permission

- Minors who are not state residents, such as children who live out of state with one parent during the school year and visit the other parent in California during the summer

- Children who work for their parents

 A **work permit** sets limits on the maximum number of days and hours of work as well as the spread of hours allowed for that minor. It may also contain limitations on other aspects of the minor's work.

How Do I Obtain a Work Permit?

1. Complete a *Statement of Intent to Employ a Minor and Request for a Work Permit - Form B1-1*, described in Table 4 on page 62. The minor's supervisor and parent/guardian must both sign the form.

2. File *Form B1-1* with the minor's school district.

3. The minor's school district completes and issues a *Permit to Employ and Work - Form B1-4*, described in Table 4 on page 62.

You must keep the work permit on file the entire length of employment. For more information on handling these forms, see Table 4 on page 62.

What Circumstances Don't Require a Work Permit?

Direct all questions regarding the need for work permits to the minor's school district (or to the school district in which the minor would go to school if he/she does not currently attend, or if he/she attends a private school). You don't need a work permit for minors who:

- Graduated from high school, though in certain hazardous occupations even these minors need a work permit unless they completed a certificate program for that industry

- Work irregularly at odd jobs, such as yard work and babysitting, in private homes

- Participate in any horseback riding exhibition, contest or event

- Are self-employed

- Are at least 14 years of age and deliver newspapers to consumers

- Work for a parent or guardian in connection with property he/she owns, operates or controls for agriculture, horticulture, viticulture or domestic labor

Penalties for Incorrectly Employing Minors

Violations of child labor laws carry serious penalties. California law provides civil penalties for violations of child labor laws.

Under California law:

- Treble damages are allowed if an individual is discriminated or retaliated against because he/she filed a claim or civil action alleging a violation of employment laws that occurred while he/she was a minor.

- The statute of limitations for claims that arise from violations of employment laws is tolled, in other words, delayed or suspended, until the minor is 18 years of age.

- Employers face a penalty of $25,000 to $50,000 for Class A violations involving minors 12 years of age or younger.

Employment Contracts

One of the most important hiring missteps to be aware of is accidentally creating an employment contract: this may lead to a wrongful termination lawsuit at the end of the employment relationship.

California is an at-will employment state. In brief, this means that you can hire, demote, amend an employee's job description or schedule, or terminate an employee whenever you want as long as you don't break a law or violate a specified public policy when you make those employment decisions.

At-will employment also means that workers can accept or leave employment whenever they want. To emphasize the at-will nature of employment, you should use an employment agreement that outlines the terms and conditions of employment and re-states the definition of at-will employment.

However, if you create employment that is not at-will, you create an employment "contract" that overrides the presumption of at-will employment. A simple statement that seems to guarantee future employment, such as "Do a good job and you'll always have work here," is enough to create an employment contract.

An employment contract can create explicit limitations on when, and under what circumstances, you can terminate the employment relationship because contracts usually create a promise that you will only terminate an employee for just cause.

 Just cause means a fair and honest cause or reason, acted on in good faith by the employer.

Remember, contracts can be written, oral or implied. An implied covenant exists in every employment relationship. This covenant requires you to exercise "good faith and fair dealing" in the employment relationship.

 Good faith and fair dealing means that you make decisions in a fair manner and treat in like manner employees who are similarly situated.

Written Contracts

These are the most obvious. An employee with a written and signed contract has the right to have that contract honored. Written contracts can work to your benefit if the contract clearly states how and why employment may be terminated. You should also consider adding these provisions to the contract:

- Specify the duration of the contract and the time period required for notice for termination of the contract

- State that the contract can be renewed at the option of the company

- State that the written document constitutes the entire agreement, that no representations or promises other than those documented can be relied upon, and that the contract can be modified only in writing signed by a corporate officer

Written contracts do carry disadvantages; they are less flexible and any inadvertent omissions or ambiguities in the contract will be interpreted in the employee's favor.

 Under SB 1241, an employer cannot require an employee who primarily works and resides in California:

- To agree to adjudicate a claim in another state when the claim arises in California (prohibiting choice of forum).

- To agree to apply another state's law to a controversy that arises in California (prohibiting choice of law).

This legislation applies to all employment agreements that are entered into, modified or extended on or after **January 1, 2017**, such as executive contracts and arbitration agreements. It will affect multi-state employers and out-of-state employers that have employees in California.

 Be sure to consult legal counsel if you decide to use employment contracts.

Oral Contracts

These are less obvious, but are just as binding as signed, written contracts. They are based on conversations between employer and employee. Watch what you say to an employee in every phase of the employment relationship. For details, see "Employment Contracts" on page 58.

 Provide training on this topic to managers and supervisors.

Implied Contracts

These are based upon the length of employment and indicators of job security that an employee receives. The courts determine whether an implied contract exists on a case-by-case basis. The best defense against an implied contract claim is a signed, at-will employment agreement. You should also maintain an explicit at-will employment policy in your employee handbook.

Discrimination in Hiring

Another important misstep to be aware of is making an employment decision or acting in any way that may lead to a discrimination lawsuit. Federal and state laws require that you treat all qualified candidates equally.

You can't make hiring decisions based (in whole or in part) on an applicant's race, gender, gender identity, nationality, sexuality, marital status, religion, disabilities, medical condition, age, union activity, past bankruptcy or status as an authorized immigrant or a veteran.

 California laws create more strict protections for applicants than do federal laws. The definition of disability is broader, and more classes are included as protected.

If a person files a discrimination lawsuit against you, your burden is to prove that you acted on legitimate reasons for not hiring that individual. This might be tougher than it sounds. Any documents or notes on documents can be used to prove your case, or to prove discrimination accusations against you. Only constant vigilance and consistent behavior will protect you.

For guidelines on non-discriminatory employment decisions, see "Discrimination and Employment Practices" in Chapter 7, page 258.

Minimum Compliance Elements

1. Hang your *2017 California and Federal Labor Law Poster* (available from *store.calchamber.com*), which includes mandatory postings that all employees and applicants must be able to see, in a prominent place (such as a break room). It includes the Healthy Workplaces, Healthy Families Act of 2014 Paid Sick Leave poster.

   If you have employees working in a city or county with a local minimum wage and/or paid sick leave ordinance, you may also need to post required local ordinances and provide additional notices to employees at the time of hire.

2. Use the *Hiring Checklist* to make sure you fill out all the required paperwork for every new hire. See Table 4 on page 62.

3. Look at all candidates objectively, in terms of their ability to do the job. See "Interview Candidates" on page 26.

4. Make sure you classify workers properly. See "Exempt and Nonexempt Employees" on page 51.

5. Make sure you don't control your independent contractors as if they were employees. See "How Do I Properly Classify the Individual as an Independent Contractor?" on page 54.

Forms and Checklists

The following tables describe required and recommended forms associated with the hiring process.

 TIP You can find these forms in your online formspack, described in detail in"Online Forms" on page 12.

Table 4. Forms and Checklists

Notice Or Form	What Do I Use It For?	When Do I Use It?	Who Fills It Out?	Where Does It Go?
Adverse Action Notice	To take adverse action (such as not hiring an applicant or terminating an employee) based on a credit report you have obtained.	This form is required when you know you are taking adverse action based on information in the credit report (see "Background Checks and Testing" on page 34).	The employer.	Give it to the employee. Keep a copy in a private file away from personnel file. Restrict access to the form to a "need to know" basis.
Certification to Consumer Credit Reporting Agency	To obtain a credit report of any type.	This form is required before you obtain the report (see "Background Checks and Testing" on page 34).	The employer.	Send the form to the agency creating the report. Keep it in the personnel file. Restrict access to the form to a "need to know" basis.
Confidentiality Agreement	To obtain an employee's acknowledg-ment that there is information necessary for his/her job that he/she may not disclose.	At the time of hire or change in duties of an employee.	The employer prepares the agreement and it's reviewed by an attorney. The employee signs the agreement.	The original agreement goes in the employee's personnel record. Give the employee a copy.

Table 4. Forms and Checklists (continued)

Notice Or Form	What Do I Use It For?	When Do I Use It?	Who Fills It Out?	Where Does It Go?
DE4 - California Employee's Withholding Certificate	All employees. This is the California tax withholding form if employees want different federal and state tax withholding.	Before employee's first pay date.	The employee.	Keep the form in the employee's personnel record. If you send the original to payroll, keep a copy of the form.
Direct Deposit Authorization	To get employees' permission to deposit paychecks directly into their bank account instead of receiving a paper check.	As part of the hiring process or whenever an employee requests direct deposit.	The employee.	Keep in personnel and/or payroll file (if separate).
Direct Deposit Authorization - Spanish	To get permission from employees whose primary language is Spanish to deposit paychecks directly into their bank account instead of receiving a paper check.	As part of the hiring process or whenever an employee requests direct deposit.	The employee.	Keep in personnel and/or payroll file (if separate).
Emergency Information	Recording important medical information and contacts in case of an emergency.	At the time of hire. Keep the form updated throughout employment.	The employee.	Keep emergency information readily accessible. You may keep the forms in your personnel records, but you might want to use a separate binder for quicker access.

Table 4. Forms and Checklists *(continued)*

Notice Or Form	What Do I Use It For?	When Do I Use It?	Who Fills It Out?	Where Does It Go?
Emergency Information - Spanish	Recording important medical information and contacts in case of an emergency for employees whose primary language is Spanish.	At the time of hire. Keep the form updated throughout employment.	The employee.	Keep emergency information readily accessible. You may keep the form in your personnel records, but you might want to use a separate binder for quicker access.
Employee Orientation Checklist	Tracking completed orientation tasks.	In the first weeks of employment.	The managers.	Keep in the employee's personnel file.
Employing Minors Checklist	Tracking legal issues to consider when hiring a minor.	During the recruiting and hiring processes.	The employer.	Keep the checklist in the minor's personnel file.
Employment Application - Long Form	To gather more detailed information and employment history, and all other necessary sections.	During the recruiting process.	The applicant.	Keep in the employee's personnel file, if the applicant is hired. If you don't hire the applicant, keep the paperwork for two years.
Employment Application – Short Form	Gathering key work history information from an applicant, obtaining authorization to check references and background, and certification that all information is truthful.	During the recruiting process.	The applicant.	Keep in the employee's personnel file, if the applicant is hired. If you don't hire the applicant, keep the paperwork for two years.

Table 4. Forms and Checklists (continued)

Notice Or Form	What Do I Use It For?	When Do I Use It?	Who Fills It Out?	Where Does It Go?
Employment Determination Guide - Form DF38	Determining employee versus independent contractor status.	During the hiring process.	The employer.	Keep in the applicant's file, or if the applicant is hired, in the personnel file.
Employment Interview Checklist	Listing which questions to ask applicants during an interview.	During the applicant's interview.	The interviewer.	Keep in the employee's personnel file, if hired. If you don't hire the applicant, keep the paperwork for two years.
Employment Letter	Informing an applicant that he or she has been selected for employment.	When the employment decision has been made.	The employer.	Mail to the applicant. Keep a copy in the employee's personnel file.
Exempt Analysis Worksheet – Administrative Exemption	Determining whether an employee's duties meet the requirements for exempt status.	During the hiring process.	The employer.	Keep in the employee's personnel file.
Exempt Analysis Worksheet – Computer Professional Exemption	Determining whether an employee's duties meet the requirements for exempt status.	During the hiring process.	The employer.	Keep in the employee's personnel file.
Exempt Analysis Worksheet – Executive Managerial Exemption	Determining whether an employee's duties meet the requirements for exempt status.	During the hiring process.	The employer.	Keep in the employee's personnel file.

Table 4. Forms and Checklists *(continued)*

Notice Or Form	What Do I Use It For?	When Do I Use It?	Who Fills It Out?	Where Does It Go?
Exempt Analysis Worksheet – Professional Exemption	Determining whether an employee's duties meet the requirements for exempt status.	During the hiring process.	The employer.	Keep in the employee's personnel file.
Exempt Analysis Worksheet – Salesperson Exemption	Determining whether an employee's duties meet the requirements for exempt status.	During the hiring process.	The employer.	Keep in the employee's personnel file.
Fair Credit Reporting Act - Summary of Your Rights	To obtain a credit report of any type.	This form is required when you give the employee a copy of the credit report.	N/A	Give it to applicant.
General Notice of COBRA Continuation Coverage Rights - California Employees	To inform California employees of their rights to continuation of health care coverage. Applies only to employers with 20 or more employees, and only to employees in California.	This form is required on the day the employee enrolls for the benefit.	N/A	Include this notice in the group health plan's Summary Plan Description. Send a copy of the notice to the spouse of a married employee, preferably by registered mail. Keep a record of the mailing and/or distribution at hire of this notice to both employee and spouse on the *Hiring Checklist*.

Table 4. Forms and Checklists *(continued)*

Notice Or Form	What Do I Use It For?	When Do I Use It?	Who Fills It Out?	Where Does It Go?
General Notice of COBRA Continuation Coverage Rights - Outside California	To inform employees outside California of their rights to continuation of health care coverage. Applies only to employers with 20 or more employees, and only to employees outside California.	This form is required on the day the employee enrolls for the benefit.	N/A	Include this notice in the group health plan's Summary Plan Description. Send a copy of the notice to the spouse of a married employee, preferably by registered mail. Keep a record of the mailing and/or distribution at hire of this notice to both employee and spouse on the *Hiring Checklist*.
Guide for Pre-Employment Inquiries	Outlining what you can and can't ask during the recruiting process.	During the recruiting process.	N/A	Use as a reference.
Hiring Checklist	Tracking completion of recommended and required hiring procedures and forms.	During the recruiting and hiring process.	The manager or other person in charge of hiring employees.	Keep in the employee's personnel file.

Table 4. Forms and Checklists *(continued)*

Notice Or Form	What Do I Use It For?	When Do I Use It?	Who Fills It Out?	Where Does It Go?
Form I-9 - Employment Eligibility Verification	To verify the employment eligibility of **all** employees.	Section 1: At the time of hire. Section 2: Within three business days after the employee's first day of work. Section 3: On or before the expiration date in Section 1.	Section 1: The employee fills out. Section 2: The employer fills out. Section 3: The employer fills out if necessary for updating or reverifying.	Keep the forms for all employees in a common file rather than separate personnel records.
Independent Contractors Report - DE542	All new independent contractors. The District Attorney uses the information in this form to locate parents who owe child support funds.	This form must be completed and submitted as soon as possible after signing the contract.	The employer.	Mail or fax the form to: Employment Development Department P.O. Box 997350 MIC 96 Sacramento, CA 95899-7350 Fax: 916-319-4410
Letter to Applicants Not Hired	Informing an applicant that he or she wasn't selected for employment.	When the employment decision has been made.	The employer.	Mail to the applicant. You should keep a list of the applicants to whom the letter is mailed.

Table 4. Forms and Checklists *(continued)*

Notice Or Form	What Do I Use It For?	When Do I Use It?	Who Fills It Out?	Where Does It Go?
New Employees Report - Form DE34	All new employees. Permits registered domestic partners to file joint state income tax and have their earnings treated as community property on par with married couples. The District Attorney uses the information in this form to locate parents who owe child support funds.	This form must be completed and submitted within 20 days of hire.	The employer.	Mail or fax the form to: Employment Development Department Document Management Group P.O. Box 997016, MIC 96 West Sacramento, CA 95799 7016 Fax: 916-319-4400
New Health Insurance Marketplace Coverage Options and Your Health Coverage - for Employers That Do Not Offer a Health Plan	Under the Affordable Care Act, employers must provide a notice of coverage options to employees.	The U.S. Department of Labor provided this model notice for use by employers who do not offer a health plan.	The employer.	Keep a record of the distribution at hire of this notice to the employee on the *Hiring Checklist*.
New Health Insurance Marketplace Coverage Options and Your Health Coverage - for Employers That Offer a Health Plan	Under the Affordable Care Act, employers must provide a notice of coverage options to employees.	The U.S. Department of Labor provided this model notice for use by employers who offer a health plan to some or all employees.	The employer.	Keep a record of the distribution at hire of this notice to the employee on the *Hiring Checklist*.

Table 4. Forms and Checklists *(continued)*

Notice Or Form	What Do I Use It For?	When Do I Use It?	Who Fills It Out?	Where Does It Go?
Notice and Authorization to Obtain Consumer Credit Report	To obtain a credit report of any type.	This form is required before you obtain the report (see "Background Checks and Testing" on page 34).	The employer.	Keep in personnel file. Restrict access to the form to a "need to know" basis.
Paid Family Leave pamphlet (available in the **2017 Required Notices Kit**)	To provide notice to employees of their rights to paid family leave benefits.	This pamphlet must be given it to all new employees and any employees taking leave for a covered reason.	N/A	Give the pamphlet to employees and make sure they understand its contents.
Permit to Employ and Work - Form B1-4	To obtain permission to employ a minor.	This is required before the minor begins working [and after the *Statement of Intent to Employ a Minor and Request for Work Permit - Form B1-1* has been approved]. See the form's description following in this table.	The minor's school district fills out and issues the permit.	Keep form (permit) on file as long as the minor is employed. Keep it in your personnel records or in a common binder for all minor employees.
Pre-Adverse Action Disclosure	To notify an employee or potential employee of the possibility of adverse action.	This form is required when you know you're taking adverse action based on information in the credit report (see "Background Checks and Testing" on page 34).	The employer.	Give to the employee. Keep a copy in a private file away from personnel file. Restrict access to the form to a "need to know" basis.

Table 4. Forms and Checklists *(continued)*

Notice Or Form	What Do I Use It For?	When Do I Use It?	Who Fills It Out?	Where Does It Go?
Pre-Hire Checklist	Organizing the process of finding and preparing to hire an employee.	During the recruiting process.	The employer.	Keep the checklist in the employee's personnel file, if the applicant is hired.
Property Return Agreement	Obtaining employee acknowledgment that he/she received property from you (tools, uniforms, etc.) and agrees to return the property.	When your property is issued to the employee.	The employee signs the form.	Keep the original agreement in your personnel records.
Recruiting Checklist	Use this checklist to guide you through the recruiting process for new and existing positions.	When you need to advertise and recruit for a new position.	The employer.	In your files.
Sexual Harassment Hurts Everyone pamphlet (available in the **2017 Required Notices Kit**)	This form describes the problem and the penalties of sexual harassment.	You must provide this pamphlet whenever you hire a new employee. It's recommended that this form is given to independent contractors.	N/A	Give a copy to your workers and make sure they understand its contents.

Table 4. Forms and Checklists *(continued)*

Notice Or Form	What Do I Use It For?	When Do I Use It?	Who Fills It Out?	Where Does It Go?
*State Disability Insurance Provisions (SDI) pamphlet (available in the 2017 **Required Notices Kit**)*	The SDI pamphlet notifies employees of their right to disability insurance benefits should they sustain a non-work related injury.	Give to an employee upon hire and when an employee takes a leave of absence for a reason that is covered.	N/A	Give a copy to your workers and make sure they understand its contents.
Statement of Intent to Employ a Minor and Request for a Work Permit - Form B1-1	To obtain permission to employ a minor. Be sure to finish the permit process with the *Permit to Employ and Work (Form B1-4),* supplied by the minor's school district.	Before the minor begins working.	Each completes the appropriate part: • Minor; • Employer; • Parent; and • School district.	File it with the minor's school district. Keep a copy in your personnel records.
W-4 – Employee's Withholding Allowance Certificate	All employees.	Before an employee's first pay date.	The employee.	Keep the form in the employee's personnel record. If you send the original to payroll, keep a copy of the form.

Table 4. Forms and Checklists *(continued)*

Notice Or Form	What Do I Use It For?	When Do I Use It?	Who Fills It Out?	Where Does It Go?
Wage and Employment Notice to Employees (Labor Code section 2810.5)	To notify nonexempt employees of their hourly or piece rate of pay, pay dates, mandatory paid sick leave, and other information required by law.	At the time of hire, or on an employee's first day of employment.	The employer.	Give a copy to the new employee and keep a copy in the employee's personnel file.
Your Rights to Workers' Compensation Benefits and How to Obtain Them pamphlet (available in the **2017 Required Notices Kit**)	To provide notice to employees of their right to workers' compensation benefits should they sustain an on-the-job injury.	This must be given to all new employees at hire.	The employee fills out the *Personal Physician Designation Form* or the *Personal Chiropractor or Acupuncturist Designation Form*, then gives it to his/her physician to sign, accepting the pre-designation; the rest is informational.	Put the designation form in the employee's regular personnel file and send a copy to your contact at your insurer or claims administrator. The employee keeps the rest of the brochure for reference.

Where Do I Go For More Information?

CalChamber and federal and state government agencies offer a variety of resources to help you hire employees in compliance with the law.

Table 5. Additional Resources

For information on	Check out these resources
General	From CalChamber: • The **2017 California Labor Law Digest**, the most comprehensive, California-specific resource to help employers comply with complex federal and state labor laws and regulations • **store.calchamber.com; www.hrcalifornia.com**
Equal opportunity	The Equal Employment Opportunity Commission (EEOC) offers prepared guidelines for the types of disability-related pre-employment questions that you may and may not ask of a job applicant under the ADA. The guidelines also address the effect of the ADA on medical examinations given to applicants and employees. You can review the enforcement guidelines at **www.eeoc.gov/policy/docs/preemp.html**. You can request publications at no cost to you, including posters, fact sheets, manuals, pamphlets and enforcement guidelines. For a list of EEOC publications, or to order publications, write, call or fax: U.S. Equal Employment Opportunity Commission Clearinghouse P.O. Box 541 Annapolis Junction, MD 20701 Toll-free: (800) 669-3362 TTY: (800) 800-3302 FAX: (301) 206-9789 California's Department of Fair Employment and Housing (DFEH) also offers informational material on discrimination in employment. Its reach is generally much broader in California than that of the EEOC. Department of Fair Employment and Housing, Headquarters 2218 Kausen Drive, Suite 100 Elk Grove, CA 95758 Telephone: (916) 478-7251 Toll-free: (800) 884-1684 *Disability Under the Fair Employment & Housing Act: What you should know about the law (DFEH-208 DH)* at **www.dfeh.ca.gov/res/docs/Publications/dfeh-208dh.pdf**

Table 5. Additional Resources *(continued)*

For information on	Check out these resources
Consumer reporting agencies	Federal Trade Commission Consumer Response Center 600 Pennsylvania Ave, NW Room H-130 Washington, D.C. 20580 (202) 326-2222 **www.ftc.gov** *Using Consumer Reports: What Employers Need to Know* at **http://business.ftc.gov/documents/bus08-using-consumer-reports-what-employers-need-know**
Immigration	The USCIS established a 24-hour toll-free hotline to provide information regarding the IRCA. Call (800) 375-5283 or (800) 767-1833 (hearing impaired). **www.uscis.gov/portal/site/uscis** Handbook for Employers at **www.uscis.gov/files/form/m-274.pdf**
Workers' compensation	California Workers' Compensation Institute 1111 Broadway, Suite 2350 Oakland, CA 94607 Telephone: (510) 251-9470 FAX: (510) 251-9485 **www.cwci.org** California Division of Workers' Compensation **www.dir.ca.gov/dwc/dwc_home_page.htm**
Fingerprinting information	California Department of Justice **http://caag.state.ca.us/fingerprints/index.htm**

CalChamber also provides many ongoing and comprehensive educational opportunities for small business owners, HR beginners and experienced HR professionals alike. These include online training, and special HR seminars and webinars. For more information, please visit our website at **store.calchamber.com**.

Chapter 3

Leaves of Absence

A complicated mix of California and federal laws govern how employers administer leaves of absences.

In general, leaves of absence fall into two categories: mandatory and optional. This chapter describes mandatory and optional leaves of absence, and guides you through the processes of administering and providing them.

You'll get answers to questions about:

- Family and medical leaves

- Pregnancy disability leave

- Mandatory paid sick leave in California

- Vacation

- Other mandatory and optional leaves of absence

When an employee goes on leave, make sure you know (and the employee knows) which type of leave it is. For example, if you fail to establish that the employee is taking leave under the Family and Medical Leave Act (FMLA) or the California Family Rights Act (CFRA), then the leave taken doesn't count toward the enforceable limit.

California employers must provide paid sick leave benefits. For more information on the interaction between mandatory paid sick leave and family and medical leaves, see "Pay and Benefits During Family and Medical Leave" on page 81.

Please continue to look for guidance from the state Labor Commissioner at *www.dir.ca.gov*.

Required and Optional Leaves of Absence

California and federal laws mandate employers to provide some leaves of absence, such as family and medical leaves and pregnancy disability leave. Certain leaves of absence are required only for companies over a certain size.

Employers have the option to offer other leaves of absence, such as bereavement leave or unpaid personal leave. Because different types of leaves, both required and optional, can interact with each other, it is important to understand the different types of leaves and any legal requirements that apply to them. See "Does This Employment Law Apply to Me?" in Chapter 1, page 1.

Required Leaves of Absence

Under California and federal law, you must provide certain leaves of absence to your employees:

- Family and medical leave, page 79

- Pregnancy Disability Leave (PDL), page 87

- Mandatory paid sick leave, page 94

- Disability leave, page 104

- Organ and bone marrow donor leave, page 109

- Crime victims' leave, page 110

- Domestic violence, sexual assault and stalking victims' leave, page 114

- Jury/witness duty leave, page 116

- Military service leave, page 117

- Military spouse leave, page 118

- School activities leave, page 119

- School appearance leave, page 121

- Volunteer emergency duty leave, page 121

- Volunteer Civil Air Patrol leave, page 122

- Voting leave, page 123

Optional Leaves of Absence

You have the option to offer a range of other leaves of absence to your employees, at your discretion:

- Vacation, page 92
- Floating holidays and personal days, page 94
- Paid holidays, page 102
- Paid time off (PTO), page 102
- Bereavement leave, page 123
- Personal leaves of absence, page 124

Family and Medical Leaves

The federal Family and Medical Leave Act (FMLA) and the California Family Rights Act (CFRA) provide for overlapping as well as separate leaves.

 CFRA regulations were updated, effective July 1, 2015. Make sure that you're using up-to-date posters, forms and guidance to comply with FMLA and/or CFRA rules and requirements.

An employee can use FMLA and/or CFRA in the following circumstances:

- The employee's own serious health condition (FMLA/CFRA)
- A qualifying exigency relating to a close family member's military service (FMLA only)
- Up to 26 weeks per 12-month period to care for an ill or injured servicemember (FMLA only)
- Pregnancy-related disability (FMLA only)
- Bonding with a newborn, an adopted child or a child placed in foster care with an employee (FMLA/CFRA or CFRA only)
- Caring for a family member (parent, child, spouse) with a serious health condition (FMLA/CFRA)
- Caring for a registered domestic partner with a serious health condition (CFRA only)

The interaction of FMLA/CFRA leaves with other types of leaves can be confusing. For more information, see "Leave Interactions" on page 107. If you fail to comply with these laws, you face civil lawsuits which could result in compensatory and punitive damages, reinstatement and back pay, court costs and attorneys' fees.

Eligibility Requirements

Family and medical leave laws cover private-sector employers with 50 or more employees on the payroll during each of any 20 or more calendar weeks in the current calendar year or the preceding calendar year.

This includes employees on the payroll who received no compensation, part-time employees, commissioned employees and employees on leave who are expected to return to active employment. Employees on layoff do not count.

Family and medical leave laws cover all public-sector employers, regardless of the number of employees.

Employee Eligibility

Employees eligible for family and medical leave are those who worked:

- For a covered employer for at least 12 months (not necessarily 12 consecutive months)

- At least 1,250 hours in the past 12 months

- At a worksite with at least 50 or more company employees within a 75-mile radius

 The 12 months of service does not have to include any employment prior to a break in service of seven years or more, unless the break was due to military service.

Employees are also eligible for FMLA if they provide care to a member of the Armed Forces (including a member of the National Guard or Reserves) undergoing medical treatment, recuperation or therapy, and veterans undergoing medical treatment, recuperation or therapy for a serious illness or injury and who was a member of the Armed Forces at any time during the five years preceding the date the medical treatment began.

Pilots and flight attendants are also eligible for FMLA benefits to the same extent as other U.S. workers. The changes allow flight crews to qualify more easily for family and medical leave by specifying how hours of service requirements are met.

An employee who is part of a same-sex marriage is also eligible for FMLA. Employers must allow employees to take FMLA leave to care for their same-sex spouse with a serious health condition, for a qualifying exigency and for other qualifying reasons.

Visit the Department of Labor's FMLA page at ***http://www.dol.gov/whd/fmla/*** for updated information.

Employees who intend to assume the responsibilities of a parent of a child (stand *in loco parentis*) are eligible for FMLA.

If you are in doubt about the standing of an employee who wishes to take leave under FMLA, consult with legal counsel before denying the leave.

Pay and Benefits During Family and Medical Leave

Family and medical leaves are generally unpaid. You can, as a matter of policy, require or allow employees to use accrued sick pay, vacation or PTO while they are on FMLA and CFRA leaves.

California employers must provide mandatory paid sick leave benefits. These mandatory paid sick days may be treated the same as optional employer-provided sick days were treated in the past. In other words, you could have a policy requiring an employee to use the mandatory paid sick leave days during unpaid FMLA/CFRA leave. However, the Healthy Workplaces, Healthy Families Act does not address the use of paid sick leave in conjunction with family and medical leaves. The interaction of the paid sick leave mandate with other leave laws is uncharted territory.

Employees may also be eligible for Paid Family Leave (PFL). For more information, see "Paid Family Leave Benefits" on page 132. If the employee is pregnant, she may also be covered by PDL. For more information, see "Pregnancy Disability Leave" on page 87.

If the employee becomes disabled, he/she may be eligible for SDI benefits. For more information, see "State Disability Insurance (SDI)" on page 134. If the employee is on FMLA and receives any disability benefits (state disability insurance, workers' compensation insurance or other disability benefit payments), you may not require the use of paid sick leave, vacation or other accrued paid time off benefits.

Employees may supplement disability benefits with any available sick pay, vacation or PTO.

Benefits

If you provide health benefits under any group health plan, you must continue providing those benefits during an employee's family and medical leave. The following rules apply:

- You must maintain and pay for the employee's health coverage at the same level and under the same conditions as coverage would have been provided if the employee was continuously employed during the entire leave period (up to 12 weeks or up to 26 weeks during a leave to care for an ill or injured servicemember).

- If your group health plan includes dental care, vision care, mental health counseling, etc., or if it includes coverage for the employee's dependents and for the employee, you also must continue this coverage to the same extent.

- Your obligation to continue benefits may extend longer than 12 weeks if you provide more than 12 weeks of benefits to employees on other types of leave.

- If the leave is also for pregnancy disability, you must continue health benefits for a maximum of four months in a 12-month period.

If the employee pays a portion of the premium, the employee is responsible for payment of that portion during the leave. Under the CFRA regulations, an employer must provide an employee with advance written notice regarding the terms and conditions under which the employee's portion of the premium must be paid.

The employer may not add additional charges to the employee's premium payments for administrative expenses while the employee is out on unpaid leave.

If the CFRA leave is paid, the premiums should be paid through the method normally used during paid leave, such as payroll deductions, unless the employee voluntarily agrees to pay the premium in another manner.

 The CFRA regulations provide extensive guidance and detail regarding providing health benefits to employees and how they are to be maintained and paid for and the consequences for untimely or missed payments.

Duration and Timing of Family and Medical Leave

If an employee is eligible for FMLA/CFRA leave, he/she can take up to 12 workweeks of family and medical leave in a 12-month period. He/she can take all 12 weeks at once, or take leave in shorter increments of hours, days or weeks.

FMLA and CFRA each provide up to 12 weeks of leave. They run concurrently for all purposes except:

- Leave to care for a registered domestic partner (CFRA only). Registered domestic partners enjoy the same rights under California law as a spouse. An eligible employee who needs time off to care for his/her registered domestic partner would be entitled to a maximum of 12 weeks of leave under CFRA. FMLA does not cover registered domestic partners. For more information about registered domestic partner rights, see "Registered Domestic Partner Rights" in Chapter 4, page 145.

- Disabilities due to pregnancy or pregnancy-related condition (FMLA only)

- Leave for a qualifying exigency related to a family member's military service (FMLA only). If the leave is for a "qualifying exigency" relating to an employee's spouse, parent, son or daughter serving in the military, the employee will be eligible for 12 weeks of leave in a 12-month period. These 12 weeks may be in addition to 12 weeks the same employee is eligible for under CFRA.

- Leave to care for an ill or injured servicemember (FMLA only). If the leave is to care for a close family member injured during military service, the leave is a maximum of 26 weeks in a 12-month period. The 12-month period begins on the first day of leave for this purpose, regardless of how the 12-month period is defined for other types of FMLA leave.

For more information on how these different leaves interact, see "Leave Interactions" on page 107.

 Regulations defining "qualifying exigency" are described in the *FMLA - Family Member Leave for a Qualifying Exigency* form, available in your online formspack.

Employer and Employee Notice Requirements

State and federal laws create specific posting and notice obligations for employers to explain employees' family and medical leave rights.

Employers may require employees to provide advance notice before FMLA/CFRA leaves begin.

Employer Requirements

Covered employers have both posting and notice obligations. You must post general family and medical leave notices in a conspicuous place where applicants and employees tend to congregate.

There are two separate general notices; one for the federal FMLA and one for the state CFRA. Both describe employees' rights to leave under these laws. For more information, see "Required Posters" in Chapter 1, page 5.

When an employee requests FMLA/CFRA leave or when you learn that an employee's leave may be for a FMLA/CFRA qualifying reason, you must notify the employee of his/her eligibility to take FMLA/CFRA leave and of his/her rights and responsibilities within **five business days**, absent extenuating circumstances.

Use the *FMLA/CFRA Designation Notice*, described in Table 7 on page 125, to respond to the leave request. If the employee is eligible for both PDL and FMLA concurrently, use the *FMLA/PDL Designation Notice*, described in Table 7 on page 125, to respond to the leave request.

The *FMLA - Notice of Eligibility and Rights and Responsibilities* must state whether the employee is eligible for leave. If the employee is not eligible for FMLA/CFRA leave, the notice must state at least one reason why. For example, the notice may inform the employee that he or she is ineligible because the employee worked less than 1,250 hours in the preceding 12 months.

You must notify employees of the method you use to calculate the 12-month period in which the 12 weeks of entitlement occurs. The method that allows you the most control uses a "rolling" 12-month period measured backward from the date the employee first uses any leave.

You can require medical certification within 15 calendar days of your request. If you wish, you may require a second and third opinion of the employee's illness, but you must pay for them. See the *Certification of Health Care Provider - Employee's or Family Member's Serious Health Condition* form, described in Table 7 on page 125.

Under CFRA regulations, employers are required to notify employees of the consequences (such as denial of CFRA leave) if employees fail to provide a medical certification. The CFRA regulations provide a sample medical certification form that's updated consistent with new regulations.

Employee Requirements

Generally, you can require that employees give you 30 days' notice when requesting family or medical leave (for example, the expected birth of a child or a planned medical treatment). The employee must consult with you and make a reasonable effort to schedule any planned medical treatment or supervision to minimize disruption of company operations (subject to the health care provider's approval).

If the condition is not planned or foreseeable, employees must provide the notice as soon as practical. Employees must state the reason for the leave request. You cannot deny leave for an emergency or unforeseeable personal or family circumstances because the employee did not provide advance notice of the need for the leave.

California regulations require an employee to provide at least verbal notice requesting a CFRA-qualifying leave and the anticipated timing and duration of the leave. An employee need not explicitly claim rights under, or even mention, CFRA or FMLA. However, the employee must communicate that the leave is needed for a protected reason to meet the notice requirement.

The employer can inquire further to determine if the employee is seeking family and medical leave. The employee is required to respond to the employer's questions to determine if the leave qualifies for protection. Failure to respond may result in denial if the employer can't determine if the leave qualifies.

Designating Family and Medical Leave

Employers need to designate leave as family and medical leave, based on information provided by the employee or the employee's spokesperson, and to give the employee notice of the family and medical leave designation. If you do not believe you have sufficient information to evaluate the request, notify the employee and request additional information.

When you have enough information to determine if the leave is being taken for a FMLA/CFRA qualifying reason, you must notify the employee in writing whether the leave will be designated and counted as FMLA/CFRA.

FMLA and CFRA regulations require employers to notify an employee whether the leave will be designated and counted as FMLA/CFRA leave within **five business days** after you have enough information to determine whether the leave is for a qualifying reason (e.g., after receiving a medical certification). If you deny the request for leave, FMLA regulations require you to state at least one reason why.

Retroactive Leave Designation

Employees may need leave for a FMLA/CFRA qualifying reason and be unable to provide advance notice. For example, a pregnant employee may deliver early or an employee and/or family member may experience a medical emergency. In these cases, you may not learn of the need for leave for a day or more.

You may be able to retroactively designate the time as FMLA and/or CFRA, depending on the type of leave and the circumstances.

For FMLA leave, employers can retroactively designate leave, or the employer and employee can mutually agree to do so, provided the failure to timely designate the leave as FMLA does not cause harm or injury to the employee.

Under the CFRA regulations, employers may not retroactively designate leave after the employee returns to work unless:

- The employer provides notice to the employee that the leave will be designated as CFRA; and

- The failure to designate the leave in a timely manner does not cause harm or injury to the employee.

Return to Work After Family and Medical Leave

You can require a medical release to allow the employee to return to work, but only if you also require medical releases for other employees returning to work after illness, injury or disability leaves.

The release should be completed by the employee's health care provider before the employee is back at work. The *Certification of Health Care Provider for Employee Return to Work*, described in Table 7 on page 125, can be used for this purpose.

You must reinstate the employee to his/her position either by an agreed-upon date, or within two days of the employee's notification of readiness to return. You may reinstate an employee and then require the employee to take a fitness-for-duty exam if that exam is at your own expense and is job related and consistent with business necessity.

California law defines "job-related" as "tailored to assess the employee's ability to carry out the essential functions of the job or to determine whether the employee poses a danger to the employee or others due to disability." "Business necessity" is defined by California law as "vital" to the business.

Although employers are obligated under the Fair Employment and Housing Act (FEHA) to engage in the interactive process, employers have a separate obligation under the CFRA to engage in the interactive process with employees and to determine whether additional leave is an appropriate reasonable accommodation even if the employee's CFRA leave has ended.

 If you need to fire an employee on family and medical leave, seek legal counsel.

Pregnancy Disability Leave

If you employ five or more full-time or part-time employees, you must make pregnancy disability leave (PDL) available to your employees. California state government, counties, cities and any other political or civil subdivision of the state must make PDL available, regardless of the number of employees.

PDL provides pregnant employees with time off from work when disabled by pregnancy, childbirth and related medical conditions. PDL also protects pregnant employees from being discriminated against.

 PDL also protects employees who need a transfer or reasonable accommodation because of pregnancy, childbirth or related medical condition.

If you refuse to provide PDL to an eligible employee or discriminate against an employee exercising her right to PDL, you can be penalized. See "Penalties Related to Discrimination" in Chapter 7, page 275.

However, employees may not take time off from work for baby bonding under PDL. For information about baby bonding leave, see "Family and Medical Leaves" on page 79.

Eligibility Requirements

If you are a covered employer, an employee is eligible for PDL leave after the employee's first day on the job. An employee does not need to meet a length of service requirement before becoming entitled to PDL.

PDL can be used for any time an eligible employee is disabled by pregnancy, childbirth or a related medical condition.

An employee is "disabled by pregnancy" if her health care provider deems that she is unable, because of pregnancy, to perform any one or more of the essential job functions of her job, or to perform any of these functions without undue risk to herself, the successful completion of her pregnancy or to other people.

 Some employers offer "maternity leave" to pregnant employees. Employers should know that no legal definition of "maternity leave" exists. Review your pregnancy and leave policies to make sure those policies conform with the law. If you do provide "maternity leave," make sure that your policy clearly defines what is meant by "maternity leave" and that this leave is offered in addition to any legally required leave, such as PDL.

Pay and Benefits During PDL

PDL is unpaid. You are not required to pay an employee on PDL unless you pay for other temporary disability leaves for similarly situated employees. However, an employee on PDL may be eligible for State Disability Insurance (SDI) benefits during the time the employee is disabled by pregnancy. For more information, see "State Disability Insurance (SDI)" on page 134.

 You can require or permit the employee to use accrued sick leave during the otherwise unpaid portion of PDL. You can also require or permit the use of sick leave benefits to supplement SDI benefits. The employee may choose to use accrued vacation (see page 92) or PTO (see page 102) during PDL, before using unpaid PDL.

Benefits and PDL

Employers must continue health benefits for employees taking PDL. When an employee takes PDL, an employer who provides health insurance under a group health plan (medical, dental, vision) must continue to maintain a pregnant employee's coverage under the plan as if she had not taken pregnancy disability leave.

An employer must maintain health benefits for the duration of the pregnancy disability leave, up to a maximum of four months in a 12-month period. The 12-month period begins on the date the leave is taken. The benefits are at the same level and under the same conditions as if the employee had continued working during the leave period.

If an employer provides greater health benefits or health benefits for a longer period of time for other types of disability, the same level of benefits must be provided to the employee on PDL.

If the employee works for a state agency, the collective bargaining agreement governs the continuation of health care under the employer's group health plan.

An employer cannot use the time that it maintains and pays for group health coverage during PDL to meet the obligation to pay for 12 weeks of group health coverage during leave under CFRA. The continuation of group health care coverage during PDL and during CFRA are two separate and distinct entitlements.

COBRA/Cal-COBRA coverage may be triggered if the employee is disabled by pregnancy for more than the four months.

During PDL, an employee continues to accrue seniority to the same extent and under the same conditions as would apply to any other unpaid leave not related to pregnancy, and is also entitled to participate in the following:

- Employee benefit plans, including life, short-term and long-term disability or accident insurance;

- Pension and retirement plans;

- Stock options; and

- Supplemental unemployment benefit plans.

Whether an employee on PDL will accrue sick leave, vacation and PTO will depend on your policy.

Duration and Timing of PDL

PDL starts when the employee's health care provider determines that she is disabled by pregnancy, childbirth or related medical conditions.

PDL covers the actual period of disability, up to four months, even if your policy for other temporary disability leaves allows less. The four months' leave is the number of days or hours the employee would normally work in four calendar months (17 and 1/3 weeks):

- If the employee works 40 hours per week, she is entitled to up to 693 hours of leave (40 hours per week x 17 1/3 weeks = 693 hours)

- If the employee works 20 hours per week, she is entitled to 346.5 hours of leave (20 hours per week x 17 1/3 weeks = 346.5 hours)

- If the employee works 48 hours per week, she is entitled to 832 hours of leave (48 hours per week x 17 1/3 weeks = 832 hours)

If your policy provides for a longer period of leave, you must allow the employee the extra time off. Also, an employee can use the leave intermittently, in increments as small as one hour.

The employee must provide you with verbal or written notice of the need for PDL, when it will start and approximately how long it will last. Use the *Request for Leave of Absence - FMLA/CFRA/PDL* form, described in Table 7 on page 125.

This time off also covers severe morning sickness and prenatal care, including doctors' visits.

Notice Requirements

Employers and employees both must follow notice requirements relating to PDL.

Requirements for Employers

Employers of five or more employees must post the PDL notice *Your Rights and Obligations As A Pregnant Employee* from the California Department of Fair Employment and Housing (DFEH). The poster is available in English or Spanish.

The PDL poster includes information about:

- An employee's right to request reasonable accommodation, transfer, or a pregnancy disability leave.

- Employees' notice obligations to provide advance notice to the employer if the employee needs reasonable accommodation, transfer, or a pregnancy disability leave.

- Any employer requirement that the employee provide medical certification of the need for pregnancy disability leave, reasonable accommodation, or transfer.

The poster must be posted in conspicuous places on the employer's premises and must contain fully legible text that is large enough to be easily read. An electronic posting may be used to meet the posting requirement, as long as it is posted electronically in a conspicuous place or places where employees would tend to view it in the workplace.

If 10 percent or more of your workforce at any location speaks a language other than English, you must translate the PDL notice into every language that is spoken by at least 10 percent of the workforce.

You must also give a copy of the PDL Notice to any employee who requests a pregnancy disability leave, a transfer or reasonable accommodation.

Requirements for Employees

An employee must provide at least verbal notice to make you aware that she needs PDL, a reasonable accommodation or a transfer, and the expected timing and duration of the leave, reasonable accommodation or transfer.

If possible, the employee must provide 30 days' advance notice whenever the need for PDL is foreseeable. The employee must consult with you and make a reasonable effort to schedule any planned medical treatment or supervision so as to minimize disruption to your operations. Any scheduling must be approved by the employee's health care provider.

If 30 days' advance notice is not possible, the employee must notify you as soon as possible.

Responding to a Request for PDL

Respond to the request as soon as possible, but no later than 10 calendar days after the request.

 If the pregnancy leave would also qualify as a leave under the FMLA, you must respond no later than five (5) business days, unless "extenuating circumstances" exist.

You should attempt to respond to the leave request before the date the leave is due to begin. Once the request for leave has been approved, it is retroactive to the first day of the leave.

You are required to give a copy of the PDL Notice, *Your Rights and Obligations As A Pregnant Employee*, to any employee who requests a pregnancy disability leave, a transfer, or reasonable accommodation.

Use the *Employee Letter - PDL Only*, described in Table 7 on page 125, to respond to an employee's notice of absence due to PDL. If you are an employer covered by the FMLA (see page 79), and the employee is eligible for FMLA running concurrently with PDL, give the employee a copy of the *FMLA/PDL Designation Notice*, described in Table 7 on page 125.

You can require a medical certification for the leave if you advise the employee of this requirement. See the *Certification of Health Care Provider for Pregnancy Disability Leave, Transfer Or Reasonable Accommodation*, described in Table 7 on page 125.

Return to Work After PDL

When you grant an employee's request for PDL, you must guarantee to reinstate the employee to the same position or to a virtually identical position. This guarantee must be put in writing if the employee requests a written guarantee. You can refuse to honor the guarantee of reinstatement only under very limited circumstances.

Under most circumstances, you must reinstate an employee returning from PDL to the same job she held before the leave, with no less seniority than she had when her PDL began. This includes seniority for the purposes of layoff, recall, promotion, job assignment and seniority related benefits, such as vacation.

You must resume benefits upon the employee's reinstatement in the same manner and at the same levels as provided when the leave began without any new qualification period, physical exam, etc.

You can require a medical release to allow the employee to return to work if you require releases for other disability leaves. See the *Certification of Health Care Provider for Employee Return to Work*, described in Table 7 on page 125.

Vacation

If you choose to offer paid vacation time to employees, you must follow California law concerning vacation benefits.

Eligibility Requirements

You decide which employees are eligible to accrue vacation. Be consistent. Similarly situated employees should accrue vacation at the same rate.

You can allow employees to start accruing vacation from the day they start work. Or you can set a reasonable waiting period (30 days or 90 days, for example) before vacation begins to accrue.

Accrual and Usage

Vacation is any paid time off earned as a benefit. Paid vacation leave constitutes a form of wages. Paid vacation time accrues, or "vests," as the employee renders services, so employees earn a portion of the annual vacation each day.

> **Example:** If your employees earn three weeks of vacation a year (120 hours), then vacation accrues at a rate of approximately 0.45 hours daily. If your employees receive one week of vacation per year (40 hours), vacation accrues at a rate of approximately 0.15 hours daily.

You can require employees to use their accrued vacation for some types of leave. For other leaves, you can't require employees to use vacation, but they can choose to do so. See:

- "Pregnancy Disability Leave" on page 87
- "Family and Medical Leave" on page 79
- "Disability Leave" on page 104
- "Workers' Compensation" on page 139

Importance of a Policy

Because paid vacation leave is a form of wages, paid vacation is also part of the "employment contract" between you and the employee. As part of that contract, the employee performs specific duties in exchange for compensation, which, in this situation, includes both regular wages and vacation time earned.

Due to a contract being created, it is critical that you clearly state your vacation policy. The policy should include how much vacation you offer and the rate at which vacation days are earned. The policy should also state whether an employee earns vacation days beginning on the first day of employment or after some period of time has passed.

Duration and Timing

You have the right to determine when employees may or may not take vacations and the length of the vacations.

You may institute a cap on vacation accrual, but the cap must be "reasonable." Under a reasonable cap plan, after an employee accrues a certain level of vacation, but does not take the time, vacation no longer accrues until the employee takes some of the previously accrued time. After the employee takes some vacation, he/she begins to accrue time at the usual rate.

The cap should be reasonable, and should be based on factors such as:

- The amount of vacation offered;
- The opportunity for employees to take vacation during the year; and
- The type of business or industry involved.

"Use it or Lose it Policies"

After an employee earns vacation, you can't take it away. California courts and the Labor Code prohibit a "use it or lose it" policy, in which employees lose earned vacation if it is not taken by a specific time.

You can't require employees to forfeit accrued vacation for any reason. You can require that your employees cash out their unused vacation once a year or that they stop accruing vacation after reaching a certain cap.

Floating Holidays/Personal Holidays/Personal Days

The way your vacation policy defines floating holidays/personal holidays/personal days determines how you need to treat the time off. You must treat time off associated with an event, such as an employee's anniversary of his/her hire date, as a holiday (see "Paid Holidays" on page 102). You must treat time off that an employee may take any time and for any reason as vacation (see "Vacation" on page 92).

You may place a cap on the accrual of these days off. But you must give employees reasonable opportunity to take the days off so that they can stay below the cap.

Accrued Vacation and Final Pay

When an employee leaves, you must pay out any accrued but unused vacation to the employee at the same time as the final paycheck. See "Calculating a Final Paycheck" in Chapter 9, page 314.

Paid Sick Leave

With the enactment of the Healthy Workplaces, Healthy Families Act of 2014, California became the second state in the nation to provide mandatory paid sick leave (PSL).

Eligibility Requirements

The paid sick leave law applies to private and public employers regardless of size. There is no small employer carve out.

All employees who, on or after July 1, 2015, have worked in California for the same employer for 30 or more days within a year from the commencement of employment will be entitled to paid sick leave. Part-time and full-time employees are covered, as well as exempt and nonexempt employees.

Out-of-state employees can be covered if they spend enough time working in California. If a business is headquartered in Oregon but an employee routinely works in California for one week out of every month, the employee will be covered under the paid sick leave law because he/she will be working in California for 30 or more days in one year.

 There are several narrow exemptions from the PSL law. Employers with questions regarding whether they are covered should consult legal counsel.

Accrual Methods

Employers have several different methods for providing PSL to employees; four different accrual methods and one lump-sum approach.

Statutory accrual method. Under the statutory accrual method, employees earn one hour of PSL for every 30 hours worked. Both regular and overtime hours are counted toward the accrual rate of one hour for every 30 hours worked. Employees exempt under the administrative, executive or professional exemption are deemed to work 40 hours a week, but if they don't, then accrual will be based on their normal workweek.

Optional accrual method that provides employees with no less than 24 hours by the 120th day. An employer may use a different accrual method, other than one hour for each 30 hours worked, if the accrual is on a regular basis so that the employee will have no less than 24 hours of accrued sick leave by the 120th calendar day of employment, or each calendar year or in each 12-month period.

Alternative accrual for new hires. An employer may use an accrual method other than the statutory accrual method of one hour for every 30 hours worked if the employer provides no less than 24 hours or three days of paid sick leave that is available to use by the completion of the 120th calendar day of employment. This option applies only to paid sick leave — not paid time off (PTO) — and the time must be provided by the 120th calendar day of employment.

Pre-Existing Employer Policy (policy in effect prior to January 1, 2015). If your organization already had a policy that provided paid sick leave or PTO to a class of employees before January 1, 2015, you can continue using your pre-existing accrual method instead of the statutory accrual method of one hour per 30 hours worked, as long as the accrual method meets certain requirements.

Accrual under the pre-existing policy must be on a regular basis and meet both of the following requirements:

- An employee has no less than one day or eight (8) hours of accrued sick leave or PTO within three months of employment, each calendar year or each 12-month period.

- The employee was eligible to earn at least three days or 24 hours of sick leave or PTO within nine months of employment.

Employers can't change the pre-January 1, 2015, accrual method under this option. If an employer makes modifications to the accrual method in the pre-existing policy, the employer will be required to select from one of the other accrual options or the lump-sum method. Employers can, however, increase the accrual rate.

"Lump-sum" method. Under the lump-sum method, employees do not accrue paid sick leave. Instead, the employer places the full amount of leave (three days/24 hours) in the employee's leave bank at the beginning of each year of employment, calendar year or 12-month period.

Under the lump-sum method, employers do not need to track accrual and there is no carryover from year-to-year. Instead of having sick leave carry over to the next year, any time left in the employee's leave bank at the end of the 12-month period goes away and the employee simply gets three new sick days/24 hours placed into his or her leave bank at the beginning of the following 12-month period.

PSL and Nontraditional Schedules

Some employers have questions relating to how to provide "24 hours or three days" of PSL when employees don't work a traditional eight-hour day schedule. For example, what about workers with an alternative workweek schedule of four, 10-hour days? Or part-time employees who work six-hour shifts?

The Labor Commissioner issued an opinion letter to address such questions. The Opinion Letter clarifies that the accrual and usage method most beneficial to the employee is advised.

For example, if an employee works 10-hour days, that employee will get three days or 30 hours of paid sick time. Or, if an employee works six-hour days, he/she will get four days or 24 hours of paid sick time.

Limits or Caps

Employees can't start using accrued paid sick days until the 90th day of employment, after which the employee can use paid sick leave as it is accrued.

If you use one of the accrual methods, accrued paid sick days will carry over to the following year of employment. The carry-over provision allows an employee to have paid sick days available at the start of the next year, depending on how much he/she has already used and accrued.

However, you can cap the employee's total accrual amount at 48 hours/six days. If an employer does not cap the accrual amount, a full-time employee (40 hours per week with no overtime) could potentially accrue more than 69 hours of PSL per year under the statutory accrual method, and be allowed to carry that over to the next year.

You can also limit the amount of paid sick days an employee can use in each year of employment to 24 hours/three days.

 If you choose to impose any of these limits on PSL, make sure that your policy clearly explains what limits and/or caps you put in place and communicate that policy to employees.

You can choose to have a more generous plan, allowing the employee to use and accrue more than the minimum amounts required under the Act.

Importantly, you can avoid having to calculate the accrual and the carry-over amounts by using the "lump-sum method" providing the full amount of leave (24 hours or three days) to the employee at the beginning of each year of employment, calendar year, or each 12-month period.

Usage

An employee can use paid sick time for an existing health condition or preventive care for themselves or a "family member." Family member has a broader definition than the current one found in the Family and Medical Leave Act/California Family Rights Act (FMLA/CFRA).

Under the PSL law, a family member is a:

- Child
- Parent (or parent-in-law)
- Spouse or registered domestic partner

- Grandparent (outside of FMLA/CFRA laws)

- Grandchild (outside of FMLA/CFRA laws)

- Sibling (outside of FMLA/CFRA laws)

An employee who is a victim of domestic violence, sexual assault or stalking may also use PSL.

PSL must be provided upon an employee's verbal or written request. If the need for paid sick leave is foreseeable, an employee must provide reasonable advance notice. If not, the employee must provide notice as soon as practicable. You can't require an employee to search for or find a replacement worker for the days off.

Unless certification is required pursuant to another leave law, no provision in the PSL law allows an employer to require medical certification for paid sick time. According to the Department of Industrial Relations, an employer can't condition taking paid sick leave on a doctor's note. Moreover, an employer who denies leave because an employee failed to provide details about the leave can end up facing a claim for violating the PSL law.

An employee may determine how much paid sick leave he/she needs to use. An employer, however, can set a "reasonable minimum increment," not to exceed two hours, for the use of paid sick leave.

Paying Employees

Paid sick leave must be paid no later than the next payday for the next regular payroll period after the sick leave was taken. The PSL amendments clarified the methods for paying employees who use their paid sick time.

Employers can use any one of the following three methods to calculate how to pay employees who take paid sick time:

- Calculate paid sick time for a nonexempt employee in the same manner as the "regular rate of pay" for the workweek in which sick leave is taken, regardless of whether the employee actually works overtime in that workweek

- Calculate paid sick time for a nonexempt employee by "dividing the employee's total wages, not including overtime premium pay, by the employee's total hours worked in the full pay periods of the prior 90 days of employment"

- Calculate paid sick time for an exempt employee in the same manner as wages are calculated for other forms of paid leave time

Documentation and Notice Requirements

The paid sick leave law contains several notice and posting requirements:

1. Pay Stub Notice: You must provide an employee with a written notice setting forth the amount of paid sick leave available to the employee each pay period. You can either provide this notice to the employee on the already required itemized wage statement or in a separate written document provided to the employee with the payment of wages.

   Employers with unlimited leave policies are in compliance if they note "unlimited" on employee pay stubs or in the separate written document.

2. The *Wage and Employment Notice (Labor Code section 2810.5)* contains information about an employee's right to accrue and use paid sick leave and about employee protections under the paid sick leave law. Employers are required to provide information about paid sick leave to all new hires and existing employees.

3. Poster: The Labor Commissioner produced a required poster advising employees of their sick leave rights. This poster must be placed in a conspicuous location. The poster is included in CalChamber's *2017 California and Federal Labor Law Poster*, which can be purchased at *store.calchamber.com*.

Recordkeeping Requirements

You will need to keep records that document the number of hours that employees worked and paid sick days accrued and used by the employees. You need to keep these records for at least three years. If you do not keep adequate records, there is a presumption that the employee is entitled to the maximum number of hours accruable.

An employer is not obligated to inquire into or record the purposes for which an employee uses paid leave or PTO.

Paid Sick Leave and Final Pay

Unlike unused, accrued vacation, which is treated like wages, paid sick leave does not need to be paid out at the end of employment. However, if you combine the sick leave and vacation into a paid time off (PTO) policy, you will have to follow the rules relating to vacation and PTO, including paying out accrued but unused PTO upon termination.

Previously accrued and unused paid sick days must be reinstated if an employee leaves employment and then is rehired within one year, and the rehired employee must be allowed to use those previously accrued sick days and begin accruing additional paid sick days upon rehire.

Employers are **not** required to reinstate any PTO that is paid out to an employee at the time of separation.

Local Ordinances

In addition to the California PSL law, many cities have passed ordinances that also require paid sick leave benefits. Employers in cities with PSL ordinances will need to review them carefully.

Many of the local PSL ordinances provide more generous benefits and protections in some areas, while the state law is more generous in others. You will have to give whichever provision or benefit is more generous to the employee.

For a comparison of state and local paid sick leave laws, see the *Comparison of California State and Local Paid Sick Leave Laws* chart in your online formspack, described in detail in "Online Forms" on page 12.

Cities that have PSL laws include, but are not limited to:

- Emeryville
- Long Beach (applies to the hospitality industry, specifically hotels with more than 100 beds)
- Los Angeles
- Oakland
- San Diego
- San Francisco
- Santa Monica

 Local PSL ordinances also contain posting and notice requirements that employers must comply with.

Penalties for Noncompliance

The paid sick leave law forbids employers from denying employees the right to use accrued paid sick days. You can't discriminate or retaliate against an employee for using or attempting to use accrued sick days, filing a complaint or cooperating in an investigation alleging a violation of the paid sick leave law.

You face stiff fines and penalties for not providing sick days, ranging from $50 to $4,000 aggregate. In addition, you can be required to compensate the state up to $50 for each day or portion of a day where a violation occurs or continues. This sum can be assessed for each employee and there is no maximum aggregate. There is also fine for willfully violating the posting requirement of up to $100 for each offense.

The paid sick leave law authorizes the Labor Commissioner or the Attorney General to bring a civil action to enforce the law and to seek financial relief on behalf of any employee, including back pay, payment of sick days unlawfully withheld, penalties, liquidated damages, attorneys' fees and costs.

Isolated, unintentional payroll errors or notice errors that are clerical or inadvertent mistakes will not be considered violations.

Other Benefits

Any sick leave payment you provide to your employees can reduce the amount of SDI benefits they receive. For more information, see "State Disability Insurance (SDI)" on page 134.

Pregnant employees must be allowed to use accrued sick leave during PDL. For more information, see "Pregnancy Disability Leave" on page 87.

Kin Care

Under California's kin care law, if you offer accrued sick leave or PTO, you must also allow employees to take up to half of their annual accrued sick leave or PTO for "kin care."

California's kin care law now conforms to the mandatory PSL law and allows employees to use kin care for the same purposes specified in the mandatory PSL law. The kin care law uses the same definition of "family member" as the PSL law. For more information, see "Usage" on page 97.

Kin care may still apply in certain situations. To the extent an employer provides optional sick leave or PTO beyond what is required under the mandatory PSL law, the employer may be able to limit employees to only using half of that additional sick leave to care for family members as defined in the kin care law.

Denying an employee the right to take leave for kin care or discriminating against an employee who exercises this right can create liability. This includes reinstating an employee to a previous position, and paying back wages, other damages and attorneys' fees.

You can't discipline, discharge, demote or suspend an employee for taking time off for kin care. You also can't count time off for kin care against an employee in accordance with any absence control policy you may have.

Paid Time Off

Some employers choose to lump various combinations of vacation, sick leave, holidays and personal days and/or floating holidays together into a benefit called "paid time off" (PTO). This allows employees a certain number of days off per year to use for planned and unplanned days off for illness, vacation, holidays and personal needs.

Though PTO is an acceptable benefit, be aware that California law treats the entire sum of accrued PTO like accrued vacation time because PTO is not tied to a specific event and may be taken at whatever time the employee chooses. For more information, see "Vacation" on page 92.

You must pay out the entire amount of accrued but unused PTO at the termination of the employment relationship. If you offer PTO, you must allow employees to use half of their annual PTO accrual for kin care.

Paid Holidays

You are not required to offer employees paid time off for holidays, but many employers do so as an employment benefit. If you do offer paid holidays, you may choose the holidays that you observe.

Common holidays include New Year's Day, Presidents' Day, Memorial Day, the Fourth of July, Labor Day, Thanksgiving and the Friday after, and Christmas.

At the beginning of each year, announce which holidays you will grant, if any, and if you will pay for the time. You may need to accommodate religious holidays in certain circumstances (see "Religion" in Chapter 7, page 268).

Eligibility Requirements

You also may determine eligibility requirements for paid holidays. For example, you can require that nonexempt employees be employed for some specified period of time before being eligible for holiday pay. All similarly situated employees should receive the same holiday benefits.

Pay and Benefits During Paid Holidays

The law doesn't require you to pay nonexempt employees for holiday time, although many employers do.

Exempt employees must be paid if they are ready, willing and able to work and no work is available, such as on a holiday when the company is shut down. You cannot withhold holiday pay from an exempt employee as you would for a nonexempt employee. Exempt employees who perform any work during the workweek in which a holiday occurs must be paid their full weekly salary, whether or not they work on the holiday.

If you provide paid holidays, you will need to explain what will happen if an employee is required to work on a day you designate as a paid holiday. The courts interpret the policy of giving a paid day off as a contract to do so. Therefore, you must make up the lost benefit to the employee in some manner.

Certain leaves may have an affect on holidays:

- "Pregnancy Disability Leave" on page 87
- "Family and Medical Leave" on page 79
- "Disability Leave" on page 104

Holidays and Final Pay

Employees can't accrue or vest holiday pay. You don't need to pay a departing employee for any future holidays.

Paid holidays must be distinguished from "floating holidays" (which is paid time off that an employee can use at any time for any reason). Because an employee can take a floating holiday at any time, a floating holiday is treated like PTO or vacation. The floating holiday time must accrue, vest and must be paid out at termination. For more information, see "Floating Holidays/Personal Holidays/Personal Days" on page 94.

Disability Leave

State and federal disability laws require covered employers to reasonably accommodate the disability of any individual if the employer knows of the disability. A leave of absence could be one form of a reasonable accommodation.

Employers must engage in the interactive process to determine what type of reasonable accommodation would enable an employee to perform the essential functions of a job.

Eligibility Requirements

Certain leaves for disability are mandated by law. See "Pregnancy Disability Leave" on page 87 and "Family and Medical Leaves" on page 79.

A leave of absence for an employee with a disability may be a reasonable accommodation if the leave is likely to be effective in allowing an employee to return to work at the end of the leave and if the leave does not create an undue hardship for the employer.

An employee who is disabled and can perform the essential functions of his/her job with or without reasonable accommodation is eligible.

Check to see if you're covered under the FMLA, CFRA, FEHA or the ADA. See "Glossary of Terms, Laws and Agencies" on page 331 and "Does This Employment Law Apply to Me?" in Chapter 1, page 1 for details about these laws.

For information on workers' compensation, see "Workers' Compensation" in Chapter 4, page 139.

Pay During Leave

Your policy dictates whether an employee is allowed to use any accrued but unused vacation, sick leave or paid time off (PTO).

Duration and Timing

Disability leave will most likely start if one of your employees becomes disabled. He/she will notify you of the need for leave either verbally or in writing. Although you are not required to provide an indefinite leave of absence, a disability-related leave of absence could last weeks or months.

When you learn that an employee has a disability that may require reasonable accommodation, engage in the interactive process to determine a reasonable accommodation.

You must make a reasonable accommodation to the known physical or mental limitations of a qualified applicant or employee with a disability unless you can show that the accommodation would cause an undue hardship on the operation of your business.

 If the need for leave may be related to a reasonable accommodation for a disability or if you have any questions on whether an employee's impairment requires accommodation, consult with legal counsel.

The Interactive Process

The Fair Employment and Housing Act (FEHA) requires you to engage in a timely, good-faith interactive process to determine effective reasonable accommodations for an employee.

The interactive process is a collaborative effort between the employer and the employee to determine what accommodation, if any, can help the employee perform the essential functions of his/her position. The employer and the employee must exchange essential information during the interactive process.

The law does not explain to what extent you must go in engaging in a timely, good-faith interactive process. At a minimum, you should meet with the employee to discuss possible reasonable accommodations and ask the employee for a note from his/her treating physician stating that the employee has a medical condition and, preferably, any of the physician's proposed accommodations.

Be open to the employee's suggestions, and be willing to try various accommodations in an attempt to find one that is successful. Document the process that you and the employee go through.

Employer Responsibilities

To comply with FEHA, an employer may either grant the employee or applicant's requested accommodation or reject the initial accommodation and initiate discussion regarding alternatives.

In consultation with the employee and in conjunction with a review of the employee's job description, the employer should identify potential accommodations for the employee, and consider the effectiveness of the accommodations to allow the employee to perform essential functions and to the employee's preference in implementing an accommodation.

If the employer considers reassigning the employee to another position, the employer may ask an employee about his or her qualifications for that position. This does not mean that an employer must put an employee into a position that he/she is not qualified for. Also, an employer is not required to continue to employ the person on an open-ended leave of absence while waiting for an appropriate vacant position to arise.

For more information on accommodations related to pregnancy, see "Pregnancy Disability Leave" on page 87.

Employee Responsibilities

Employees must cooperate in good faith in the reasonable accommodation process and provide medical documentation where a disability or need for accommodation is not obvious and the documentation is requested by the employer.

Employees must also give their employers information about education or work history that might qualify them for alternative positions.

 If you need to fire an employee on disability leave, seek legal counsel.

Other Benefits

If you determine that a disability leave is appropriate, the employee may use up any accrued but unused vacation, sick leave or PTO.

The employee may be eligible for SDI benefits. For more details, see "Required and Optional Benefits" in Chapter 4, page 131.

Leave Interactions

California and federal laws mandate employers to provide several different types of leave, some of which overlap. This section provides an overview of the ways FMLA/CFRA, PDL and disability leaves interact.

If you need help understanding the exact impact on your company, consult legal counsel.

 You must provide notice to the employee taking the leave as soon as possible before he/she takes the leave, or once you learn the employee is on a protected type of leave that runs concurrently with FMLA and/or CFRA. **Concurrently** means that as a week of leave type "A" is used up, so is a week of leave type "B."

You may be required to provide employees a leave of absence as a reasonable accommodation. For more information, see "Disability Discrimination" in Chapter 7, page 272.

Table 6. Types Of Leaves and Benefits and How They Interact

This Leave	Runs Concurrently With	Under These Conditions
PDL (see page 87)	FMLA	Always, if you notify the employee
	CFRA	Never
	Workers' Compensation	Never

Table 6. Types Of Leaves and Benefits and How They Interact *(continued)*

This Leave	Runs Concurrently With	Under These Conditions
FMLA (see page 79)	CFRA	For all leaves except: • Leave due to pregnancy disability • Leave to care for a registered domestic partner; see "Duration and Timing of Family and Medical Leave" on page 82 • Leave due to a qualifying exigency related to a family member's service in the military or to care for a servicemember, see "Family and Medical Leaves" on page 79
	Workers' Compensation	If there is a work-related injury or illness, the employee can't work, and you notify the employee
	PDL	If the employee takes leave due to pregnancy disability and you notify the employee
CFRA (see page 79)	FMLA	For all leaves, except leave due to pregnancy disability, to care for a registered domestic partner or military related; see "Duration and Timing of Family and Medical Leave" on page 82
	Workers' Compensation	If there is a work-related injury or illness, the employee can't work, and you notify the employee
	PDL	Never
Workers' Compensation (see "Workers' Compensation" in Chapter 4, page 139)	FMLA/CFRA	Always, if there is a work-related injury or illness, the employee can't work, and you notify the employee
	PDL	Never

Organ and Bone Marrow Donor Leave

All employers with 15 or more employees must provide leave for employees who choose to donate organs and bone marrow.

Eligibility Requirements

The employee must take the leave to donate an organ or bone marrow to another person. The employee must provide you with written verification of the need for donation leave. The verification must state that the employee is a bone marrow or organ donor and that the donation is medically necessary. The employee must have worked for you for at least 90 days prior to taking leave.

Duration and Timing of Leave

Bone marrow donors may take up to five business days of leave in a one-year period. Organ donors may take up to 30 business days of leave in a one-year period.

The "one-year period" starts the day the leave begins and consists of 12 consecutive months.

Pay and Benefits During Leave

Employees who take leave to donate bone marrow or an organ are entitled to be paid for the full leave, unless the employer's policy requires the use of vacation or sick leave.

You may require that bone marrow donors use up to five days of paid sick leave, vacation time or paid time off. You may require organ donors to use two weeks of paid sick leave, vacation time or paid time off. After that, or if the employee does not have any accrued time, the employer must provide paid leave up to the time limits provided.

If you will require the use of paid sick leave/ vacation/paid time off, be sure to state the requirement in your employee handbook policy.

The employer must continue the employee's health benefits coverage and pay for the coverage during the leave of absence. The time off for donor leave is not a break in service for the purpose of salary adjustments, sick leave, vacation, paid time off, annual leave or seniority.

Donor leave does not run concurrently with leave under the CFRA or the FMLA.

Employees returning from donor leave must be reinstated to the position held when the leave began, or to a position with equivalent seniority status, employee benefits, pay, and other terms and conditions of employment.

You cannot terminate, discriminate or retaliate against an employee for exercising their right to use this type of protected leave.

Crime Victims' Leave

State law creates protected time off for employees who are victims of crime and who meet the eligibility requirements to take crime victims' leave to attend judicial proceedings related to the crime.

State law also creates protected leave for crime victims to attend any proceeding in which the rights of the victim are at issue (for more information on this leave, see "Leave for a Proceeding Involving Victims' Rights" on page 112).

Leave to Attend Judicial Proceedings Related to the Crime

All employers must grant leave for eligible employees to attend judicial proceedings related to a:

- Violent felony.

- Serious felony.

- Felony theft or felony embezzlement.

Eligibility Requirements

You must allow an employee to take time off from work to attend judicial proceedings related to one of the above crimes if the employee is:

- A victim of a crime

- A crime victim's immediate family member

- A crime victim's registered domestic partner

- A child of a registered domestic partner who is a crime victim

Immediate family members include the employee's:

- Spouse
- Child or stepchild
- Brother or stepbrother
- Sister or stepsister
- Mother or stepmother
- Father or stepfather

Pay and Benefits During Leave

This leave is unpaid. Employees may choose to use accrued paid vacation, PTO or sick leave.

Duration and Timing of the Leave

An employee notifies you in some way that he/she, or someone listed in the section above, is a crime victim. There are no restrictions on the length of time. However, the time off from work must be used to attend judicial proceedings related to the violent crime.

Notice Requirements

Before taking leave to attend the judicial proceeding, the employee must give you a copy of the notice of each scheduled proceeding. These notices are provided to the victim by the pertinent government agency. Documentation can come from any of the following sources:

- The court or government agency setting the hearing
- The district attorney or prosecuting attorney's office
- The victim or witness assistance office advocating on the victim's behalf

When advance notice is not feasible or if an unscheduled absence occurs, you can't take action against the employee if, within a reasonable time after the absence, he/she provides documentation from one of the above sources confirming the judicial proceeding.

You cannot terminate, discriminate or retaliate against an employee for exercising their right to use this type of protected leave.

Leave for a Proceeding Involving Victims' Rights

California law provides protections for crime victims to take time off from work, at the victim's request, to appear in court to be heard at any proceeding in which a right of the victim is at issue.

Labor Code section 230.5 prohibits an employer from discriminating against an employee who takes such time off. A violation of this leave law entitles the employee to reinstatement and reimbursement for lost wages and work benefits. Refusal to reinstate someone wrongfully fired under this law is a misdemeanor.

Eligibility Requirements

For this particular leave, you are required to provide time off from work to a "victim," or to an employee whose immediate family member is a victim. "Victim" is defined as "any person who suffers direct or threatened physical, psychological, or financial harm as a result of the commission or attempted commission of a crime or a delinquent act."

"Immediate family member" includes the employee's:

- Spouse
- Parent
- Child
- Sibling
- Guardian

The employee, or the employee's family member, must be a victim of one of the following covered offenses:

- Vehicular manslaughter while intoxicated
- Felony child abuse likely to produce great bodily harm or a death
- Assault resulting in the death of a child under eight years of age
- Felony domestic violence
- Felony physical abuse of an elder or dependent adult
- Felony stalking
- Solicitation for murder
- A serious felony, such as kidnapping, rape or assault

- Hit-and-run causing death or injury

- Felony driving under the influence causing injury

- Specified sexual assault

Pay and Benefits During Leave

Leave to attend proceedings involving victims' rights is unpaid. Employees can use available vacation or personal leave while on leave. Unlike crime victims' leave, sick leave is not specifically included.

Duration and Timing of Leave

The leave can be of any length.

Unlike crime victims' leave, this leave can be initiated at the victim's request and does not need to be initiated by a notice from a government agency.

The law protects time off to attend any "proceeding," including any delinquency proceeding, involving a post-arrest release decision, plea, sentencing, post-conviction release decision; or any proceeding in which a right of the victim is at issue.

Notice Requirements

Before taking this type of leave, the employee must give you reasonable advance notice of his/her intention to take the time off.

When advance notice is not feasible, or if an unscheduled absence occurs, you cannot take action against the employee if he/she, within a reasonable time after the absence, provides you with certification.

Any one of the following forms will be sufficient:

- A police report indicating that the employee was a victim of one of the specified offenses

- A court order protecting or separating the employee from the perpetrator of one of the specified offenses

- Documentation verifying that the employee was undergoing treatment for physical or mental injuries or abuse as a result of being a victim of one of the specified offenses. Documentation must be accepted from a:

  - Medical professional

- Domestic violence advocate

- Victims of sexual assault advocate

- Health care provider

- Counselor

You cannot terminate, discriminate or retaliate against an employee who is absent to attend judicial proceedings involving his/her victim rights.

Domestic Violence, Sexual Assault and Stalking Victims' Leave

An employee who is victimized by domestic violence, sexual assault or stalking may request time off from work to attend legal proceedings or medical treatment, and to ensure his/her health, safety or welfare, or that of his/her children.

Employers must maintain the confidentiality of any employee who requests leave as a result of domestic violence, sexual assault or stalking.

In addition, state law contains a reasonable accommodation requirement for employers with employees who are victims of domestic violence, sexual assault or stalking. Reasonable accommodations under the statute may include implementation of safety measures.

You cannot terminate, discriminate or retaliate against an employee for exercising their right to use this type of protected leave.

Eligibility Requirements

An eligible employee is any employee who is victimized by domestic violence, sexual assault or stalking.

All employers, regardless of size, must provide eligible employees with time off work to appear in court to comply with a subpoena or other court order or to serve as a witness in any judicial proceeding.

Employers must also provide employees with time off to obtain or attempt to obtain any relief, such as a temporary restraining order, or other court-ordered relief to help ensure the health, safety or welfare of the employee or his/her child.

Employers with 25 or more employees must also provide eligible employees with time off for the following reasons:

- To seek medical attention for injuries caused by domestic violence, sexual assault or stalking

- To obtain services from a domestic violence shelter, program or rape crisis center as a result of domestic violence sexual assault or stalking

- To obtain psychological counseling related to domestic violence sexual assault or stalking

- To participate in safety planning and take other actions to increase safety from future domestic violence, sexual assault or stalking, including temporary or permanent relocation time off from work

Pay and Benefits During Leave

Under California's mandatory paid sick leave law, employees who are victims of domestic violence, sexual assault or stalking may use available sick time to attend legal proceedings or seek medical treatment.

Additionally, employees may use available vacation, personal leave or PTO.

Notice Requirements

New 2017

AB 2337 requires employers with 25 or more employees to provide employees with written notice about the rights of victims of domestic violence, sexual assault and stalking to take protected time off for medical treatment or legal proceedings.

A required form must be given to all new hires and to other employees upon request. The Labor Commissioner is required to develop the form on or before **July 1, 2017.** When the form becomes available, it will be part of your online formspack, described in detail in "Online Forms" on page 12.

Employers are not required to comply with this section until the Labor Commissioner posts the new form on its website.

If feasible, your employee will provide you with reasonable advance notice of his/her intent to take time off. If your employee is unable to provide reasonable advance notice and an unscheduled absence occurs, you may not take any action against the employee.

However, the employee must provide one of the following within a reasonable time after the absence:

- A police report regarding the domestic violence, sexual assault or stalking

- A court order protecting or separating the employee from the abuser, or other evidence from the court or prosecuting attorney that the employee appeared in court

- Documentation from a medical professional, domestic violence advocate, health advocate, health care provider or counselor that the employee underwent treatment for injuries resulting from domestic violence

Duration and Timing of the Leave

There is no limit on the amount of leave that can be taken to attend legal proceedings. Leave for medical treatment does not give an employee the right to take leave that exceeds or is in addition to the leave available under FMLA (12 weeks in a 12-month period).

Time Off for Jury/Witness Duty

According to state law, a person called to serve on a jury or participate as a witness in a trial must do so, unless the court releases him/her from service.

California law requires that all employers provide employees with time off to serve as a juror or as a witness. The duration of leave depends on how long the court proceeding lasts, or how long the employee's responsibilities as a witness last.

Your employee will receive a summons for jury duty or a subpoena to appear in court as a witness. Your employee then gives you notice that he/she received a summons for jury duty or a subpoena to appear in court as a witness.

Time off for jury duty or to serve as a witness is unpaid. However, an employee can use available vacation or PTO while taking this leave. You may not terminate or discriminate against any employee who takes time off to serve as a juror or a witness, provided he/she gives reasonable notice.

Military Service Leave

All employers must provide this leave. When your employees serve in the military during their employment, you must either hold their jobs or re-employ them in similar positions when they return.

You cannot terminate, discriminate or retaliate against an employee for exercising their right to use this type of protected leave.

The Veterans Benefits Improvement Act requires all employers to provide a notice of rights under the Uniformed Services Employment and Reemployment Rights Act (USERRA) to all persons entitled to rights and benefits under USERRA. The only official version of this poster is provided in English because the federal Department of Labor (DOL) stated that all military service personnel must be able to read and understand English.

The most efficient way to comply is to post the notice in a prominent place where employees customarily check for such information.

 The notice is part of CalChamber's ***California and Federal Labor Law Poster***. You can purchase this product, available in English or Spanish, at ***store.calchamber.com***.

Eligibility Requirements

An eligible employee is virtually anyone absent from work due to "service in the uniformed services." "Service" includes active duty, active duty for training, initial active duty for training, inactive duty training, full-time National Guard duty and examinations to determine fitness for duty.

"Uniformed services" include:

- The Army, Navy, Air Force, Marine Corps and Coast Guard (and the Reserves for each of those branches)

- The Army National Guard, Air National Guard and commissioned corps of the Public Health Service

- The National Disaster Medical System

- Any other category of persons designated by the president in time of war or emergency

Pay and Benefits During the Leave

This leave is unpaid.

The employee is entitled to all rights and benefits as if he/she had remained continuously employed. The employee can also choose COBRA-like health care coverage.

Existing California law provides protections and return rights for members of the National Guard ordered into active state service for emergency purposes and for reservists called to active duty.

These protections are extended to California employees who are members of the National Guard in another state and are called into service by the other state or by the president, causing them to leave a private job in California.

Duration and Timing of Leave

Military service leave may take almost any length, with a maximum of a cumulative five years. Ask your employee to notify you as soon as he/she learns of the need for military leave.

When the service is over, he/she will provide notice of intent to return. Under most circumstances, you must reinstate the employee. For exceptions, see the USERRA website at *www.dol.gov/elaws/userra.htm*.

Military Spouse Leave

State law provides for a leave of absence for military personnel spouses if employed by a covered employer. All California employers with 25 or more employees must provide an unpaid leave of absence for employees whose spouses are in the military and on leave from deployment during a time of military conflict.

You cannot terminate, discriminate or retaliate against an employee for exercising their right to use this type of protected leave. You must reinstate any employee to his/her position upon return from military spouse leave.

Eligibility Requirements

To be eligible for the leave, an employee must work an average of 20 hours or more per week and have a spouse in the United States Armed Forces, National Guard or Army Reserve who was deployed during a period of military conflict.

Pay and Benefits During the Leave

This leave is unpaid.

You can allow an employee to use accrued sick time, vacation or PTO during this leave, but you can't require him/her to do so.

Duration and Timing of the Leave

The leave lasts for up to 10 days. The employee must provide the employer with notice within two business days of receiving official notice that their spouse will be on leave from deployment.

School and Child Care Activities Leave

Parents or guardians of a child in school may occasionally need to participate in school activities, such as parent/teacher conferences, field trips or meetings.

California law requires employers with 25 or more employees at the same location to provide employees with time off to participate in certain school or child care activities.

An employer cannot terminate, or in any way discriminate against, an employee for taking this time off. An employer who violates this law may be required to rehire the employee and/or reimburse the employee for lost wages and work benefits. Willful failure to rehire can lead to a penalty of three times the amount of lost wages and work benefits.

Eligibility Requirements

An eligible employee is any employee who is the parent, guardian, step-parent, foster parent, grandparent or a person who stands *in loco parentis* to a child who is in grades K–12 or who is with a licensed day-care provider.

An employee can take time off to:

- Find, enroll, or re-enroll his or her child in a school or with a licensed child care provider;

- Participate in activities of the school or licensed child care provider; or

- Address a "child care provider or school emergency."

A "child care provider or school emergency" means that the employee's child cannot remain in a school or with a child care provider due to one of the following:

- The school or child care provider has requested that the child be picked up, or has an attendance policy (excluding planned holidays) that prohibits the child from attending or requires the child to be picked up from the school or child care provider;

- Behavioral or discipline problems;

- Closure or unexpected unavailability of the school or child care provider, excluding planned holidays; or

- A natural disaster, including, but not limited to, fire, earthquake or flood.

Pay and Benefits During the Leave

School activities leave is unpaid.

 Employees can use paid sick leave under the Healthy Workplaces, Healthy Families Act for this time off.

If the employee is on company paid leave, then sick pay, vacation and PTO continue to accrue. If on unpaid leave, they only accrue if your other policies require.

Duration and Timing of the Leave

You must provide up to 40 hours off per calendar year for school activities. You can limit the use of this time off to no more than eight hours in any one calendar month.

However, you can't limit the use of this time off to eight hours per month when the time off is necessary to address a childcare provider or school emergency.

Notice Requirements

If an absence for school or child care activities is planned, the employee must give reasonable prior notice. If there is a child care provider or school emergency, the employee need only give notice.

You can require employees to provide documentation from the school or child care provider that the employee was participating in school or child care activities. Acceptable documentation is any written verification of participation that the school or licensed child care provider deems appropriate and reasonable.

School Appearances Leave

Parents or guardians of a child in school may need time off work to appear at school when a child has been suspended from school. All employers must provide employees with unpaid leave for this purpose.

You cannot terminate, discriminate or retaliate against an employee for exercising their right to use this type of protected leave.

The parent or guardian should receive a written notice from the school stating that they must attend a class. You can require a copy of the notice or some other certification from the school stating that the employee's presence is required.

Volunteer Civil Service and Training Leave

You may employ people who also volunteer to provide emergency services in times of crisis. They may be called away during work hours to help in an emergency or go through training.

You cannot terminate, threaten with termination, demote, suspend or otherwise discriminate against an employee who takes time off to engage in emergency civil service duty or training. An employee who suffers any of these consequences is entitled to reinstatement and reimbursement for lost wages and work benefits.

Time Off for Emergency Civil Service Duty

All employers must provide unpaid time off for employees who are required to perform emergency duty. The leave extends to volunteer firefighters, reserve police officers and emergency rescue personnel.

"Emergency rescue personnel" is defined as any person who is:

- An officer, employee or member of a fire department, fire protection or firefighting agency of the federal government, California state government, local government, special district or other public or municipal corporation or political subdivision of California

- An officer of a sheriff's department, police department or private fire department

- An officer, employee or member of a disaster medical response team sponsored or requested by the state

An employee who is a health care provider, as defined, is required to notify his/her employer when he/she is designated as emergency rescue personnel and also to notify the employer at the time that the employee learns that he/she will be deployed for emergency duty.

The leave lasts for the duration of the emergency duty. The leave is unpaid.

Time Off for Civil Service Training

If you employ 50 or more people, you must allow an employee who is a volunteer firefighter, reserve peace officer or emergency rescue personnel to take temporary leaves of absence, up to a total of 14 days per calendar year, to engage in fire, law enforcement or emergency rescue training. The leave is unpaid.

Civil Air Patrol Leave

California law requires all employers with more than 15 employees to provide leave to participate in Civil Air Patrol duty. The leave is not paid.

You cannot discriminate against or discharge an employee because of membership in the Civil Air Patrol. You cannot prevent the employee from performing service. Employees must be reinstated to the position held when the leave began, or to an equivalent position.

An eligible employee is any employee who is a volunteer member of the California Wing of the civilian auxiliary of the U.S. Air Force (Civil Air Patrol), responding to an emergency operation mission. The employee must have been employed for at least 90 days before the start of the leave.

Employees who take leave under this law can't be required to exhaust all accrued vacation, personal, sick, disability or other leave available to the employee.

The employer and employee can negotiate for the employer to maintain the benefits of the employee at the expense of the employer during the leave. The leave can't result in a loss of benefits accrued before the date on which the leave began.

An employee is entitled up to 10 days of leave per year. The leave for a single emergency mission can't exceed three days, unless the emergency is extended by the entity in charge of the operation and the extension of leave is approved by the employer.

Voting Leave

All employers must allow an employee up to two hours of paid time off to vote in a statewide election if the employee does not have sufficient time outside of work to do so.

Employees must notify you at least two working days in advance to arrange time off for voting. You can grant time off at the beginning or end of the employee's regular working shift, whichever allows the most free time for voting and the least time off from work.

You must grant up to two hours of leave on election days. The time off is paid. You also must post the voting leave requirements in a conspicuous place at least 10 days before every statewide election.

Bereavement Leave

When an employee experiences the death of a family member or friend, he/she may request time off for a funeral or for mourning. Bereavement leave is not required by law

Whether you provide this leave is entirely a matter of company policy. If you do provide this leave, your policy should communicate how much time is allowed, which family members are covered by your policy, whether the time off is paid, and what notice or documentation employees must provide.

You can determine eligibility requirements for this leave. You might designate bereavement leave as applicable only to family deaths, or you might extend it for other circumstances.

Personal Leaves of Absence

Employers are not legally required to provide time off for employees who want to take a leave of absence for personal reasons. Whether you grant a personal leave of absence is entirely a matter of company policy. If you do allow personal leaves, be consistent in how you apply your personal leave policy.

 If you provide this benefit for one employee, you set a precedent for other employees and could create the potential for a discrimination claim if you deny another employee's request for the same type of leave.

Minimum Compliance Elements

1. Hang your *2017 California and Federal Labor Law Poster* (available from *store.calchamber.com*), which includes mandatory postings that all employees and applicants must be able to see, in a prominent place (such as a break room). It includes the Healthy Workplaces, Healthy Families Act of 2014 Paid Sick Leave poster.

   If you have employees working in a city or county with a local minimum wage and/or paid sick leave ordinance, you may also need to post required local ordinances and provide additional notices to employees at the time of hire.

2. Provide employees with a written notice setting forth the amount of paid sick leave available to them each pay period. Also, the *Wage and Employment Notice (Labor Code section 2810.5)* needs to contain information about an employee's right to accrue and use paid sick leave and about employee protections. See "Paid Sick Leave" on page 94.

3. Give employees information on their workers' compensation, paid family leave and disability insurance benefits (all located in the *Required Notices Kit*, available at *store.calchamber.com*).

4. Pay particular attention to the overlapping requirements of pregnancy disability leave, family and medical leave and workers' compensation. For more information, see:

   - "Pregnancy Disability Leave" on page 87;

   - "Family and Medical Leaves" on page 79;

   - "Leave Interactions" on page 107; and

   - "Workers' Compensation" on page 139.

Forms and Checklists

The following table describes forms associated with leaves of absence.

 TIP You can find these forms in your online formspack, described in detail in "Online Forms" on page 12.

Table 7. Forms and Checklists

Notice Or Form	What Do I Use It For?	When Do I Use It?	Who Fills It Out?	Where Does It Go?
Certification of Health Care Provider for Employee Return to Work	To obtain physician or medical practitioner approval for the employee to return to work.	Just before the employee returns to work.	The employee's physician or medical practitioner.	Keep a copy in the employee's confidential medical file, separate from his/her personnel file.
Certification of Health Care Provider - Employee's or Family Member's Serious Health Condition	To obtain physician or medical practitioner certification that the employee or family member is disabled due to "a serious health condition."	At the time of the medical leave.	The patient's health care provider. (The patient could be either the employee or a family member.)	Keep a copy in the employee's confidential medical file, separate from his/her personnel file.
Certification of Health Care Provider for Pregnancy Disability Leave, Transfer Or Reasonable Accommodation	To obtain physician or medical practitioner certification that the employee requires a leave.	At the time of a disability leave related to pregnancy, childbirth or a related medical condition.	The employee's physician or medical practitioner.	Keep a copy in the employee's confidential medical file, separate from his/her personnel file.

Table 7. Forms and Checklists

Notice Or Form	What Do I Use It For?	When Do I Use It?	Who Fills It Out?	Where Does It Go?
COBRA Administration Guide	To ensure you use the proper, required forms relating to COBRA (20 or more employees) and Cal-COBRA (2 to 19 employees), as applicable.	Use when an employee is hired and refer back to it when a qualifying event occurs.	N/A	N/A
Employee Letter - PDL Only	To respond to notice of an employee's absence due to Pregnancy Disability Leave (PDL).	Respond within 10 calendar days of the request or no later than the following payday, whichever is sooner.	The employer.	Send a copy to the employee and keep a copy in the employee's confidential medical file, separate from his/her personnel file.
FMLA/CFRA Designation Notice	To notify the employee of the type of leave granted.	At the beginning of the leave.	The employer.	Send a copy to the employee and keep a copy in the employee's confidential medical file, separate from his/her personnel file.

Table 7. Forms and Checklists

Notice Or Form	What Do I Use It For?	When Do I Use It?	Who Fills It Out?	Where Does It Go?
FMLA/PDL - Designation Notice	To notify the employee of the type of leave granted.	At the beginning of the leave.	The employer.	Send a copy to the employee and keep a copy in the employee's confidential medical file, separate from her personnel file.
Leave Interaction	Use this form to determine the relation-ships among the various state-mandated leaves of absence and benefits during the time off.	When an employee considers a leave.	N/A	Your employee would also benefit from this information.
Military Spouse Request for Leave - 25 or More Employees	For employees to request mili-tary spouse leave in writing.	At the time an employee requests military spouse leave.	The employee.	In the employee's personnel file.
Request for Leave of Absence - FMLA/CFRA/ PDL	Give to employees who request or may need a leave of absence under FMLA, CFRA or PDL.	Provide this form when an employee requests a leave of absence or you recognize the need.	The employee.	The employee's personnel file - medical file if the request for leave is for the employee's own medical condi-tion.

Table 7. Forms and Checklists

Notice Or Form	What Do I Use It For?	When Do I Use It?	Who Fills It Out?	Where Does It Go?
Request for Leave of Absence - FMLA/CFRA/ PDL - Spanish	Give to employees who request or may need a leave of absence under FMLA, CFRA or PDL.	Provide this form when an employee requests a leave of absence or you recognize the need.	The employee.	The employee's personnel file - medical file if the request for leave is for the employee's own medical condition.
Temporary Modified Duty Agreement	To document a temporary modified duty assignment.	When an employee can't perform the essential functions of a job without accommodation.	The employee.	Keep a copy in the employee's confidential medical file, separate from his/her personnel file.
Wage and Employment Notice to Employees (Labor Code section 2810.5)	To notify employees about mandatory paid sick leave.	Provide this form to all nonexempt employees at the time of hire. If any change is made to the information on this form, notify employees of the change in writing within seven calendar days after the time a change was made unless notice is provided in another writing required by law within seven days of the change.	You do.	In your files.
Workers' Compensation Insurance Shopper's Checklist	Use this form to ask potential brokers and carriers important questions as you shop for a workers' compensation policy.	When shopping for a workers' compensation insurance policy.	N/A	In your files.

Where Do I Go for More Information?

CalChamber and federal and state government agencies offer a variety of resources to help you develop written employee policies.

Table 8. Additional Resources

For Information On	Check Out These Resources
General	From CalChamber: • *2017 California Labor Law Digest* • *Employee Handbook Creator* • *Required Notices Kit with Poster* • *www.hrcalifornia.com* • *store.calchamber.com*
Paid family leave	• *www.edd.ca.gov*
Military leave	• Veterans' Employment and Training Service "eLaws Advisor" *www.dol.gov/elaws/userra.htm* • Employer Support of the Guard and Reserve (ESGR) at *www.esgr.org/* 4800 Mark Center Dr., Suite 03E25 Alexandria, VA 22350-1200 (800) 336-4590 • Non-technical Resource Guide to the USERRA at *www.dol.gov/vets/whatsnew/userraguide0903.rtf* • *www.dol.gov/vets/programs/userra/main.htm*

TIP CalChamber also provides many ongoing and comprehensive educational opportunities for small business owners, HR beginners and experienced HR professionals alike. These include online training, webinars and special HR seminars. For more information, please visit our website at *store.calchamber.com*.

Chapter 4

Providing Benefits

This chapter describes mandatory and optional benefits, and guides you through the processes of administering and providing them. Make sure that you offer benefits evenly. Don't discriminate amongst your employees.

You'll get answers to questions about:

- Required and optional benefits
- Paid family leave
- State disability insurance
- Unemployment insurance
- Workers' compensation
- Commuter benefits

Required and Optional Benefits

Employers must offer certain benefits, such as Unemployment Insurance or State Disability Insurance. Certain benefits are required only for companies over a certain size. See "Does This Employment Law Apply to Me?" in Chapter 1, page 1.

California recognizes same-sex marriages as lawful and same-sex marriage is also lawful in all 50 states. In addition, it is unlawful to exclude same-sex spouses from the definition of "spouse" under federal law.

California employers should be aware that this impacts federal benefits, such as coverage under the Consolidated Omnibus Budget Reconciliation Act (COBRA) and eligibility for Employee Retirement Income Security Act (ERISA) benefit plans, for partners in same-sex marriages.

Employers have the option to offer extra benefits, such as health care and retirement plans. You must comply with certain legal guidelines that expand your employees' rights to use the optional benefits you offer. California and federal law regulate how you provide benefits.

Required Benefits

Under federal and California law, you must provide certain benefits to your employees:

- Paid Family Leave (PFL) Benefits, page 132
- State Disability Insurance (SDI), page 134
- Unemployment Insurance (UI), page 137
- Workers' Compensation, page 139
- Health care, if you are covered by the employer mandate of the Affordable Care Act, page 149

Optional Benefits

You have the option to offer a range of other benefits to your employees, at your discretion:

- Health care, if you are not covered by the employer mandate of the Affordable Care Act, page 149
- Voluntary disability insurance, page 150
- Bonuses, page 151
- Retirement and pension plans, page 151

Paid Family Leave Benefits

Employees may apply for wage replacement benefits under California's Paid Family Leave (PFL) program when they take a leave of absence to care for certain seriously ill family members or bond with a new baby.

Employers with one or more employees are covered by PFL. PFL is not a leave of absence. It does not give employees the right to take time off work.

California's Employment Development Department (EDD) administers the PFL program. Employers do not fund PFL; employee payroll deductions fund the program.

Eligibility Requirements

To be eligible for PFL benefits, an employee must suffer a wage loss because he/she is taking a leave of absence to:

- Care for a seriously ill child, spouse, parent, registered domestic partner, grandparent, grandchild, sibling or parent-in-law (a parent of a spouse or of a registered domestic partner)

- Bond with the employee's new child or the new child of the employee's spouse or domestic partner

- Bond with a child in connection with the adoption or foster care placement of the child with the employee, the employee's spouse or domestic partner

PFL does not give employees the right to take a leave. Applicable state and federal laws or your own policy determines whether the employee is eligible for a leave of absence.

The EDD determines eligibility and administers the benefit.

Duration and Timing of the Benefits

Employees who meet all of the eligibility requirements can receive PFL benefits for up to six weeks in a 12-month period. The weekly benefit amount is based on the employee's wages in the highest quarter of the employee's base period, and wage replacement benefits under PFL represent approximately 55 percent of the employee's regular wages.

There is a one-week waiting period before benefits begin. Employers must provide all new employees and employees absent for a qualifying reason with a copy of the *Paid Family Leave* pamphlet.

 Effective **January 1, 2018**, AB 908 increases the amount of PFL benefits an employee can receive from 55 percent of earnings to either 60 percent or 70 percent of earnings, depending on the employee's income. There still will be a maximum weekly benefit on the amount received. The new law also will remove the current seven-day waiting period that exists before an employee is eligible to receive PFL benefits.

 The notice is part of CalChamber's **Required Notices Kit**. You can purchase this product at **store.calchamber.com**.

When an employee files a PFL claim, the EDD will contact you and provide you with any paperwork required from you.

The law doesn't require you to hold the employee's job merely because he/she collects PFL benefits. However, other laws, such as the Family and Medical Leave Act (FMLA) and the California Family Rights Act (CFRA), may protect the employee's job.

PFL and Other Benefits

PFL covers loss of earnings not covered by workers' compensation and SDI benefits. If a person receives Unemployment Insurance benefits, he/she can't receive PFL benefits for the same period.

If the employee receives full replacement wages, such as sick leave and paid time off (PTO), then he/she is ineligible for PFL benefits during that time. Employers can coordinate sick leave and PTO benefits with the EDD to maximize PFL payments.

An employee receiving vacation pay doesn't affect PFL benefits. However, employers may require that employees take up to two weeks of accrued, unused vacation before PFL payments begin. The first week of vacation would be the seven-day waiting period for PFL payments.

For information about specific leave benefits, see "Required and Optional Benefits" on page 131.

State Disability Insurance (SDI)

California's State Disability Insurance (SDI) program provides wage-replacement benefits for California employees who are unable to work due to a non-work-related illness, injury or disability, including pregnancy and pregnancy-related conditions.

SDI provides short-term benefits to eligible workers who suffer a loss of wages when unable to work due to a non-work-related illness or injury, or when medically disabled due to pregnancy or childbirth.

California's EDD administers the SDI program. Employers do not fund SDI; employee payroll deductions fund the program. For more information, visit the EDD's website at **www.edd.ca.gov/**.

Eligibility Requirements

An employee is eligible for SDI benefits if the employee:

- Is unable to perform his/her regular or customary work;

- Has suffered a loss of wages because of a disability;

- Is disabled at least eight calendar days; and

- Is under the care and treatment of a physician or practitioner who certifies that the individual is disabled.

An employee seeking SDI benefits must submit a claim within 49 days from the date of becoming disabled. The EDD can extend this time if the individual can establish good cause for filing late.

The Unemployment Insurance Code was amended effective July 1, 2016, to reflect that a second disability claim filed within 60 days of the initial claim will be considered one disability benefit period. Also, the seven-day waiting period before disability benefits begins is waived for someone who has already served the waiting period for an initial disability and then files a second disability benefits claim for the same or related condition within 60 days after the first claim.

The employee must be employed or actively looking for employment when the disability began. The employee must also have earned at least $300 during a previous 12-month base period, from which SDI taxes were withheld.

The EDD determines eligibility and administers the benefit.

Duration and Timing of the Benefits

Employees who meet the eligibility requirements will receive a weekly benefit amount that is approximately 55 percent of the wages the employee earned in the highest quarter of the base period. There is a one-week waiting period before benefits begin. Employees can receive benefits for up to a maximum of 52 weeks.

If you are covered by the SDI and Unemployment Insurance (UI) programs, you must post and maintain the EDD's *Form DE 1857A - Notice to Employees - Unemployment Insurance, State Disability Insurance and Paid Family Leave* in places readily accessible to employees to inform employees of their rights to UI and disability insurance.

If you are covered only by disability insurance, you must post the *Form DE 1858 - Notice to Employees Disability Insurance, Paid Family Leave.*

You also must provide the EDD pamphlet *Disability Insurance Provisions* pamphlet, which summarizes the state disability program, to:

- Each new employee at the time of hire

- Each employee who becomes disabled due to pregnancy or who becomes ill, injured or hospitalized due to causes unrelated to work

 The *Disability Insurance Provisions* pamphlet is part of the **Required Notices Kit**. You can purchase this product at **store.calchamber.com**.

Employees who are placed on a leave of absence must be given a *DE 2320 - For Your Benefit, California's Programs for the Unemployed* pamphlet.

Failure to comply with these requirements constitutes a misdemeanor. You can download disability insurance forms and publications from the EDD's website. When an employee files an SDI claim, the EDD will contact you and provide you with the appropriate paperwork. You fill out the employer portion of the form.

The law doesn't require you to hold the employee's job merely because he/she collects SDI benefits. However, other laws, such as the FMLA, California's pregnancy disability leave (PDL) law or the Americans with Disabilities Act (ADA), may protect the employee's job.

SDI and Other Benefits

SDI covers loss of earnings not covered by workers' compensation. If someone receives workers' compensation, then he/she is only eligible for SDI benefits in the amount of the difference between normal wages and workers' compensation.

If a person receives unemployment insurance (UI) benefits, he/she can't receive SDI benefits for the same period.

When employees receive full pay, they are ineligible for SDI benefits during that time. The employee may choose to take accrued vacation or PTO, or you may require that the employee do so. Employers can coordinate sick leave, PTO benefits or other pay (excluding vacation) with the EDD to maximize SDI payments.

If you pay out accrued sick leave, the employee's SDI benefits get reduced by the amount of sick pay. To avoid reduction of SDI benefits, you may coordinate the payment of sick leave with SDI benefits. An employee's receipt of vacation pay doesn't affect SDI benefits.

For information about coordinating SDI with specific leaves of absence or other benefits, see:

- "Leave Interactions" in Chapter 3, page 107

- "Pregnancy Disability Leave" in Chapter 3, page 87

- "Family and Medical Leaves" in Chapter 3, page 79

- "Disability Leave" in Chapter 3, page 104

- "Workers' Compensation" on page 139

Unemployment Insurance

The unemployment insurance (UI) system is a state program required by federal law. Typically funded by taxes paid by employers, UI payments are sometimes extended by federal law, particularly during times of high unemployment.

Almost all California employers must pay the tax, and employers face steep penalties for failing to pay their share. Employers with employees that work in multiple states should contact legal counsel or the EDD to determine how to file. For more information, visit the EDD's website at *www.edd.ca.gov*.

Eligibility Requirements

To be eligible for UI, a claimant must:

- Make a claim for benefits in accordance with the regulations

- Be unemployed through no fault of his/her own, including circumstances where an employee leaves employment to protect his/her family, or himself/herself from domestic violence

- Be going through a reduction in hours because of lack of work through no fault of his/her own

- Have earned $1,300 in one quarter, or have high quarter wages of $900 and total base period earnings of 1.25 times that amount

- Be able to work and available for work (including part-time work, if appropriate)

- Be actively looking for work

- Register for work and conduct a search for suitable work, as directed

A claimant is *not* eligible if he/she is out of work for one of the following reasons:

- A voluntary quit without just cause

- Termination for willful misconduct

- Refusing to perform suitable work

 If an employee challenges his/her eligibility for UI benefits after being terminated for willful misconduct, consult legal counsel.

For further information, see Chapter 9, "Terminating Employment."

Duration and Timing of the Benefits

An employee may file for UI benefits when he/she is out of work or when his/her hours get significantly reduced. The EDD will then send you a "Notice of Unemployment Insurance Claim Filed." Respond to the EDD's request for information.

UI benefits get paid every two weeks (after a one-week waiting period) for up to 26 weeks. However, this time is often extended depending on the unemployment situation.

You face penalties for providing false information as to the reason for an employee's termination in connection with a UI claim. For the steps to follow when the employment relationship ends, see "Ending the Employment Relationship" in Chapter 9, page 312.

Keep records of employee pay as required by state and federal law. For more information, see "What Sort of Records Must I Retain?" in Chapter 5, page 196.

If you disagree with EDD's determination, you can protest the claim. You must appeal in a timely manner. You can use the *Unemployment Insurance - Responding to a Claim Checklist*; the *Unemployment Insurance Claim - Appealing to an Administrative Law Judge Checklist*; and the *Unemployment Insurance Claim - Appealing to the Appeals Board Checklist*, described in Table 23 on page 329.

UI and Other Benefits

An unemployed person can't draw both UI and SDI or PFL benefits. For details, see "State Disability Insurance (SDI)" on page 134 and "Paid Family Leave Benefits" on page 132.

Workers' Compensation

Every employer, including nonprofit organizations, government entities and every person employing another person, must carry workers' compensation insurance.

Workers' compensation insurance provides payments without regard to fault for any injury or death "arising out of and in the course of employment."

An employer must maintain coverage at all times while its business is in operation. If an employer fails to provide coverage and an injury occurs, the employer still has to pay the employee's medical costs, in addition to penalties and possible financial damages from lawsuits.

Injured workers receive the necessary medical care, at no cost to them, to cure or relieve the effects of the injury. Employees generally give up their rights to sue you for civil damages in exchange for certain, though limited, benefits, which may include pay for time away from work.

 An employer doesn't pay any benefits directly to an employee. The employee may receive temporary disability benefits, medical expenses and possibly a permanent disability award from the workers' compensation insurance carrier.

For information on preventing injuries at work, see Chapter 6, "Ensuring Workplace Safety."

Eligibility Requirements

Just about all workers, including non-U.S. citizens, casual workers (if they work at least 52 hours in a 90-day period) and minors, are eligible for workers' compensation. Independent contractors are excluded. For more information about independent contractors, see "Independent Contractors" in Chapter 2, page 53.

Employees are protected as soon as they start performing work on your behalf. You must provide all new employees with the current *Your Right to Workers' Compensation Benefits and How to Obtain Them* pamphlet, described in Table 4 in Chapter 2, page 62.

 This pamphlet is part of the **Required Notices Kit**. You can purchase this product at **store.calchamber.com**.

If you are in a Medical Provider Network (MPN), you must follow additional requirements. You must give a complete written MPN employee notification about coverage under the MPN to covered employees at the time of injury or when an employee with an existing injury begins treatment under the MPN.

As soon as you get workers' compensation insurance, you should identify health care providers and hospital facilities designated by the insurance company or that are familiar with occupational injuries and the workers' compensation system.

In most circumstances, you may designate the treating physician for the first 30 days after an injury. An employee can predesignate a personal physician. If the employee has made a valid predesignation, then the personal physician may immediately assume treatment for a work-related injury.

Predesignating a Personal Physician, Chiropractor or Acupuncturist

Before an injury occurs, each employee has the right to designate a personal physician as well as a personal chiropractor and a personal acupuncturist. Unless the employee works for an employer who has a medical provider network (MPN), the employee may choose to be treated by a physician of his/her own choice. The employee must predesignate, in writing, before an injury occurs, his/her personal physician.

After an injury occurs, the predesignated physician becomes the medical provider for injury-related treatment. Within the first 30 days following an injury, the employee may make a one-time request for a change of physician. After the first 30 days, the employee may choose his/her own treatment provider, subject only to any applicable MPN.

Employees that properly predesignate a personal physician are entitled to be treated by that physician. Employees may make a valid physician predesignation if:

- The employee has health care coverage for injuries or illnesses that are not work related.

- The physician is the employee's regular physician, who limits his/her practice of medicine to general practice or is a board-certified or board-eligible internist, pediatrician, obstetrician/gynecologist or family practitioner. In addition, the physician must have previously directed the employee's medical treatment and must maintain the employee's medical records.

- Prior to the injury, the employee's physician agrees to treat him/her for work injuries or illnesses.

- Prior to the injury, the employee provided you the following information in writing:

  - Notice that the employee wants his/her personal physician to treat him/her for a work-related injury or illness

  - The employee's personal physician's name and business address

Employers must notify employees of the right to predesignate a personal physician and must provide new employees with a physician predesignation form upon hire or by the end of the first pay period.

Employers must notify employees in writing of the right for employees to request a change to a treating physician of their choice 30 days after reporting an injury if the original treating physician was selected by the employer or its insurer.

Some employees may want to predesignate a personal chiropractor or acupuncturist, instead of a medical doctor. Unless covered by an MPN, the rules also require employers to provide their employees with a form for predesignating a personal chiropractor or acupuncturist, upon hire or by the end of the first pay period.

The chiropractor or acupuncturist must:

- Have previously directed treatment of the employee

- Be licensed under the Business and Professions Code

- Retain the employee's treatment records and history

There is no requirement for acceptance by the health care provider as there is with the personal physician. For injuries after January 1, 2004, the personal chiropractor may be designated as the treating physician for a maximum of 24 visits per injury, unless additional visits are authorized in writing. After that, the employee must choose a non-chiropractic treating physician.

Injuries Covered by Workers' Compensation

Workers' compensation law covers four types of injuries:

- Specific physical injury

- Cumulative physical injury

- Specific mental/psychiatric injury

- Cumulative mental/psychiatric injury

Workers' compensation law covers all of these injuries, regardless of whether first aid or surgery is required, so long as the injury is either work-disabling or medical treatment is required.

An injury is deemed job-related when:

- It arises out of and in the course of employment.

- The job played an "active" role and was a "positive" factor in the injury.

- The injury was caused by something to which the employee was exposed during his/her employment period.

- The employment brought the employee to the place where the accident occurred.

- The injury happened at home, if the employee's work duties require tasks at home.

Typically, courts will resolve any reasonable doubt about whether an injury occurred in the course of employment in favor of the injured claimant.

If an employee suffers from a specific injury and a cumulative injury, regardless of when the injury occurred, the employee is entitled to two separate awards — one for each injury — but not a combined award with a longer payout period.

Psychiatric injuries fall under slightly different standards. Work-related stress must be "predominant as to all causes of the psychiatric injury combined." Unless a "sudden and extraordinary" employment condition is involved, the employee must have worked for you for at least six months.

Work-related stress (not stress from the employee's family, health or other issues) must account for more than half of the employee's injury. Psychiatric injuries must meet *all* of the following criteria:

- Diagnosis as a mental disorder, based on the published criteria of the American Psychiatric Association;

- Determination that the mental disorder results in disability or requires medical treatment; and

- Proof that the "actual events of employment were predominant as to all causes combined," except in situations involving a significant violent act.

Exclusions From Workers' Compensation

In some cases, an employee could be disqualified from receiving workers' compensation benefits even if the employee was injured on the job.

An injury is not covered by workers' compensation law if the employee was:

- Under the influence of alcohol or drugs at the time of the injury

- Intentionally inflicting the injury or committing suicide

- Engaging in an "altercation" in which he/she was the initial physical aggressor

- Committing a felony for which he/she was later convicted

- Engaging in horseplay

- Voluntarily participating in off-duty recreational, social or athletic activity not constituting his/her work-related activities (unless those activities are expected of employees)

- Going to or coming from work, unless you control the route or mode of transportation

Duration and Timing of the Benefits

This is determined by the workers' compensation carrier and the treating physician. You should take steps to keep informed about your employee's progress and monitor whether the employee can return to work, even in a modified duty capacity.

What to do if an Injury Occurs

1. Should a work-related injury or illness occur, your company's first duty is to provide the employee with first aid or emergency medical care, if needed.

   To meet the obligation to furnish medical care, you or your insurance carrier can designate the physician who provides medical treatment for the first 30 days after an injury.

   An employee can predesignate a personal physician. If the employee has made a valid predesignation, then the personal physician may immediately assume treatment for a work-related injury.

 Need help finding a medical provider? Visit the State Compensation Insurance Fund's website at *http://statefundca.com/claims/mpnforers.asp*.

2. If the injury requires more than first aid, give the employee the *Workers' Compensation Claim Form - DWC 1* as soon as possible after the incident.

   Although you can postpone acceptance of a workers' compensation claim for up to 90 days, pending an investigation to determine if the injury is work-related, you must provide all appropriate medical care immediately upon learning of the injury. Your potential liability for medical care costs is limited to $10,000 for treatment prior to the decision to accept or reject the claim.

3. File the *Employer's Report of Occupational Injury or Illness - Form 5020* with your insurance company.

4. Conduct an investigation into the circumstances surrounding the injury. Document any findings and use this information to prevent future injuries.

5. If the law requires you to record and report injuries on the Cal/OSHA *Log 300* forms, fill out the forms appropriately. To find out if these requirements apply to you, see "Reporting and Recording Work-Related Injuries and Illnesses" in Chapter 6, page 239.

6. Communicate with your injured employee and focus on his/her recovery and return to work. Make sure the employee knows about available benefits and when the benefit services will be furnished. Make sure that employees receive the benefit checks they're entitled to. Stay informed.

7. Take corrective action to eliminate any workplace hazards discovered during the injury investigation.

8. Respect employee confidentiality. Like most types of medical information, workers' compensation claim information must be kept private.

Workers' Compensation and Discrimination

Don't take adverse action against an employee involved in a workers' compensation claim, unless you first consult legal counsel. The law explicitly prohibits you from discharging, threatening or discriminating in any way against an employee because he/she received an award from, filed or intends to file a workers' compensation claim.

If the employee decides to leave the company (voluntary quit), workers' compensation leave ends. The workers' compensation carrier handles medical treatment and disability benefits, which may continue even if the employee no longer works for you.

If you need to fire an employee on workers' compensation leave, consult legal counsel. If you need to lay off an employee on workers' compensation leave, remember that the employee enjoys the same rights and seniority that he/she would have earned if he/she was at work. For more information, see "Layoff" in Chapter 9, page 310.

Workers' Compensation and Other Benefits

Workers' compensation leave may run concurrently with family and medical leave for eligible employees. During the time workers' compensation runs concurrently with family and medical leave, the employee may receive the following health benefits:

- Up to 12 weeks of continued health benefits as if the employee was still at work

- COBRA coverage, if triggered by absences related to the workers' compensation injury. Contact your insurance provider for information

Workers' compensation covers the following employee benefits:

- Seniority — employees continue to accrue seniority as defined by your paid and unpaid leave policies.

- Holidays — you determine whether an employee on workers' compensation receives holiday pay. Treat the employee on workers' compensation the same as you treat employees on other types of disability leave.

- Sick leave, vacation and PTO — if the employee takes company-paid leave, these benefits continue to accrue. If unpaid leave, they only accrue if your other disability policies allow.

You may allow the use of sick pay ("Paid Sick Leave" in Chapter 3, page 94), vacation time ("Vacation" in Chapter 3, page 92) or PTO ("Paid Time Off" in Chapter 3, page 102) to supplement workers' compensation benefits.

The employee may now be a "qualified person with a disability" requiring reasonable accommodation as a result of his/her injury. See "What Is a Reasonable Accommodation?" in Chapter 7, page 273.

Registered Domestic Partner Rights

California law requires equal civil rights, legal status and benefits for registered domestic partners as for spouses. Registered domestic partners are opposite-sex couples with one partner over the age of 62 or same-sex couples who have registered their relationship with the California Secretary of State.

California law:

- Gives registered domestic partners the same rights, protections and benefits as those granted to, and imposed on, spouses

- Subjects registered domestic partners to the same responsibilities, obligations and duties under law — whether they derive from statutes, administrative regulations, court rules, government policies, common law or any other provisions or sources of law — as those granted to and imposed on spouses

- Provides registered domestic partners with the same rights, with respect to a child of either of them, as spouses would have with respect to a child of either of the spouses

- Gives registered domestic partners the same rights for leave under the California Family Rights Act (CFRA) as that given to spouses and their children. See "Duration and Timing of Family and Medical Leave" in Chapter 3, page 82

Employers with state contracts for $100,000 or more must certify that they comply with legislation regarding benefits for registered domestic partners. If you want to contract with the state, you must provide the same benefits to registered domestic partners of employees as those provided to spouses of employees.

If you do business with the state, consult with your legal counsel and benefits expert.

Health Insurance

Some employers offer health insurance plans covering medical, dental, vision, prescription drugs and mental health care. These types of benefit are complicated; consult a benefits expert when setting up your plan.

This section does not address requirements under the Patient Protection and Affordable Care Act (ACA). For more information, see "Federal Health Care Reform" on page 149.

Providing Health Insurance

Unless you are covered by the ACA's employer mandate, the law does not require you to provide health insurance to your employees. If you do offer it, you must offer it in accordance with the applicable laws.

See "Glossary of Terms, Laws and Agencies" on page 331 for details about COBRA, the Health Insurance Portability and Accountability Act (HIPAA) and ERISA.

You decide whether you want to offer this benefit. Your insurance carrier can offer advice and suggestions. You also decide who is eligible. Make sure that similarly situated employees are similarly eligible.

If you offer a health insurance plan, you may fall under ERISA regulations relating to notifying your employees about changes to benefits and to other employer duties. Check with your legal counsel. ERISA is very complicated.

Continuing Health Insurance After the Employment Relationship Ends

If you offer health insurance, you must give ex-employees the opportunity to continue coverage by paying their own premiums. Employers with between two and 19 employees are covered by Cal-COBRA, and employers with more than 20 employees are covered by COBRA.

For details, see Chapter 9, "Terminating Employment."

Health Insurance and Other Benefits

During certain leaves, health insurance benefits must be extended to cover the leave. For details, see "Family and Medical Leaves" in Chapter 3, page 79 and "Pregnancy Disability Leave" in Chapter 3, page 87.

Registered Domestic Partners and Health Insurance Plans

The California Insurance Equality Act amended the Health and Safety Code and the Insurance Code regarding registered domestic partner coverage.

The carrier must provide the same coverage to registered domestic partners as is provided to a spouse. This law may result in carriers offering employers only plans that provide registered domestic partner and spousal benefits. The employer still has the option to offer only employee coverage, and no spouse or registered domestic partner coverage.

Every group health care service plan contract and every group health insurance policy that is marketed, issued or delivered to a California resident is subject to the requirement to provide equal coverage to registered domestic partners as is provided to spouses.

California law requires health care service plans and health insurance policies to provide group coverage to the registered domestic partner of the employee or insured equal to the coverage provided to the spouse of those persons. State law was amended to close a loophole that allowed employers operating in multiple states to discriminate by not providing the same health coverage for registered domestic partners as they provide for spouses.

As a result of the amendments, employers operating in multiple states can't discriminate against same-sex couples by not providing the same insurance coverage for registered domestic partners as they do for spouses.

Even if the employer's principal place of business and majority of employees are located outside of California, no policy or certificate of health insurance marketed, issued or delivered to a California resident may discriminate between spouses or registered domestic partners of a different sex and spouses or registered domestic partners of a same sex.

A willful violation of this provision by a health care service plan is a crime.

Registered Domestic Partners and COBRA

A registered domestic partner is not a qualified beneficiary under COBRA because federal law does not treat a registered domestic partner the same as a spouse. COBRA covers employers with 20 or more employees. A former employee's registered domestic partner may be enrolled as a dependent at open enrollment time, but the duration of that coverage is determined by that of the former employee.

> **Example:** If an employee in your health plan terminates employment, the employee is eligible for COBRA, followed by Cal-COBRA, for a total of 36 months. The employee's registered domestic partner is not eligible for COBRA. If the employee was married, his/her spouse would have an independent right to COBRA.
>
> At open enrollment, the employee on COBRA may choose to add his/her registered domestic partner as a dependent. This does not give the registered domestic partner any COBRA rights. The registered domestic partner is entitled to dependent coverage only for the remaining length of time that your former employee is entitled to COBRA coverage. If the former employee and his/her registered domestic partner end their relationship, the dependent coverage for the registered domestic partner also ends.

However, the child of a registered domestic partner has COBRA rights independent of the former employee if the child was covered as a dependent under the former employee's plan on the day before the COBRA-qualifying event.

Registered Domestic Partners and Cal-COBRA

Registered domestic partners are qualified beneficiaries under Cal-COBRA, which covers employers with between two and 19 employees. If a registered domestic partner was a health plan participant on the day before a qualifying event, he or she would be entitled to continuation benefits.

The Cal-COBRA extension of federal COBRA continuation benefits does not apply to a registered domestic partner. A person must have been a COBRA-qualified beneficiary to be entitled to this extension, and COBRA doesn't cover registered domestic partners. Once COBRA benefits are exhausted, a registered domestic partner may be eligible to continue benefits by converting to an individual policy.

Mental Health and Substance Abuse

The federal Mental Health Parity and Addiction Equity Act of 2008 does not apply to group plans for 50 or fewer employees. The act requires covered group health plans to offer mental health plan parity with health and surgical benefits. A similar California law has been in effect for some time. Consult a benefits expert if you employ more than 50 staff and want to know how the act applies to the health plans you offer as employee benefits.

Federal Health Care Reform

The Patient Protection and Affordable Care Act, as amended by the Health Care and Education Affordability Reconciliation Act (together the Act or ACA), was signed into law by President Obama in March 2010.

The ACA includes the most sweeping changes to the health care laws in generations and will significantly affect not only health insurers, but also employers who sponsor group health plans and employees who participate in them.

The ACA's employer mandate requires all employers with more than 50 full-time employees (including full-time equivalent (FTE) employees) to provide health insurance for their full-time employees, or pay a per-month "employer shared responsibility payment" on their federal tax return.

 The final regulations establish a "full-time" employee as someone who works an average of 30 or more hours per week.

The ACA also imposes plan design mandates applicable to insurance plans, including requirements related to restrictions on annual and lifetime limits, dependent coverage of children to age 26, rescissions, and pre-existing condition exclusions.

In addition, under the ACA, the maximum eligibility waiting period for group health plan participation is no more than 90 days.

CalChamber members can get detailed information about federal health care reform on *HRCalifornia.com*.

Other Benefits

Employers can also choose to add other benefits to the total benefits package offered to employees. These optional benefits — such as life insurance, voluntary disability insurance plans, bonuses and retirement plans — can help employers attract and retain employees.

Life Insurance Plans

Many employers include life insurance among the benefits they offer to their employees. This type of benefit is complicated. Consult a benefits expert when setting up your plan.

Voluntary Disability Insurance Plans

Most employers must contribute to the SDI program. Employers can establish their own voluntary disability insurance program with the EDD and employee approval. A voluntary disability insurance plan must offer coverage, benefits and rights equal to the state program in all aspects, and better in at least one.

Your employees can still opt into the state program. See "Required and Optional Benefits" on page 131. Check with your legal counsel if you want to set up a voluntary program.

Bonuses

A bonus is money promised to an employee in addition to the salary or hourly rate usually due as compensation. Bonuses can be based on various factors, such as a company's overall production numbers or annual revenue.

Employers can choose to pay "objective" or "discretionary" bonuses:

- An objective bonus is tied to certain goals (such as working a certain number of hours or making a certain dollar amount of sales)

- A discretionary bonus is awarded at the employer's discretion (such as a holiday bonus)

This type of benefit is complicated. Consult a benefits expert when setting up your plan. For additional information, see "Bonuses" in Chapter 5, page 175.

Retirement or Pension Plans

Although not required by law, a company-sponsored qualified retirement plan (one that meets IRS specifications) is an excellent benefit that can attract and reward employees and provide you with tax advantages.

You can choose from a wide range of options, from complex plans requiring advice from experts to simple plans that you can establish without any outside consultants. Some examples:

- Individual Retirement Accounts (IRAs);

- Simplified Employee Pensions (SEPs);

- Profit-sharing plans (including 401(k) plans); and

- Employee Stock Ownership Plans (ESOPs).

Retirement plans fall into two general categories:

- Defined benefit plans — a predetermined formula determines the benefits received, tied to the employee's salary, length of service or both. You bear the responsibility for funding and investment risks.

- Defined contribution plans — a specified amount is placed in a participant's account. The amount of funds accumulated and the investment gains or losses determine the benefit received at retirement. You bear no responsibility for investment returns, but you must provide a good selection of sound investment options.

ERISA regulates retirement plans. See "Glossary of Terms, Laws and Agencies" on page 331 for more details about ERISA. Consult legal counsel to make sure you establish and maintain your plans according to this complex and technical area of the law.

Commuter Benefits

Offering commuter benefits is voluntary in California, unless your business is located in the San Francisco Bay Area. Employers with 50 or more full-time employees in the San Francisco Bay Area are required to offer commuter benefits under the Bay Area Commuter Benefits Program to employees who walk or bike to work, or use public transportation, car sharing or vanpools.

Under the program, covered employers must select a commuter benefit; register via the program website; and implement their program. For more information, see the Bay Area Commuter Benefits website at *http://511.org/employers/commuter/overview*.

If an employer reaches the 50-employee threshold after the program goes into effect, the employer will have six months to comply with the program.

Minimum Compliance Elements

1. Hang your *2017 California and Federal Labor Law Poster* (available from *store.calchamber.com*), which includes mandatory postings that all employees and applicants must be able to see, in a prominent place (such as a break room). It includes the Healthy Workplaces, Healthy Families Act of 2014 Paid Sick Leave poster.

   If you have employees working in a city or county with a local minimum wage and/or paid sick leave ordinance, you may also need to post required local notices and provide additional notices to employees at the time of hire.

2. Provide employees with a written notice setting forth the amount of paid sick leave available to them each pay period. Also, the *Wage and Employment Notice (Labor Code section 2810.5)* needs to contain information about an employee's right to accrue and use paid sick leave and about employee protections. See "Paid Sick Leave" on page 94.

3. Give employees information on their workers' compensation, paid family leave and disability insurance benefits (all located in the *Required Notices Kit*, available at *store.calchamber.com*).

4. Pay particular attention to the overlapping requirements of pregnancy disability leave, family and medical leave and workers' compensation. For more information, see:

   - "Pregnancy Disability Leave" on page 87;
   - "Family and Medical Leaves" on page 79;
   - "Leave Interactions" on page 107;
   - "Paid Family Leave Benefits" on page 132;
   - "Workers' Compensation" on page 139.

Forms and Checklists

The following table describes forms associated with leaves of absence and other benefits.

You can find these forms in your online formspack, described in detail in "Online Forms" on page 12.

Table 9. Forms and Checklists

Notice Or Form	What Do I Use It For?	When Do I Use It?	Who Fills It Out?	Where Does It Go?
COBRA Administration Guide	To ensure you use the proper, required forms relating to COBRA (20 or more employees) and Cal-COBRA (2 to 19 employees), as applicable.	Use when an employee is hired and refer back to it when a qualifying event occurs.	N/A	N/A
Leave Interaction	Use this form to determine the relationships among the various state-mandated leaves of absence and benefits during the time off.	When an employee considers a leave.	N/A	Your employee would also benefit from this information.

Table 9. Forms and Checklists

Notice Or Form	What Do I Use It For?	When Do I Use It?	Who Fills It Out?	Where Does It Go?
Personal Physician Designation Form This form is also a tear-out in the **Workers' Compensation Rights and Benefits** pamphlet (in the **Required Notices Kit**).	To notify employees of their right to choose medical treatment by their personal physician.	Give it to the employee at the time of hire.	The employee.	Keep a copy in the employee's personnel file, and send a copy to your contact at your insurer or claims administrator.

Table 9. Forms and Checklists

Notice Or Form	What Do I Use It For?	When Do I Use It?	Who Fills It Out?	Where Does It Go?
Personal Chiropractor or Acupuncturist Designation Form This form is also a tear-out in the **Workers' Compensation Rights and Benefits** pamphlet (in the **Required Notices Kit**).	To notify employees of their right to choose medical treatment by their personal chiropractor or acupuncturist.	Give it to the employee at the time of hire.	The employee.	Keep a copy in the employee's personnel file, and send a copy to your contact at your insurer or claims administrator.
Workers' Compensation Insurance Shopper's Checklist	Use this form to ask potential brokers and carriers important questions as you shop for a workers' compensation policy.	When shopping for a workers' compensation insurance policy.	N/A	In your files.

Where Do I Go for More Information?

CalChamber and federal and state government agencies offer a variety of resources to help you develop written employee policies.

Table 10. Additional Resources

For Information On	Check Out These Resources
General	From CalChamber: • *2017 California Labor Law Digest* • *Employee Handbook Creator* • *Required Notices Kit with Poster* • *HRCalifornia.com* • *store.calchamber.com*
San Francisco-specific benefits	• For current information on San Francisco's Health Care Security Ordinance, visit *http://sfgsa.org/index.aspx?page=418* • For information on the Bay Area Commuter Benefits Program, please visit *https://commuterbenefits.511.org/*
Self-insured employers	• Department of Industrial Relations Office of Self Insurance Plans 11050 Olson Dr., Suite 230 Rancho Cordova, CA 95670 Telephone: (916) 464-7000 FAX: (916) 464-7007; and • The Department of Industrial Relations website *www.dir.ca.gov/osip*
State Disability Insurance	• *www.edd.ca.gov/Disability/More_Employers_Information.htm* • 2014 California Employer's Guide at *www.edd.ca.gov/pdf_pub_ctr/de44.pdf*
Unemployment Insurance	• The Benefit Determination Guide California on the EDD website at *www.edd.ca.gov/UIBDG/* • *www.edd.ca.gov/Unemployment/More_Employer_Information.htm* • 2014 California Employer's Guide at *www.edd.ca.gov/pdf_pub_ctr/de44.pdf*

Table 10. Additional Resources *(continued)*

For Information On	Check Out These Resources
Workers' Compensation	• CalChamber's *2017 Labor Law Digest* • The Division of Workers' Compensation within the Department of Industrial Relations will provide assistance and advice; *www.dir.ca.gov/dwc/contactdwc.htm* • The Equal Employment Opportunity Commission (EEOC) at *www.eeoc.gov/policy/docs/workcomp.html* • State Compensation Insurance Fund at *www.statefundca.com* • Workers' Compensation Offices 455 Golden Gate Avenue, 2nd Floor San Francisco, CA 94102-7014 (415) 703-5020 (800) 736-7401
Work Sharing	EDD Special Claims Office P.O. Box 419076 Rancho Cordova, CA 95741-9076 (916) 464-3343 • *Guide for Work Sharing Employers* at *www.edd.ca.gov/pdf_-pub_ctr/de8684.pdf*

 TIP

CalChamber also provides many ongoing and comprehensive educational opportunities for small business owners, HR beginners and experienced HR professionals alike. These include online training, webinars and special HR seminars. For more information, please visit our website at *store.calchamber.com*.

Chapter 5

Paying Employees

In California, an exhaustive set of rules govern employee pay. In this chapter you can find answers to questions about:

- California Wage Orders
- Work schedules
- Wages and salaries
- Other compensation
- Paid non-work time
- Overtime
- Pay rules
- Deductions

California Wage Orders

California's Department of Industrial Relations (DIR) regulates wages and hours of nonexempt employees. California's Wage Orders define the minimum wages, hours and working conditions for nonexempt employees in a specific industry.

Currently, California law contains 17 Wage Orders, plus a Wage Order Summary and a Minimum Wage Order. Each of the Wage Orders is specific to the industry or occupations it covers, and each Wage Order contains different requirements for different occupations. Wage Orders are numbered 1 through 17, with each number followed by the year in which the Wage Order was last amended and reprinted.

California employers must comply with one or more of 17 Wage Orders, plus a Minimum Wage Order, as well as any applicable statute. Be sure you understand which Wage Order applies to your business. In some cases, more than one Wage Order will apply — depending on the type of work performed.

Each Wage Order contains regulations on the following topics:

- Hours and days of work

- Minimum wages

- Overtime

- Alternative workweeks

- Reporting time pay

- Special licenses for disabled employees

- Record retention

- Cash shortage and breakage

- Uniforms and equipment

- Meals and lodging

- Meal periods

- Rest periods

- Changing rooms and resting facilities

- Temperature

- Seats

Wage Order Provisions

Although each Wage Order includes comparable information, pay special attention to some of the more obscure provisions of the Wage Orders. For example, a provision in many Wage Orders requires "suitable seats when the nature of the work reasonably permits the use of seats."

If work allows the employee to sit, you must provide suitable seats. If the work does not allow for sitting, you must provide seats close to the work area and permit employees to use them. If an employer fails to provide suitable seating, employees can sue under the Private Attorneys General Act of 2004.

 In 2016, the California Supreme Court issued a decision affirming these requirements. Employers must perform a case-by-case analysis of tasks performed at various locations, such as check-out aisles, to determine if a seat is required at a particular location.

CalChamber®

Employers will need to look at the tasks at a particular work station, as opposed to all the tasks an employee performs during the day. For instance, an employee who stocks shelves but also cashiers may need a seat at the cashiering work station. There is no bright line — "Yes, seats are required" or "No, seats are not required." Instead, employers will need to be ready to defend their decisions using the guidelines discussed by the court.

If an employer argues no suitable seat is available, the burden is on the employer to prove unavailability. In other words, employers who want to be excused from the requirement of providing a seat must show that compliance is not feasible because no suitable seating exists.

 As a result of the guidelines issued by the California Supreme Court, as well as continuing litigation in this area, employers with any questions on their obligations should seek advice of legal counsel.

The purpose of your business determines which Wage Order applies to you. For help determining the correct wage order for your business, use CalChamber's web-based wizard at ***https://www.calchamber.com/hrcalifornia/forms-tools/wizards/Pages/wage-order-wizard-home.aspx***.

Setting Work Schedules

You can set a work schedule that suits your company or a particular job in your company. Base your work schedule(s) on workdays and workweeks. You can start the workday and workweek at a specific date and time of your choosing, but from then on you must follow this schedule as a uniform rule.

The schedule you choose and how you set up that schedule will have an affect on pay-related issues, such as overtime pay for nonexempt employees. Your schedule must comply with the day and hour limits and overtime regulations for your industry.

Defining Workdays and Workweeks

Employers must keep certain facts in mind when defining workdays and workweeks:

- Workday: A workday is not simply the hours an employee normally works; for example, 8 a.m. to 5 p.m. A "workday" is any consecutive 24-hour period starting at the same time each calendar day.

  - Note: If you don't define the workday, California's Labor Commissioner will presume a workday of 12:01 a.m. to midnight.

- Workweek: Similarly, a workweek is not just the days that an employee normally works; for example, Monday through Friday. A "workweek" is any seven consecutive 24-hour periods starting on the same calendar day each week.

  - Note: If you don't define the workweek, California's Labor Commissioner will presume a workweek of Sunday through Saturday.

Whatever schedule you set, it must follow regulations that govern day and hour limits, overtime, paydays and meal and rest breaks for nonexempt employees. California's Wage Orders explain these regulations for various industries.

Effects of Workday and Workweek Definitions

Generally, every employee is entitled to at least one day off in a seven-day workweek or, under some circumstances, the equivalent to one day's rest in seven during each calendar month.

You can't require employees who work under Wage Orders 4 and 13 to work more than 72 hours per week. Other limits are placed on daily and weekly hours of work for certain types of employees, such as minors, truck drivers, pharmacists, train crews and health care employees.

Overtime

The definition of workweek becomes extremely important when calculating overtime under the "seventh-day" rule. This rule applies only on the last day of your defined workweek, not any time an employee works seven days in a row.

In a Sunday through Saturday workweek, the seventh day rule applies only if an employee works each day, Sunday through Saturday. Even if the employee works each day beginning on Monday of the first workweek and ending on Sunday of the next workweek (seven consecutive days), Sunday does not count as the seventh consecutive day in that "workweek"— Sunday starts the new workweek. In the first workweek, the employee worked only six days — Monday through Saturday.

For more information, see "Overtime Pay" on page 183.

Scheduling Options

You can choose from a variety of scheduling options for your employees. You may define different workdays or workweeks for different groups of employees if all the employees in the group follow the same schedule. Make sure to observe meal and rest break requirements, whatever schedule you choose. For more information, see "Meal and Rest Periods" on page 176.

Regular Workweek

A regular workweek is a seven-day workweek where anything over eight hours in one workday or 40 hours in one workweek is considered overtime. See "Defining Workdays and Workweeks" on page 161.

Flexible Schedule

A flexible schedule is a workweek schedule of eight hours per day where some employees begin the shift early in the day and others begin their work later in the day.

Split Shift

A split shift is any two distinct work periods established by the employer that are separated by more than a one-hour unpaid break. You must pay the employee at least one hour's pay, at no less than minimum wage, for the time between shifts. Any hourly amount the employee earns above minimum wage can be used to partially or fully offset the split shift requirement.

Alternative Workweek

An alternative workweek is any regularly scheduled workweek requiring an employee to work more than eight hours in a 24-hour period. Common schedules include:

- 4/10 — a four-day workweek of 10 hours per day
- 9/80 — a two-week schedule of nine-hour days with every other Friday off

Employees on an alternative workweek earn overtime differently than those employees eligible for overtime after eight hours per day.

Use extreme caution when setting up an alternative workweek. Consult your industry's Wage Order to learn the specific steps you must follow to create, implement, follow and repeal an alternative workweek.

Wages and Salaries

What you pay your workers depends on what type of workers they are classified as (see "Properly Classify Workers" in Chapter 2, page 21 for more information) and what type of earnings you designate for the job, such as an hourly rate or a salary.

California and federal law create minimum wage and overtime requirements for nonexempt employees and minimum salary requirements for exempt employees. You must adhere to these requirements.

California law prohibits employers from paying any employees at wage rates less than the rates paid to opposite-sex employees for "substantially similar work," as opposed to equal work or the exact same job title. Employees may file complaints alleging pay gaps between people doing substantially similar jobs at different work-sites.

 New 2017 SB 1063 prohibits an employer from paying any of its employees wage rates that are less than the rates paid to employees of another race or ethnicity for substantially similar work.

Nonexempt Employees

Nonexempt workers are typically paid an hourly rate and receive at least the minimum wage for each hour they work.

California regulates nonexempt employees' wages and hours through Wage Orders. Get to know the Wage Order for your industry. You can find this information at **https://www.calchamber.com/hrcalifornia/forms-tools/wizards/Pages/wizards.aspx**. Local ordinances can also affect nonexempt employees' wages. For more information, see "Local Minimum Wage Ordinances" on page 170.

Exempt Employees

Exempt employees are typically paid on a salary and receive a fixed amount for each payroll period, whether weekly, bi-weekly, semi-monthly or monthly. Salary is limited to cash wages. It may not include payments "in kind," such as the value of meals and lodging.

If you fail to pay an exempt employee the minimum salary or misclassify an exempt employee who should be nonexempt, the employee's exempt status can change, which would force you to pay for overtime worked and any missed meal and rest breaks.

Executive, Administrative and Professional Exemptions

Under California law, the most common exemptions (the executive, administrative and professional exemptions) require employees to earn a minimum monthly salary of no less than two times the state minimum wage for full-time employment, and the salary must be a pre-determined sum. There are different rules for some employees, such as hourly physicians, computer professionals and outside salespersons.

 The exempt minimum salary requirement is based on the current state minimum wage, **not** any applicable local minimum wage.

 The 2017 minimum salary threshold for the executive, administrative and professional exemptions is as follows:

- For employers with **26 or more employees**, the state minimum wage increases on January 1, 2017, to $10.50 per hour. Accordingly, the minimum monthly salary test for these exemptions will be $3,640 per month ($43,680 per year) as of January 1, 2017.

- For employers with **25 or fewer employees**, the minimum wage does not increase. It remains at $10 per hour in 2017. Accordingly, the minimum monthly salary test remains at $3,466.67 per month ($41,600 per year).

The minimum salary calculation for employers with 26 or more employees is:

- California minimum wage = $10.50/hour

- Number of hours a full-time employee works in a week = 40

- Number of weeks in a year = 52

- Number of hours a full-time employee works in a year = 40 x 52 = 2,080

- Minimum annual salary for a full-time exempt employee beginning January 1, 2017 = $10.50 x 2 = $21 x 2,080 = $43,680

- Minimum monthly salary for a full-time exempt employee beginning January 1, 2017 = $43,680 ÷ 12 = $3,640

The minimum salary calculation for employers with 25 or fewer employees is:

- California minimum wage = $10 per hour

- Number of hours a full-time employee works in a week = 40

- Number of weeks in a year = 52

- Number of hours a full-time employee works in a year = 40 x 52 = 2,080

- Minimum annual salary for a full-time exempt employee beginning January 1, 2017 = $10 x 2 = $20 x 2,080 = $41,600

- Minimum monthly salary for a full-time exempt employee beginning January 1, 2017 = $41,600 ÷ 12 = $3,466.67

State legislation passed in April 2016 created two minimum wage rates in California: one for employers with 25 or fewer employees, and another for employers with 26 or more employees. The minimum wage in California will gradually increase to $15 per hour by 2022. There is a one-year implementation delay for companies employing 25 or fewer people. For a schedule of increases, see Table 11 on page 169.

Because the minimum wage and salary requirements will change annually, each year employers should evaluate their exempt employees' pay to ensure it complies with the upcoming year's minimum salary requirements.

Federal Salary Test

Federal overtime laws also impose a salary test. In the past, federal overtime requirements generally did not apply to California employees because California overtime law was stricter in both the duties and salary tests. That changed when the federal Department of Labor (DOL) announced its final rule updating the federal overtime regulations.

The new federal overtime rule was supposed to go into effect on December 1, 2016. The rule would have changed the salary test for the white-collar exemptions (administrative, executive and professional).

The rule would have raised the federal salary test to $47,476 annually ($913 per week) for administrative, executive and professional employees, which is higher than California's minimum salary. For an employee to be exempt under both federal and California law, he/she would have needed to meet this higher minimum salary threshold.

However, in November 2016, a federal court issued a nationwide preliminary injunction blocking the new federal overtime rule. At of the time of this *Quick Guide's* publication, the rule was stopped while litigation continued. The rule cannot be implemented or enforced.

The future of the rule is uncertain. The court will have to decide in the future whether the rule should be permanently stopped. In addition, with a new federal administration, the federal government's position on pursuing implementation of the federal overtime rule may also change. Employers should monitor the status of the federal overtime rule to ensure compliance with both California and federal overtime requirements.

As long as the federal overtime rule cannot be enforced, California employers should continue to use the California minimum salary test of two times the state minimum wage to determine whether an employee can be classified as exempt under the executive, administrative and professional exemptions. Employers must also continue to meet California's stricter duties test.

Computer Professional Exemption

Employees exempt under the computer professional exemption may be paid on a salaried basis, either monthly or annually. This exemption allows for salaried pay without having to break down the payment by hour. These rates usually change annually, based on the California Consumer Price Index for Urban Wage Earners and Clerical Workers.

The hourly rates for the computer professional exemption increased, effective **January 1, 2017**:

- The minimum hourly rate of pay exemption increased to $42.35 from its previous rate of $41.85.

- The minimum monthly salary increased to $7,352.62 from its previous rate of $7,265.43.

- The minimum annual salary exemption increased to $88,231.36 from its previous rate of $87,185.14.

Computer professionals must meet separate exemption requirements regarding their job duties (see the *Exempt Analysis Worksheet – Computer Professional Exemption* in Table 4 in Chapter 2, page 62).

Computer professionals who meet the job duties and minimum wage requirements of this exemption are exempt from overtime pursuant to Labor Code section 515.5; they must still take mandatory meal and rest breaks. For more information see "Meal and Rest Periods" on page 176.

Outside Salesperson Exemption

Outside salespeople are exempt from overtime pay, minimum wage, and meal and rest breaks if they meet both of the following criteria:

- Are 18 years of age or older

- Customarily and regularly work more than 50 percent of his/her working time away from your place of business selling tangible or intangible items or obtaining orders or contracts for products, services or use of facilities

Outside salespeople do not need to meet the minimum salary requirement that covers the executive, administrative and professional exemptions.

Commissioned Inside Sales Employee Exemption

Wage Order 4, Professional, Technical, Clerical, Mechanical and Similar Occupations, and Wage Order 7, Mercantile Industry, contain exemptions for some commissioned sales employees. However, the exemption is from overtime, not from the other requirements of the wage orders — such as minimum wage, meal and rest breaks and tracking hours worked.

Generally, the exemption applies if:

- The employee earns more than 1.5 times the state minimum wage; and

- More than half of the employee's compensation represents commission earnings.

This is a narrow exemption. Consult legal counsel with any questions regarding whether your inside sales employees meet the commission exemption.

Licensed Physicians and Surgeons

 The hourly rate for the licensed physician or surgeon exemption increased, effective **January 1, 2017**. The minimum hourly rate of pay exemption increased to $77.15 from $76.24.

The exemption applies to a licensed physician or surgeon primarily engaged in performing duties that require a license. This exemption does not apply to employees in medical internships or resident programs, physician employees covered by collective bargaining agreements or veterinarians.

California Minimum Wage

 California's minimum wage increased to $10.50 per hour on **January 1, 2017**. Legislation passed in April 2016 will gradually increase the minimum wage in California to $15 per hour by 2022.

Employers with 26 or more employees must pay the $10.50 minimum wage in 2017, but there is a one-year implementation delay for companies employing 25 or fewer people.

Table 11. Increases to California's Minimum Wage

Dates	Employers with 25 or Fewer Employees	Employers with 26 or More Employees
01/01/2017	$10 per hour	$10.50 per hour
01/01/2018	$10.50 per hour	$11 per hour
01/01/2019	$11 per hour	$12 per hour
01/01/2020	$12 per hour	$13 per hour
01/01/2021	$13 per hour	$14 per hour
01/01/2022	$14 per hour	$15 per hour
01/01/2023	$15 per hour*	$15 per hour*

*Once the minimum wage reaches $15 per hour for all businesses, wages could then be increased each year up to 3.5 percent (rounded to the nearest 10 cents) for inflation as measured by the national Consumer Price Index.

The federal minimum wage is $7.25 per hour. When state and federal law differ, you must comply with the more restrictive requirement. The California minimum wage is higher so you must pay employees that rate in California.

If your company policies create special pay rates determined by applying the minimum wage rate, those policies will need to be updated. For example, a policy that stipulates that travel pay is paid at minimum wage will need to be changed.

Not paying the minimum wage can get you in trouble (see "What Happens If I Fail to Pay the Minimum Wage?" on page 204).

Local Minimum Wage Ordinances

Some cities and counties in California have adopted their own local minimum wage rates that are separate from the state rate. This is part of a growing trend. Keep in mind that the minimum salary requirement for exempt employees is based on the current state minimum wage, not any applicable local minimum wage.

 Cities in California continue to pass local ordinances relating to the minimum wage. Eligibility rules may vary from city to city. The minimum wages rates in these cities may change at any time; employers should closely monitor them. Check with your local city government as to whether any local minimum wage ordinance might apply to your workforce.

At the date of this book's publication, the following localities have passed minimum wage ordinances:

- Berkeley
- Cupertino
- El Cerrito
- Emeryville
- Long Beach
- Los Altos
- Los Angeles City
- Los Angeles County
- Malibu
- Mountain View
- Oakland
- Palo Alto
- Pasadena
- Richmond
- San Diego
- San Francisco
- San José
- San Mateo
- Santa Clara

- Santa Monica

- Sunnyvale

For a list of local minimum wages, please see the *Local Minimum Wage and Paid Sick Leave Ordinances* chart in your online formspack, described in detail in "Online Forms" on page 12.

"Living Wage" Ordinances

Many California cities and counties adopted local "living wage" ordinances. These ordinances generally require employers who contract with a city or county to pay their employees at a higher rate than the state (or local) minimum wage for work that's performed related to the contract. See "Where Do I Go for More Information?" on page 214 for information on where to check if a living wage ordinance applies to your city or community.

Paying Less Than the Minimum Wage

California's Wage Orders and the federal Fair Labor Standards Act (FLSA), which is the governing law for most wage-and-hour issues, contain provisions for paying less than the minimum wage to certain types of employees and under certain circumstances. For more information about Wage Orders and the FLSA, see "Glossary of Terms, Laws and Agencies" on page 331.

Federal and state laws create certain exceptions to minimum wage requirements. You must follow the most restrictive rule.

California's Wage Orders permit you to pay learners 85 percent of the minimum wage, rounded to the nearest nickel. State law allows for the subminimum wage for the first 160 work hours, after which the employee must be paid at least minimum wage. "Learners" are employees who have no previous similar or related experience in the occupation.

Federal law allows payment of a subminimum wage — called an opportunity wage — for employees younger than 20 years of age, for their first 90 consecutive calendar days of employment. You cannot displace employees or reduce employees' hours, wages or employment benefits to hire a youth at subminimum wage.

The following table summarizes subminimum wage laws. The most restrictive rules are in bold and must be followed in California.

Table 12. Subminimum Wage Rules

	Federal	State
Hourly rate of pay	$4.25	$8.50
Age requirements	**Must be younger than 20 years old**	None
Length of time lower payments can be made	First 90 consecutive calendar days of employment	**First 160 work hours**
Other restrictions	Cannot displace others or reduce hours, wages or benefits to hire a youth	Must have no previous similar related experience in the occupation

Other exceptions to the minimum wage include:

- **People with certain disabilities and apprentices:** You can obtain licenses from the Labor Commissioner to pay less than the minimum wage to learners and apprentices or to people whose productivity is affected by certain mental or physical disabilities.

- **Your parent, spouse or child:** No minimum wage laws apply to these family members if you employ them.

- **Outside salespersons:** Employees must spend more than one-half of work time away from the employer's place of business. No minimum wage laws apply to outside salespersons. For more information, see *Exempt Analysis Worksheet – Salesperson Exemption*, described in Table 4 in Chapter 2, page 62.

Other Compensation

In some businesses, tips and gratuities make up part of employees' pay in addition to wages. In other businesses, piece rates, meals and lodging, commissions and bonuses make up part of employees' pay.

Piece Rate

A piece rate is a figure paid based on completing a particular task or making a particular piece of goods. A piece rate includes only time spent producing the particular good or completing the particular task, and not time spent on non-piece-rate work.

Non-piece-rate work must be compensated separately, and at least at the minimum wage:

> **Example:** If employees have time where they are not performing the work to produce the particular good or completing the particular task but must wait at the worksite until more work is available, that time must be compensated at least at minimum wage.

Also, the piece-rate system does not include compensation for employees' rest breaks. Rest breaks must be compensated for separately, and at least at the minimum wage. At the end of the payroll period, the employee must receive at least minimum wage for each hour worked, despite slow production hours or slow production days.

Piece-rate employees are entitled to overtime wages. To determine the regular rate of pay, divide total earnings by total hours (even if more than 40 hours).

Employers paying employees on a piece-rate system must include the following information on the itemized pay statement provided to employees:

- The total hours of compensable rest and recovery periods, the rate of compensation and the gross wages paid for those periods during the pay period;

- The total hours of other nonproductive time (defined as time under the employer's control, exclusive of rest and recovery periods, that is not directly related to the activity being compensated on a piece-rate basis);

- The rate of compensation; and

- The gross wages paid for that time during the pay period.

Piece-rate employees must be compensated for rest and recovery periods and other nonproductive time at or above minimum wage, separately from any piece-rate compensation.

 If you're using a piece-rate compensation system, consult legal counsel to make sure your system complies with recent changes in the law.

Meals and Lodging (Nonexempt Employees)

Employer-provided food and lodging counts as wages and can help you meet minimum wage requirements. However, meals or lodging can't be credited against the minimum wage without a voluntary written agreement between the employer and the employee. Be sure to consult your Wage Order regarding the regulatory requirements as applied to your industry.

Meals must be varied and nutritious, and lodging must meet sanitary standards. Employees can't be required to share beds.

Tips and Gratuities

Tips and gratuities are any money left by patrons for employees only. Employers can't count tips against minimum wage requirements.

If tips get paid by credit card, payment can be delayed only until the next payday.

Tip Pools

The restaurant and hospitality industries commonly create tip pools for employees. In a tip pool, employees who receive tips share those tips with other employees. Tip pools spread the risk of low-tipping patrons among all tipped employees. Tip pools also create a way for tips to be shared with employees who aren't directly tipped by customers, such as table bussers.

California law does not specifically prohibit mandatory tip pooling, in which you require employees to pool all or a portion of their tips and then share those tips with other employees. But the employer and any supervisors may not share in the tips.

Automatic Gratuities and Mandatory Service Charges

Restaurants commonly add an automatic gratuity or mandatory service charge to bills for large parties. An example would be a 15-percent charge added to the cost of a banquet.

In most instances, mandatory service charges are not considered tips, according to the California Division of Labor Standards Enforcement (DLSE). When a business establishes a non-voluntary, flat charge or a set percentage of a bill that must be paid by the customer, that amount belongs to the business and is not classified as a tip or gratuity left for the employee.

This practice also has wage and tax implications for employers. The Internal Revenue Service treats automatic gratuities as "wages" for payroll tax purposes. Besides the payroll tax implications, the distinction between whether the amount added is a "tip" or a "service charge" can affect employee wages. A "service charge" belongs to the business; it's not left for the employee.

According to the DLSE, if an employer pays out all or a portion of the service charges to employees, these payouts must be included in the employee's regular rate of pay and must be factored into any overtime calculation.

Commissions

Commission wages are defined as compensation paid to any person for services rendered in the sale of the employer's property or services, and based proportionately on the amount or value of the property or services. An employee's main task must be selling a product or service, not making the product or rendering the service.

An inside salesperson must earn at least minimum wage for each hour he/she works. His/her commission earnings are part of his/her regular rate of pay, used to calculate overtime. Divide total earnings by total hours (even if more than 40 hours).

Employers who pay commission wages to employees working in California must put commission agreements into writing. The agreement must contain the method by which the commissions are computed and paid. Also, the agreement must specify when commissions are earned, paid out and how the employee's termination impacts the commission payment.

Employers must give the employee a signed copy of their contract, as well as obtain a signed receipt from each employee acknowledging that the employee received a copy of the agreement. If the contract expires and the employee continues working for the employer, the terms of the expired contract are presumed to be in effect.

"Commissions" do not include short-term productivity bonuses. Bonus and profit-sharing plans are not included in this requirement unless the employer offers to pay a fixed percentage of sales or profits as compensation for work.

Excluded from the contract requirement are temporary, variable incentive payments that increase, but do not decrease, payment under the written contract.

Bonuses

A bonus is money promised to an employee in addition to the salary or hourly rate usually due as compensation.

Performance based bonuses provided to a nonexempt employee must be included in the employee's regular rate of pay for purposes of determining overtime rates. Divide total earnings by total hours (even if more than 40 hours).

Meal and Rest Periods

Meal and rest break compliance has been the source of a great deal of litigation. California employers face costly consequences for violating meal and rest break rules. Court decisions have increased the potential for large financial fines.

It is imperative that you understand the complex meal and rest break requirements. You must do everything you can to communicate the legal requirements to employees and give them opportunities to take the requisite breaks.

Meal Period Requirements

Nonexempt employees are entitled to an uninterrupted, 30-minute meal period if they will work five hours or more. However, if six hours of work will complete the day's work, the employee and employer can mutually agree, in writing, to waive the meal period.

The California Supreme Court, in *Brinker Restaurant Corp. v. Superior Court*, set forth specific guidelines relating to meal breaks. The court clarified that an employer's obligation is to "provide" the meal break, and underscored the need for employers to maintain time records demonstrating that they have provided meal breaks to their employees.

According to the court in *Brinker*, the employer satisfies its legal obligation to provide an off-duty meal period to its employees if the employer:

- Relieves its employees of all duty

- Relinquishes control over their activities

- Permits them a reasonable opportunity to take an uninterrupted, 30-minute break

- Does not impede or discourage them from doing so

A meal break can be unpaid only if all of the above conditions are met. The timing for meal periods was set forth by the court in *Brinker*:

- The first meal break must be provided "no later than the end of the employee's fifth hour of work." For example, if an employee begins an eight-hour shift at 8 a.m., he/she must start the meal period no later than 12:59 p.m.

- The second meal break must be provided "no later than the end of an employee's 10th hour of work."

Refer to the Wage Order(s) for your industry for any exceptions, especially if your employees work shifts between 10 and 12 hours long.

 Wage Order 5 authorizes health care workers to waive their second meal break, even in shifts longer than 12 hours.

Employers in the health care industry can allow employees to voluntarily waive one of their two meal periods, even when an employee's shift exceeds 12 hours.

On-Duty Meal Breaks

On-duty meal breaks must be paid if you require the employee to remain on the premises. You must pay hourly wage for the meal time, and this time is included in overtime calculations. On-duty meal breaks are very difficult to legally implement, even when there is only one person available to perform the job at hand. Consult legal counsel before allowing on-duty meal breaks.

Rest Break Requirements

Nonexempt employees are entitled to a rest break of 10 consecutive minutes for each four hours (or major fraction thereof) worked. If the employee's total daily work time is less than 3.5 hours, he/she need not be given a rest break. The breaks should occur as near as possible to the middle of the work period.

This is the general rule. There is no absolute obligation to permit a rest period before a meal period. In *Brinker*, the court ruled that, "[s]horter or longer shifts and other factors that render such scheduling impracticable may alter this general rule." Employers are given some latitude as they may "deviate from that preferred course where practical considerations render it infeasible."

 New 2017 In 2016, a California court affirmed the general rule as to the timing of rest breaks and held that a departure from the general rule is allowed only if the departure can meet this two-prong test:

1. The departure will not unduly affect employee welfare; and

2. The departure is tailored to alleviate a material burden that would be imposed on the employer by implementing the preferred schedule.

A departure from the preferred schedule that is "merely advantageous" to the employer will not meet the above test. Instead, the employer must show that providing the rest break in the middle of each work period imposes a material burden and that a departure from the norm is necessary to alleviate that burden.

Employers should be cautious about departing from the general rule to provide rest breaks in the middle of each work period and should consult with counsel if practical considerations unique to their industry seem to warrant a departure from the general rule.

Missed Meal or Rest Break

You must pay an employee one additional hour of wages owed if he/she misses any part of his/her unpaid *meal* break. You must also pay one additional hour of wages if you restrict an employee's ability to take his/her 10-minute, paid *rest* break.

You must pay an employee an amount equal to the employee's hourly rate of pay, up to a maximum of two hours a day (one for any missed meal breaks and one for any rest breaks the employee was not allowed to take.)

This time is **not** included in overtime pay calculations.

Meal and Rest Break Policies

Following the *Brinker* decision, the employer's responsibility to maintain and follow meal and rest break policies and to document that the meal break was provided is even more important.

You should draft break policies for your specific operation. Vague policies that are subject to interpretation by the employee increase your risk of liability.

Meal and rest break policies should stress the timing of the breaks. Consider formally scheduling breaks for your employees as evidence that the rest breaks have been provided. Distribute the policies to all employees and periodically remind employees of your policy. Train all supervisors and managers to make sure breaks are taken and employees are not discouraged from taking all required breaks.

A court ruling in a California case relating to meal and rest breaks highlights the dangers of not maintaining formal policies related to meal and rest breaks and discouraging employees from taking meal and rest breaks.

The court found substantial evidence that the employees were routinely and consistently prohibited from taking meal periods and rest breaks in violation of California law and the *Brinker* standard. Seventy-three present and former employees will share an award of $964,557, and the company was also required to pay roughly another half-million dollars in other costs.

In another case, the employer successfully defended itself against a class-action lawsuit because the employer had implemented clear meal and rest break policies, trained managers to follow those policies by scheduling breaks and following up with employees who did not take their breaks, and documented all steps of the process.

Paid Non-Working Time

At times, you need to pay a nonexempt employee for time not spent performing his/her regular work duties. This might include travel time, attendance at mandatory meetings, on-duty meal breaks and other special circumstances.

If you will pay a special rate for travel time or other special circumstances, you must establish and communicate the rate to employees in advance of the event. The amount and duration depends on what he/she does during that time.

Time Spent Between Split Shifts

You must pay employees an amount equal to one hour of pay of at least the current state minimum wage if the time between shifts is more than one hour in duration. You can use any hourly amount the employee earns above minimum wage to offset the split shift requirement.

This time is **not** included in overtime calculations because the time wasn't actually spent working.

Reporting Time

You must pay reporting time when you require the employee to report to work at his/her normal work time, and you do not put him/her to work or give him/her less than half the hours he/she was scheduled to work.

The employee must be paid his/her hourly wage for at least half of the employee's scheduled hours, which must be paid for no less than two hours, and no more than four. This time is **not** included in overtime calculations.

You must also pay reporting time if you require the employee to report to work a second time in any one workday and give him/her less than two hours of work. The employee must be paid his/her hourly wage for at least two hours. Only the time the employee actually worked is included in overtime calculations.

You must also pay reporting time for on-call employees who are not being paid while they are on-call. These employees typically have the freedom to spend their on-call time as they wish and have a reasonable amount of time to report to work when called.

You do not have to pay reporting time pay if the employee is only required to respond to a telephone call, text message or other communication which does not mandate the employee's "reporting" to a specific location. You do not have to pay reporting time for on-call employees who are being paid for their on-call time. You must only pay the time employees actually work.

You also do not have to pay reporting time when your business operations are disrupted by:

- Threats to your property
- Utility failure
- Acts of God

On-Call (Standby) Time

If you require an employee to stay at home or at work on an on-call or standby status, that time may qualify as hours worked depending on the restrictions you put on his/her ability to actually have free time.

Courts typically consider the following factors in looking at whether on-call time should be paid:

- Are there excessive geographic restrictions on the employee's movements?
- Is the frequency of calls unduly restrictive?
- Is there a fixed time limit for the employee to respond to the call that is unduly restrictive?
- Can the on-call employee easily trade his/her on-call responsibilities with another employee?
- Can the employee engage in personal activities during on-call periods? If so, to what extent?
- What is the nature of the employment relationship and the industry practice?
- Are there any other limitations on the employee's ability to use the time for his/her own benefit?

The more restrictions on an employee's use of his or her time while on call, the more likely the on-call time is compensable.

You must pay on-call time for any time spent on-call that can't be used for the employee's benefit. You must also pay for time spent on call-backs and time spent traveling from the point summoned to the worksite and the return trip.

You must pay the employee at the applicable rate (straight time or overtime). This time is included in overtime pay calculations. On-call time is *not* compensable if the employee can use the time spent on-call primarily for his/her own benefit.

Travel Time

You must pay for travel time if the employee reports to the regular site and then has to go to another site. You must pay the employee at least minimum wage, for the time between sites.

You must also pay for travel time if the employee has to work at another site. In this circumstance, you must pay the employee at least minimum wage for the time in excess of the employee's normal commute.

Finally, you must pay for travel time if the employee must travel to a distant place, such as another city. You must pay the employee at least minimum wage for the time spent in transit from his/her home or office to the destination where the employee is no longer under the employer's control.

If the employee travels and then begins working, the employer may pay for travel time at a lower rate, as long as it is at least minimum wage. The employee would earn his/her usual rate of pay once work begins.

All travel time is included in overtime pay calculations. For more information, see "Calculating Overtime for Nonexempt Employees" on page 185.

Mandatory Mode Of Transportation

You must also pay for travel time if you require your employees to travel to the worksite on employer-provided transportation. You must pay employees at least minimum wage for duration of travel. This time is included in overtime pay calculations.

Uniform Changing/Washing Up

If employees must change uniforms, wash up or clean up at work, or engage in other preparatory activity that's required for the job, that time must generally be counted as hours worked in California. You must pay the employee at his/her applicable rate (straight time or overtime). This time is included in overtime pay calculations.

Federal law generally considers this time non-compensable. However, there is significant current litigation on this issue that may impact California law. When in doubt as to whether you should count the time toward an employee's pay, consult legal counsel.

This is an unsettled area of the law. For up-to-date information on this and other employment-related issues, subscribe to the CalChamber's free newsletter, *HRCalifornia Extra*, at *www.calchamber.com/hrcalifornia/cases-news/hrcalifornia-extra/Pages/subscribe-to-hrcalifornia-extra.aspx*.

Employee Meetings

You must pay employees for attending meetings if you require them to attend. This time is included in overtime pay calculations. If you schedule a meeting or require the employee to report to work for a specific amount of time on a day the employee is not normally scheduled to work, you must pay the employee only for the time he/she attended the meeting; this is to be distinguished from "reporting time" requirements.

Employer-Sponsored Activities

You must pay employees for attending training, lectures or work courses that you sponsor if you require employees' attendance or if the training relates to the employees' regular job. This time is included in overtime pay calculations.

Time Spent On Maintaining Physical Fitness

You must pay employees for time they spend maintaining their physical fitness if you require remedial fitness training for the employee's regular job. This time is included in overtime pay calculations.

Reimbursing Employees for Their Expenses

You must reimburse all employees (exempt and nonexempt) for all the expenses they incur in performing their duties, such as mileage, travel and dining expenses, and personal cell phone usage. The mileage reimbursement rate considered most reasonable in California is set by the Internal Revenue Service.

At the time of this *Quick Guide's* publication, the IRS had not yet announced the optional standard mileage rates for 2017. For the most recent rate, please visit the IRS website at ***www.irs.gov***.

The 2016 optional standard mileage rates are:

- 54 cents per mile for business miles driven

- 19 cents per mile driven for medical or moving purposes

- 14 cents per mile driven in service of charitable organizations

Under California law, an employer must reimburse an employee if the employee is required to use a personal cell phone to make work-related calls. This is true even when the employee did not incur an extra expense by making the work calls because he/she had an unlimited data plan.

The employer must pay "some reasonable percentage" of the employee's cell phone bill to comply with the Labor Code. The court did not define or clarify what a "reasonable percentage." The case is limited to situations where the employer requires an employee to use his/her personal cell phone for work-related calls.

 If you have any questions about whether you should reimburse employees, and at what rate, for using their personal cell phone to make work-related calls, consult legal counsel.

Overtime Pay

When your nonexempt employees work beyond a "normal" number of hours, you must compensate them at a higher rate. In most cases, this means you pay overtime to a nonexempt employee who works more than eight hours per day or 40 hours per week. Failing to pay overtime can get you into trouble. For more information, see "What Happens If I Fail to Pay Overtime?" on page 204.

 Remember — exempt employees do not receive overtime pay.

Employees with an alternative workweek schedule earn overtime differently (see "Alternative Workweek" on page 163). Be sure to consult the Wage Order that applies to your industry.

 Sometimes a collective bargaining agreement can affect overtime rules, so check yours if you have one.

Overtime Rates of Pay

In California, nonexempt employees must be paid overtime at the following rates:

- For hours worked beyond eight in one workday, an employee must be paid at his/her regular rate of pay, multiplied by 1.5 (time-and-one-half).

- For hours worked beyond 12 in one workday, an employee must be paid at his/her regular rate of pay, multiplied by 2.0 (double-time).

- For hours worked up to eight hours on the seventh consecutive day of the workweek, an employee must be paid at his/her regular rate of pay, multiplied by 1.5 (time-and-one-half).

- For hours worked beyond eight on the seventh consecutive day of the workweek, an employee must be paid at his/her regular rate of pay, multiplied by 2.0 (double-time).

- For hours worked beyond 40 straight-time hours in one workweek, an employee must be paid at his/her regular rate of pay, multiplied by 1.5 (time-and-one-half).

Wage Orders 3, 4, 8, 13 and 16 contain special provisions regarding required overtime:

- Wage Order 3 — an employee may work up to a maximum of 72 hours in seven consecutive days, after which the employee must receive a 24-hour period off duty.

- Wage Order 4 — no employee shall be terminated or otherwise disciplined for refusing to work more than 72 hours in any workweek, except in an emergency.

- Wage Order 8 — an employee may work up to a maximum of 72 hours in any workweek, after which the employee must receive a 24-hour period off duty. The wage order contains some exceptions. All employers who permit any employees to work more than 72 hours in a workweek must give each employee a copy of the applicable provision for exemption, in English and in Spanish, and post it at all times in a prominently visible place.

- Wage Order 13 — any work by an employee in excess of 72 hours in any one workweek must be on a voluntary basis. No employee can be discharged or in any other manner discriminated against for refusing to work in excess of 72 hours in any one workweek.

- Wage Order 16 — no employee can be terminated, disciplined or otherwise discriminated against for refusing to work more than 72 hours in any workweek, except in an emergency.

Calculating Overtime for Nonexempt Employees

1. Determine the employee's regular rate of pay:

   - For hourly workers, total the amount earned for each hour worked plus any bonuses and commissions, and divide that by the total number of actual hours worked.

   - For piece-rate workers, total the amount earned for units produced and divide that by the total number of actual hours worked, even if it's more than 40.

The **regular rate of pay** equals an employee's actual earnings, which may include an hourly rate, commission, bonuses, piece work and the value of meals and lodging. For examples of other compensation, see "Other Compensation" on page 172.

Though you need to include bonuses and commissions in the regular rate of pay, you don't need to include:

   - Hours paid but not worked (vacation, reporting time, etc.). See "Paid Non-Working Time" on page 179.

   - Reimbursement of expenses. See "Reimbursing Employees for Their Expenses" on page 182.

   - Gifts or discretionary bonuses (in recognition of services performed during a given period)

   - Benefits payments (profit sharing plan, health care plan, etc.)

For a sample calculation, see "Calculating Overtime for Nonexempt Employees With More Than One Rate of Pay" on page 186.

2. Determine how many straight-time hours the employee worked for that workweek. Straight-time hours are hours that the employee would usually work (the first eight hours of his/her workday). For information on defining your workweek, see "Setting Work Schedules" on page 161.

   Only hours worked at straight time apply to the weekly 40-hour limit. This prevents "pyramiding" of overtime, where an employee earns overtime on top of overtime already paid. Once an employee has been paid overtime for hours over eight in one day, those overtime hours do not count toward the weekly 40-hour limit.

Example: Assume the workweek is Monday through Sunday. An employee works 10 hours each day Monday through Thursday, and is owed eight hours of straight time and two hours of overtime for each of those days. When that employee comes in on Friday morning, although he/she actually worked 40 hours already in the workweek, he/she worked only 32 hours of straight time and does not begin earning weekly overtime until after he/she works eight more hours.

The employee works 10 hours on Friday. So far, the employee earned straight time hours for the eight hours worked on each of the five days, and earned overtime at the rate of time and a half for two hours on each of the five days. If the employee works on Saturday, those hours will exceed 40 straight time hours in the workweek and the employee will be entitled to overtime for up to 12 hours of work on Saturday.

3. For any overtime hours, pay the appropriate rate listed in Table 13 on page 187.

Calculating Overtime for Nonexempt Employees With More Than One Rate of Pay

Different rates may be paid for different jobs so long as the work involved is objectively different. For example, travel time pay may be paid at a lower rate than the employee's regular rate of pay, but travel time must be paid at least the minimum wage. Accurate recordkeeping is imperative in such scenarios.

When employees travel to a different time zone, be sure to ask them to track all hours based on California time — it will make the math much easier and your payroll department will sincerely appreciate it. Consistent communication by email or phone can also cut down on later disputes regarding hours actually worked.

Especially with travel time, employers should communicate with nonexempt employees regarding these obligations. In this case, there's a difference between the hourly rate and the regular rate of pay when an employee works overtime and earns:

- Time and one-half: you must pay him/her the hourly rate for the job he/she does, plus one-half of the regular rate of pay.

- Double-time: you must pay him/her two times the regular rate of pay.

CalChamber®

If your employee works an alternative workweek, you must use different calculations. See "Scheduling Options" on page 163.

Table 13. Regular Rate Of Pay For Multiple Hourly Rates

An employee normally earns $13 per hour working at trade shows for his/her employer and $10.50 per hour for travel time. In one week, the employee works 40 hours at the trade show and spends 10 hours traveling.	
Total rate 1	$13 per hour x 40 hours = $520
Total rate 2	$10.50 per hour x 10 hours = $105
Total weekly wages before overtime premiums	$520 + $105 = $625
Regular rate of pay	$625 ÷ 50 hours = $12.50
Overtime premium for time-and-one-half	$12.50 ÷ 2 = $6.25

For more than two rates, multiply the additional rates by the number of hours worked at those rates and include them in the total weekly compensation. If the employee earned commissions or bonuses in addition to his/her hourly rates, include those amounts in the total weekly compensation.

Requiring Employees to Work Overtime

With a couple of limited exceptions, employees can use no statutory or regulatory basis to refuse your request that they work overtime. You can often find employees who will voluntarily work overtime.

A good approach is to first request volunteers among qualified employees, and then require overtime only in the absence of such volunteers. You can enforce overtime requests with disciplinary action if the employee refuses.

Overtime and Agricultural Employees

 New 2017 In a major change for agricultural employers, AB 1066 will phase in overtime requirements for agricultural employees over the course of four years from 2019 to 2022.

Currently, agricultural employees are exempt from overtime, meal breaks and other working conditions and wage requirements.

Agricultural employers will initially start paying overtime when employees work more than 9.5 hours per day/55 hours per week. This number will decrease yearly until it reaches 8 hours per day/40 hours per week by January 1, 2022. Employers with 25 or fewer employees will have an additional three years to comply with the phasing in of these requirements and won't start paying overtime until 2022.

In addition to phased in overtime, AB 1066 eliminates an important existing exemption for agricultural employers. Currently, agricultural employers are exempt from the Labor Code requirement to provide one day's rest in seven worked. Effective **January 1, 2017**, agricultural employers are no longer exempt from this provision and cannot cause employees to work more than six days in seven.

Overtime for Private Elementary or Secondary School Teachers

Private school teachers in California must currently earn two times the state minimum wage to be exempt from overtime and must meet all other requirements for the exemption.

 Under AB 2230, private school employees will need to meet a new minimum earnings test that will look at the comparable salaries offered to public school teachers in the school district or county, rather than the state minimum wage. This legislation is effective **July 1, 2017**.

To qualify as exempt, the new minimum earnings standard will require the employee to earn the greater of: (1) no less than the lowest salary offered by any school district or (2) the equivalent of no less than 70 percent of the lowest schedule salary offered by the school district or county in which the private school is located.

Overtime and Non-Resident Employees

The California Supreme Court ruled that California overtime laws apply to non-resident employees when they perform work in California for California-based employers. Although the case involved full weeks of work by employees not based in California, it's possible that future decisions will find in favor of employees who work less than a full work week in California.

The court did not address meal and rest periods, pay stubs and other California issues related to nonexempt employees. The court also did not make a decision about out-of-state employees working in California for an employer based outside of California. Employers who send out-of-state employees to California to work should consult legal counsel for advice on how to pay those employees.

Makeup Time and Compensatory Time Off

You can choose to offer makeup time to your nonexempt employees if they want to request time off for a personal obligation and make up the time without receiving overtime pay.

The law doesn't require you to offer this option, but if you offer it, you must abide by these rules:

- You can't ask or encourage employees to use makeup time

- The time must be made up within the same workweek

- The employee is limited to 11 hours per day and 40 hours per week when working makeup time

- Before taking off or making up the time, the employee must provide you with a signed, written request for each occasion that makeup time is desired, unless the time off is for a recurring event, such as a college course

Make sure your time-recording system shows which hours you will pay at an overtime rate and which hours you will pay at a normal rate as makeup time. The sample *Makeup Time Checklist* and *Makeup Time Request* forms are described in Table 14 on page 210.

Compensatory time off (CTO) is lawful only for public-sector employers. CTO is time off given to employees in exchange for extra hours worked. CTO is not "makeup time."

 It is illegal for all private sector employers to provide CTO under any circumstances; not only in California, but nationwide.

Pay Rules

California has extensive rules that determine how employees are paid. It is important that you understand the laws pertaining to amount, timeliness and form of payment.

When Do I Pay My Workers?

If you fail to pay your workers in a timely manner, you face certain penalties (see "What Happens If I Fail to Pay Wages Due an Employee?" on page 205). You must pay employees according to guidelines that apply to the type of payment.

Regular Wages (Nonexempt Employees)

Nonexempt employees must be paid at least twice each calendar month on days designated in advance (see "Notifying Employees About Paydays" on page 192).

- Twice-monthly (semi-monthly):
  - For hours worked between the 1st and the 15th day of the month (no later than the 26th day of the same month)
  - For hours worked between the 16th and the last day of the month (no later than the 10th day of next month)
- Weekly or bi-weekly:
  - Within seven days of the end of the pay period

Regular Wages (Exempt Employees)

Exempt employees must be paid at least once per month by the 26th day of the month for all wages, including those yet unearned for the month.

Overtime

Overtime wages must be paid no later than the next work period's payday. For a complete discussion, please see "Overtime Pay" on page 183.

Tips/Gratuities Paid By Credit Card

Credit card tips or gratuities must be paid no later than the next scheduled payday following the date the patron authorized the credit card payment.

Expense Reimbursements

Reimbursements may be paid on any reasonable schedule.

 Expense reimbursements to terminated employees are not subject to final paycheck deadlines and can be paid at the same time as reimbursements to active employees. Put a policy or procedure in place regarding reimbursements and follow it consistently.

Vehicle Salespeople Commission Wages

These wages must be paid once per month.

Farm Labor Contractor Employees

These employees must be paid at least once every week on a day designated in advance.

 Payment must include all wages earned up to and including the fourth day.

Temporary Service Employees

These employees must be paid at least weekly, and daily if an employee is assigned to a client on a day-to-day basis or to a client engaged in a trade dispute.

There is an exception to these pay rules — employees assigned to a client for more than 90 consecutive calendar days are not subject to this requirement unless the employer pays the employee weekly.

 AB 1311 applies the weekly pay requirement to security guards employed by private patrol operators who are temporary services employers. This urgency legislation took effect on **July 25, 2016**.

 In California, employers are jointly liable for wage-and-hour and Workers' Compensation coverage violations against workers hired through temporary service employers. Exercise due diligence to make sure that the companies you hire workers through are complying with the law.

Ask legal counsel to review all contracts between you and the temporary service company and include an indemnification clause to protect your company. For more information, see "What Happens If I Use a Labor Contractor and the Contractor Violates the Law?" on page 205.

Exceptions to Payday Rules

Under certain circumstances, you can make exceptions to the payday requirements:

- Agriculture workers may be paid once per month if you lodge and board them
- Domestic employees may be paid once per month if you lodge and board them
- Striking employees may be paid on the next regularly scheduled payday when they come back to work

Notifying Employees About Paydays

You must post the day, time and place of the regular payday in a way that your employees can understand. As a convenience, the state provides a small form for this purpose, which CalChamber includes as part of the ***2017 California and Federal Labor Law Poster*** (available from ***store.calchamber.com***).

If you change the payday schedule, notify your employees of the change at least one full payroll cycle in advance.

Wage Information Notice to Employees

Nonexempt employees must be provided with specific written wage information, at the time of hire. Use the *Wage and Employment Notice to Employees (Labor Code section 2810.5)* form, described in Table 14 on page 210.

The Labor Commissioner designed a template that complies with the specific notice requirements, which include:

- The rate/rates of pay and basis — hourly, by a shift, day, week, salary, piece, commission or otherwise, including applicable overtime rates

- Allowances, if any, claimed as part of minimum wage, including meal or lodging allowances

- The regular payday designated by the employer

- The name of the employer, including any "doing business as" names used

- The physical address of the employer's main office or principal place of business, and a mailing address, if different

- The employer's phone number

- The name, address and telephone number of the employer's workers' compensation carrier

- Information about mandatory paid sick leave

- Any other information the Labor Commissioner deems material and necessary

Temporary service employers must also include the name, physical address of the main office, mailing address if different from the physical address of the main office, and the telephone number of the legal entity for whom the employee will perform work, as well as any other information the Labor Commissioner deems material and necessary. Security service companies are exempt from this requirement.

Additionally, the employer is required to notify employees in writing of any changes to the information above, within seven calendar days after the time a change is made, unless:

- All changes are reflected on a timely wage statement (must meet all legal requirements)

- Notice is provided in another writing required by law within seven days of the changes

Employees exempt from the payment of overtime wages by statute or Wage Order, employees of the state or any political subdivision (city, county, city and county or special district) and employees covered by a collective bargaining agreement are not covered by the written statement requirement.

What If a Payday Falls on a Sunday or Holiday?

If your business is closed on a payday that falls on a Saturday, Sunday or a legal holiday, you must pay wages no later than the next business day. Make sure you state your policy in your employee handbook.

What If an Employee Fails to Turn in a Time Card?

Even when a nonexempt employee fails to turn in a record of time worked, the law requires you to pay him/her on the established payday.

Since you have no time record to verify actual hours worked, pay all wages that would normally be due for the employee's work period and defer payment of overtime until the next pay period. If the payment results in an overpayment of wages, deducting the wages from the next payroll can be risky. Consult legal counsel before taking such action.

 Exempt employees should not turn in time cards for pay purposes.

What Form Can a Paycheck Take?

All paychecks must be payable in cash, on demand and without discount, at a bank that does business in California. The bank's name and address must appear on the paycheck.

At the time the paycheck is issued, and for at least 30 days after, you must maintain sufficient funds in the payroll account, or credit, for payment. Paying any wage with a check that is backed by insufficient funds is unlawful. See "What Happens If I Issue a Paycheck That Is Returned for Insufficient Funds?" on page 207.

You can also use an electronic transfer system (direct deposit) to transfer wages to a bank, savings and loan or credit union if the employee chooses to do so. You may not force employees to use a direct deposit system. Even though the money is transferred electronically, you must still provide a written statement of wages and deductions to the employee.

You may deposit final wages by direct deposit if the payment complies with existing laws concerning final payment and the employee authorizes you to do so.

Itemized Wage Statement

California employers have a legal obligation to provide employees with specified information regarding their wages. You must provide each employee an itemized statement, in writing and at the time wages are paid, that contains the following information:

- Gross wages earned

- Total hours worked (except exempt employees)

- All deductions, including taxes, disability insurance and health and welfare payments

  - Deductions ordered by the employee can be aggregated and shown as one item

- Net wages earned

- The pay period's inclusive dates

- Name of the employee and last four digits of his/her Social Security number (SSN)

  - All employers can print no more than the last four digits of an employee's Social Security number on check stubs or similar documents (they can substitute some other identifying number)

- Name and address of employer or legal entity

- All applicable hourly rates in effect during the pay period and the corresponding number of hours the employee worked at each hourly rate

- Piece rate units and applicable piece rate, if the employee is paid on a piece rate basis

- Temporary service employers must also include the rate of pay and the total hours worked for each temporary services assignment. Licensed security services companies are specifically excluded from this law

 AB 2535 amends Labor Code Section 226 and clarifies that employees who are exempt from the payment of minimum wage and overtime are not required to have their hours tracked and logged on an itemized wage statement, commonly referred to as a pay stub.

California's mandatory PSL law requires employers to provide employees with a written notice that sets forth the amount of paid sick leave available for use, or paid time off leave an employer provides in lieu of sick leave. Employers can provide the information on either:

- The employee's itemized wage statement; or

- A separate writing provided on the designated pay date with the employee's payment of wages.

Failing to provide an itemized wage statement or to include the correct information on the wage statement may subject you to a Private Attorneys General Act (PAGA) claim which contains additional penalties (for more information, see "Private Attorneys General Act (PAGA) Claims" on page 208).

California law provides employers a limited time period to fix specific technical violations (failing to list the inclusive dates of the pay period or the employer's proper legal name and address) on itemized wage statements before civil litigation begins.

The period of time is very short, so employers should respond promptly and consult legal counsel when faced with litigation from employees seeking financial penalties related to technical violations on wage statements.

Do I Need to Report any Payroll Information?

You must provide information to assist district attorneys with the enforcement of garnishments for child support. In an effort to collect child support, federal law requires all employers to report certain information on their newly hired employees to the EDD within 20 days of hire. All businesses and government entities that hire independent contractors must file similar reports. For more details, see "Independent Contractors" in Chapter 2, page 53.

What Sort of Records Must I Retain?

You must maintain an accurate record of employees' hours of work and compensation. The basic recordkeeping obligation includes the employee's:

- Name

- Home address

- Date of birth (if under 18 years of age)

- Occupation/job title

- Total wages and other compensation paid during each payroll period

- And for nonexempt employees:

    - Clock time when each work period and off-duty meal period begins and ends (for more information, see "Meal and Rest Periods" on page 176)

    - Total hours worked in each payroll period and applicable rates of pay

    - Number of piece-rate units earned, if applicable, and any piece rate paid

Access to Payroll Files

You must keep an indelible record of payments and deductions for each employee for at least three years. The employee, upon reasonable request, can inspect and/or copy these records.

 TIP **Indelible records** are records that can't be erased or deleted.

If an employee or ex-employee requests to review or receive copies of the payments and deductions listed in "Wage Garnishments" on page 198, you must comply with the request within 21 calendar days. You may charge the individual for the actual cost of reproducing the requested information.

A copy includes a duplicate of the itemized statement provided to an employee or a computer-generated record that accurately shows all of the information required by law to be included in the itemized statement.

The penalty (for actual damages) for failure to comply may be up to $4,000 plus costs and attorneys' fees for the employee. The Labor Commissioner may also impose a penalty of up to $750. For more information, see "What Happens If I Fail to Provide a Statement of Wage Deductions?" on page 207.

Execution of Release on Account of Wages Due

You can't ask or require an employee to forgo wages due or "execute a release" of wages due. The phrase "execute a release" includes requiring an employee, as a condition of being paid, to sign a false statement of the hours he/she worked during a pay period. Employers who violate this law are guilty of a misdemeanor.

Deductions From Employee Pay

You must make certain deductions from the total compensation of both exempt and nonexempt employees. You must take out taxes and wage garnishments, if any.

Federal and State Taxes

You must make certain tax deductions from employee paychecks.

Federal Income Tax

Use the *W-4 – Employee's Withholding Allowance Certificate* (described in Table 4 in Chapter 2, page 62) and the withholding methods described in the Employer's Tax Guide (Publication 15) from the IRS. You can download the Employer's Tax Guide from the IRS website at ***www.irs.gov***.

State Income Tax

Use the *DE4 - California Employee's Withholding Certificate* (described in Table 4 in Chapter 2, page 62). For information about rates, forms, exemptions and withholdings, contact the EDD or visit its website at ***www.edd.ca.gov***.

Social Security (FICA)

Both you and your employee must pay Social Security taxes. You must withhold and deposit the employee's withheld taxes and pay a matching amount.

 The withholding rate for 2017 is 6.2 percent (unchanged from 2016). However, the wage base limit for 2017 increased to $127,200.

Medicare

Both you and your employee must pay Medicare taxes. You must withhold and deposit the employee's withheld taxes and pay a matching amount at the rate of 1.45 percent (no wage base limit). The Medicare tax rate is unchanged from 2016.

State Disability Insurance (SDI) Tax

SDI provides temporary disability benefits for employees disabled by a non-work-related illness or injury. You must withhold monies from each paycheck.

 The SDI withholding rate for 2017 is 0.9 percent, unchanged from 2016. The taxable wage limit for 2017 is $110,902 for each employee per calendar year, and the annual maximum withholding is $998.12.

Paid Family Leave (PFL) Tax

PFL provides temporary disability benefits for employees who can't work because of the need to care for a family member or bond with a child. You must withhold monies from each paycheck. The SDI withholding includes the PFL tax.

Wage Garnishments

A public agency or court judgment may require you to withhold money from an employee's paycheck. This is known as a "wage garnishment."

The money is distributed to a third party pursuant to the order from a public agency or a court judgment. These third parties could be government agencies, debt collection companies or divorced spouses, for example. Make these deductions after taking out taxes.

The amount of wages exempt from garnishment is higher under the California standard than the federal standard. In California, a withholding order can't exceed the lesser of:

- 25 percent of an individual's weekly disposable earnings; or

- 50 percent of the amount by which the disposable earnings for the week exceed 40 times the state minimum hourly wage in effect.

If the employee works in a location where the local minimum hourly wage is greater than the state minimum hourly wage, the local minimum hourly wage in effect at the time the earnings are payable must be used for the calculation.

 The Consumer Credit Protection Act prohibits you from terminating an employee for having his/her wages garnished.

You must comply with garnishment orders as written until directed otherwise by the issuing agency or the court, stopping the withholdings only when ordered to do so.

When you receive the court order:

- Mark the date received on the notice and retain the postmarked envelope in case you need to prove timely compliance.

- Keep a copy of the court order in the employee's personnel file as the legal basis for making the payroll deduction.

- Advise the employee of the court order within 10 days of receiving the order, as well as the date you will make the first deduction. The first deduction must be made within 10 days of your receipt of the order, unless the order specifies otherwise.

Employers can withhold $1.50 for each payment made, in compliance with an earnings withholding order that enforces payment of support obligations.

 You must notify the appropriate agency if an employee subject to wage garnishment leaves your company.

If you have any questions about wage garnishments, please visit the Judicial Council's website at ***www.courts.ca.gov/documents/wg002.pdf*** to download the Form WG-002, which contains instructions for employers.

Child Support or Alimony

Court orders for child support take precedence over all other garnishments. If the employee has multiple child support garnishments, current support takes priority over past due support.

Regardless of the number of garnishments, you can't deduct more of the employee's disposable income than:

- 50 percent if the employee has current spouse/child dependents

- Or 60 percent if the employee has no dependents

An additional 5 percent may be garnished for support payments that are more than 12 weeks behind. Different limits apply for child support (50 percent of amount remaining after deductions).

California law imposes a penalty on an employer that helps an employee or contractor with child support obligations to evade meeting those obligations, including failure to file reports upon hiring.

The law imposes liability upon any person or business entity that knowingly helps a child support obliger with an unpaid child support obligation to escape, evade or avoid current payment of those unpaid child support obligations. The penalty is three times the value of the assistance to have been provided, up to the total amount of the entire child support obligation due.

The penalty will not apply if the unpaid obligation is satisfied. Prohibited actions, when an individual or entity knows or should have known of the child support obligation, include:

- Hiring or employing a person who owes child support without making a timely report to the EDD's New Employee Registry

- Retaining an independent contractor who owes child support and failing to file a timely report of such engagement with the EDD

- Paying wages or other forms of compensation (including cash, barter or trade) not reported to the EDD

Visit the California Department of Child Support Services website at **www.childsup.ca.gov/Portals/0/employer/docs/EmployerHndbk.pdf** for a complete guide to complying with child support orders.

Attempted Service on Employees

Employees who are embroiled in legal disputes, such as civil lawsuits or divorce and custody proceedings, may be served with legal papers at work.

Process servers have no legal right to enter an employer's premises to serve legal papers and employers can ask them to leave without fear of repercussion. An employer also has no obligation to direct an employee to meet a process server at a worksite.

Employers who have a lobby or reception area to receive visitors should make a policy decision as to whether it will cooperate with process servers and call employees to reception to be served. Reception staff should be trained to either call employees to meet a process server or to ask the process server to leave the premises.

Since service must be made personally to the individual identified in the legal documents, employers should instruct all employees, including management employees, not to accept service of process on behalf of any other employee.

Back Taxes

The amount deducted depends on how many dependents the employee has. The more dependents, the less the IRS can deduct.

Deductions and Repayment for Employee Related Items

You can make deductions from an employee's paycheck for certain items, such as meals, lodging or other facilities, because these deductions are for the employee's benefit. You can consider it part of his/her wages and include it in your calculations to ensure that you're meeting minimum wage requirements if:

- The employee entered into a voluntary agreement.

- The amounts credited do not exceed the limits specified in the applicable Wage Order.

As a result of updates to the Division of Labor Standards Enforcement's (DLSE) manual, consider the following before deducting from an employee's paycheck:

- If you loan money to an employee, ask him/her to sign a promissory note guaranteeing repayment and get the repayment by personal check or other form of payment — never through a payroll deduction.

- Discuss automatic enrollment in your 401(k) or other retirement plan with your benefits provider. Not all providers follow the automatic enrollment process.

- Review your policies and procedures regarding loans or advances, including advances on vacation and PTO, to ensure you aren't repaid by payroll deduction.

For more information, see "Wages and Salaries" on page 164.

Impermissible Employer Deductions

You can't deduct for any cash shortages (for example, if a cashier's drawer doesn't match the record), breakage or loss of equipment from employees' wages. You can't make deductions for ordinary wear and tear to uniforms and equipment. You can't deduct the cost of a uniform from employees' wages.

You also can't require them to purchase the uniform on their own, unless it would be generally worn in an occupation — for example, a nurse's uniform, or basic wardrobe items, such as white shirts, dark pants and black shoes and belts (of an unspecified design) for waitstaff.

If you require tools and equipment, you must furnish and maintain them, except for customary hand tools required of employees making at least twice the minimum wage. Be sure to consult the Wage Order applicable to your industry relating to uniforms, tools and equipment.

Voluntary Deductions

The employee can volunteer to have other monies deducted from his/her paycheck, such as:

- Charitable contributions
- 401(k)/IRA contributions
- Health insurance plans
- Union dues

Some voluntary deductions can be taken out before taxes, thus reducing the employee's taxable income. For more information, visit the IRS website at **www.irs.gov**.

Deductions From an Exempt Employee's Salary

Exempt employees receive a full week's salary for any week in which they perform any work, except in the following situations:

- If the employee is hired and begins work in the middle of the week
- If the employee is terminated in the middle of the week
- If the employee's absences are covered under the federal Family and Medical Leave Act and/or the California Family Rights Act
- If the employee's absence meets the criteria described in this section

Deductions may be made from an exempt employee's accrued vacation or paid time off (PTO) bank for partial-day absences, in accordance with your policy or practice. Never make a partial day deduction from an exempt employee's salary.

Deductions for Partial Day Absences Caused by Sickness or Injury

Partial day absences caused by sickness or injury can be charged to an exempt employee's sick pay bank, provided the employee has such sick pay available at the time of the absence.

Deductions for Absences From Vacation Pay/PTO

If the employee has accrued vacation pay/PTO:

- You may make a deduction for a complete day of absence.

 You can't require employees to use vacation/PTO for a partial week's absence for convenience only (for example, for a plant shutdown).

- You may make a deduction for a partial day of absence from accrued vacation pay/PTO in whatever increment your policy specifies. You may not make a deduction for a partial day of absence from the employee's *salary*.

If an employee has no vacation/PTO accrued or used up all his/her vacation pay/PTO:

- You may make a deduction for a complete day of absence from the employee's salary if he/she is absent for personal reasons and has no accrued benefit or used all accrued time.

- You may not make a deduction from the employee's salary if the employee is sick. Deductions from pay for full day increments if an employee is sick may be made only if the employer has a bona fide sick leave plan, the employee has exhausted all sick leave available and the employee is absent for a full day.

- You may *not* make a deduction for a partial day of absence from an exempt employee's salary.

You should give reasonable notice to exempt employees before you require them to take paid time off or vacation during a business closure or plant shutdown.

Pay and Scheduling Violations

Employee pay is a serious matter. You face steep penalties if you fail to pay employees in the proper manner and do not make required withholding deductions.

The Labor Commissioner enforces wage-and-hour laws and has the power to:

- Issue levies and liens on employer property to enforce a judgment;

- Issue a "stop order" to satisfy a final judgment for unpaid wages; or

- Deny a license to an employer in the long-term care industry for failing to pay a judgment for unpaid wages.

California law also:

- Imposes personal liability on individuals acting on the behalf of the employer who violate wage and hour provision in the Labor Code; and

- Provides joint and several liability for unpaid wages in the property services (including janitorial, security guard, valet parking, landscaping and gardening businesses) and long term care industries when judgments are not satisfied.

What Happens If I Fail to Pay the Minimum Wage?

The California Labor Commissioner can:

- Assess fines

  - First offense: $100 per employee per pay period

  - Subsequent offenses: $250 per employee per pay period

- File charges with the district attorney

If found guilty of a misdemeanor (a criminal offense that's less serious than a felony), you will have to pay the difference between the minimum wage and the wage paid during the period of violation, and pay court costs. You may also have to pay a fine of $100 or more; go to jail for 30 days; or both.

What Happens If I Fail to Pay Overtime?

The California Labor Commissioner can assess civil penalties against you or any other person acting on your behalf:

- First offense — $50 fine per underpaid employee, plus the amount of underpaid wages

- Subsequent offenses — $100 fine per underpaid employee, plus the amount of underpaid wages

What Happens If I Fail to Pay Wages Due an Employee?

This is a misdemeanor, and can bring about a claim with the Labor Commissioner. When an employee files a complaint with the Labor Commissioner to recover unpaid wages, the Labor Commissioner will:

- Investigate the complaint.

- Hold hearings and take action to recover wages (the Labor Commissioner will notify the parties whether a hearing will be held within 30 days after a complaint was filed).

- Assess penalties and make demands for compensation.

The Labor Commissioner can assess fines of up to $200 per employee per pay period, plus 25 percent of the wages not paid to each employee each pay period. All awards made by the Labor Commissioner accrue interest on all due and unpaid wages. In the event of a dispute over wages, you must pay, without condition, all of the undisputed wages.

 If you don't pay the disputed wages within 10 days after the Labor Commissioner resolves the dispute, you will have to pay triple the amount due to the employee.

If you must comply with the federal Fair Labor Standards Act, employees may initiate claims with the U.S. Department of Labor (DOL). Employers should contact legal counsel if the DOL begins an investigation. For details about the FLSA and the DOL, see "Glossary of Terms, Laws and Agencies" on page 331.

What Happens If I Use a Labor Contractor and the Contractor Violates the Law?

Under state law, an employer who contracts for labor may be held accountable for wage-and-hour violations committed by the labor contractor. The law covers any business entity with 25 or more workers that obtains or is provided at least six (6) workers to perform labor within the usual course of business from one labor contractor or various labor contractors.

If a labor contractor fails to pay its employees properly or fails to provide workers' compensation coverage for those employees, the client employer is legally responsible.

What Happens If I Fail to Give Nonexempt Employees Meal and Rest Breaks?

For each workday you fail to provide an employee a meal period, you must pay the employee one additional hour of pay at his/her regular rate. For each workday you fail to provide an employee a rest period, you must pay the employee one additional hour of pay at his/her regular rate. Premium pay for missed meal or rest breaks can raise your payroll costs by as much as 25 percent.

 You are liable for only one hour of pay even if the employee fails to take both rest periods. However, if the employee does not receive one or more meal breaks and one or more rest breaks, you owe two hours of pay at the regular rate of pay. Failure to pay the wages due may result in a civil penalties. For more information, see "What Happens If I Fail to Pay Wages Due an Employee?" on page 205.

A three-year statute of limitations applies to the "one additional hour of pay" employers must pay employees when meal and/or rest breaks aren't provided. In some cases, the statute of limitations can be four years.

The California Supreme Court in *Brinker Restaurant Corp. v. Superior Court* clarified that employers must "provide" employees with unpaid, 30-minute meal periods, but need not "ensure" such periods are taken. Once the meal period is provided, there is no duty to police meal breaks to ensure no work is being done. For more information, see "Meal and Rest Periods" on page 176.

An employee who voluntarily chooses to work during a provided meal period may be eligible for straight pay if the employer knew or reasonably should have known of the work. The employer will not be required to pay premium pay if it "provided" the meal period and the employee voluntarily did some work.

There are limited exceptions to the meal period requirement for employees in:

- Wholesale baking
- The motion picture or broadcasting industry
- Construction
- Commercial drivers
- Security guards
- Utility company employees

 Consult with your legal counsel if you have employees in one of these industries.

What Can Go Wrong With an Alternative Workweek Schedule?

The Labor Commissioner can invalidate an alternative workweek schedule for a number of reasons, including improper implementation, improper payment of overtime and changing the schedule without the required procedure, among others.

In addition, employees on public works and those in agricultural occupations under Wage Order 14 may not work alternative workweeks. Employees covered by collective bargaining agreements that pay premium rates for overtime hours and at least 30 percent more than the state minimum wage are not required to comply with the alternative workweek regulations.

What Happens If I Fail to Provide a Statement of Wage Deductions?

If you don't provide the paycheck information, the employee can recover $50 per employee for the initial violation and $100 per employee for subsequent violations, up to $4,000.

If you don't provide the statements in writing or fail to keep the records for three years, you must pay a civil penalty of $250 per employee for the first violation and $1,000 per employee for each subsequent violation. If you make a clerical error or inadvertent mistake on the first violation, the Labor Commissioner has discretionary power not to penalize you.

What Happens If I Issue a Paycheck That Is Returned for Insufficient Funds?

The penalty for issuing a nonsufficient funds (NSF) check is one day's pay for each day the wages remain unpaid, not to exceed 30 days of wages:

- The penalty applies to any wages paid with a nonsufficient funds instrument.
- If the NSF check is provided for payment of final wages owed, the employer would face penalties both for payment by NSF check and for late payment of final wages.
- The penalty provided for NSF is not applicable if the employee recovers the service charge authorized by law.

What Happens If I Don't Issue a Final Paycheck in a Timely Manner?

You are liable for a penalty of one day's wages for each day the check is late, up to a maximum of 30 days. Any penalty awarded by the Labor Commissioner is paid to the employee who was not paid on time.

What Should I Know About Wage Claims?

Employees who believe they have not been paid correctly may file a wage claim with the state Labor Commissioner or pursue a civil claim. When a claim is filed with the Labor Commissioner and a decision rendered, either party can file an appeal to a trial court.

If the party seeking the review is not successful, the court could award the non-appealing party monetary damages for court costs and attorneys' fees. The party that appealed would have to pay these costs.

An employee's claim is considered successful if he/she recovers a judgment in any amount greater than zero.

Private Attorneys General Act (PAGA) Claims

Under the Private Attorneys General Act of 2004 (PAGA), an individual aggrieved employee, acting on his/her own behalf and/or on behalf of other current and former employees, can bring a civil action for Labor Code violations.

An aggrieved employee can recover the applicable civil penalty on behalf of himself/herself and other current or former employees against whom one or more of the alleged violations was committed. Employees must comply with specific procedural and notice requirements before filing a civil suit. Employers have the opportunity to "cure" violations before the lawsuit proceeds. The law includes civil penalties of:

- $100 per aggrieved employee per pay period for the initial violation
- $200 per aggrieved employee per pay period for subsequent violations

Twenty-five percent of the penalties goes to the employee(s). If the employee prevails in the civil action, he/she is also entitled to an award of reasonable attorneys' fees and costs.

Minimum Compliance Elements

1. Hang your *2017 California and Federal Labor Law Poster* (available from *store.calchamber.com*), which includes mandatory postings that all employees and applicants must be able to see, in a prominent place (such as a break room). It includes the Healthy Workplaces, Healthy Families Act of 2014 Paid Sick Leave poster.

   If you have employees working in a city or county with a local minimum wage and/or paid sick leave ordinance, you may also need to post required local notices and provide additional notices to employees at the time of hire.

2. Require your nonexempt (hourly) employees to keep accurate records of time worked.

3. Require that your nonexempt (hourly) employees follow meal and rest period requirements.

4. Calculate overtime for nonexempt employees after eight hours worked in a day and after 40 hours in a workweek (see "Overtime Pay" on page 183).

5. Make sure you don't treat your exempt employees like nonexempt workers — remember, your exempt employees get paid to get the job done, not to work a set number of hours.

6. Get to know the Wage Order for your industry and post it in a conspicuous place (see "California Wage Orders" on page 159).

7. Comply with payday rules and notice requirements.

8. Distribute required notices and pamphlets.

Forms and Checklists

The following table describes forms and checklists associated with paying employees.

 TIP You can find these forms in your online formspack, described in detail in"Online Forms" on page 12.

Table 14. Forms And Checklists

Notice Or Form	What Do I Use It For?	When Do I Use It?	Who Fills It Out?	Where Does It Go?
Absence Request	Give this form to employees when requesting future time off or reporting previous time off. This form also gives your employees the opportunity to indicate a Family and Medical Leave absence, although it is not required.	When an employee requests time off or reports time off taken.	The employee.	In the employee's personnel file; and a copy should go to payroll.
Absence Request - Spanish	Give this form to employees when requesting future time off or reporting previous time off. This form also gives your employees the opportunity to indicate a Family and Medical Leave absence, although it is not required.	When an employee requests time off or reports time off taken.	The employee.	In the employee's personnel file; and a copy should go to payroll.

Table 14. Forms And Checklists *(continued)*

Notice Or Form	What Do I Use It For?	When Do I Use It?	Who Fills It Out?	Where Does It Go?
Makeup Time Checklist	To help you figure out if, when and how to offer the time.	When you plan your pay policies.	The employer.	Keep the checklist in your own employee pay records.
Makeup Time Request	To document requests for the time.	When an employee requests the time.	The employee.	Keep it in the employee's personnel file.
Makeup Time Request - Spanish	To document requests for the time.	When an employee requests the time.	The employee.	Keep it in the employee's personnel file.
Meal Break Waiver - Employee Shift 6 Hours or Less	Written documentation of a worker's waiver of the 30-minute meal break.	When a nonexempt employee works a shift of six hours or less; use this form when both you and the worker wish to waive the required 30-minute meal break.	You and the employee.	In the employee's file; a copy to payroll.
Meal Break Waiver - Employee Shift 6 Hours or Less - Spanish	Written documentation of a worker's waiver of the 30-minute meal break.	When a nonexempt employee works a shift of six hours or less; use this form when both you and the worker wish to waive the required 30-minute meal break.	You and the employee.	In the employee's file; a copy to payroll.

Table 14. Forms And Checklists (*continued*)

Notice Or Form	What Do I Use It For?	When Do I Use It?	Who Fills It Out?	Where Does It Go?
Meal Break - On Duty	Written documentation of an on-duty meal break.	When a nonexempt employee's work prevents him/her from being able to take a meal break; use this form when both you and the worker wish to have the worker work through the required 30-minute meal break. On-duty meal breaks are enforceable in very limited circumstances. Please consult with legal counsel before using this form.	You and the employee.	In the employee's file; a copy to payroll.
Meal Break Waiver - Second Meal	Written documentation of a second meal break waiver.	When a nonexempt employee's shift will be more than 10 hours but less than 12 hours, the worker has not waived his first meal break, and the worker wishes to waive the second required 30-minute meal break, use this form.	You and the employee.	In the employee's file; a copy to payroll.

Table 14. Forms And Checklists *(continued)*

Notice Or Form	What Do I Use It For?	When Do I Use It?	Who Fills It Out?	Where Does It Go?
Overtime Request	To document in writing employee requests to work overtime hours.	Provide these forms to supervisors, managers and employees and train all employees in using this form whenever overtime work is needed or performed.	You and the employee.	In the employee's file; a copy to payroll.
Overtime Request - Spanish	To document in writing employee requests to work overtime hours.	Provide these forms to supervisors, managers and employees and train all employees in using this form whenever overtime work is needed or performed.	You and the employee.	In the employee's file; a copy to payroll.
Wage and Employment Notice to Employees (Labor Code section 2810.5)	To notify nonexempt employees of their hourly or piece rate of pay, pay dates and other information required by law.	At the time of hire, or on an employee's first day of employment.	The employer.	Give a copy to the new employee and keep a copy in the employee's personnel file.

Where Do I Go for More Information?

CalChamber and federal and state government agencies offer a variety of resources to help you learn more about issues related to wages and hours.

Table 15. Additional Resources

For Information On	Check Out These Resources
General	From CalChamber: • The **2017 California Labor Law Digest**, the most comprehensive, California-specific resource to help employers comply with complex federal and state labor laws and regulations • **Employee Handbook Creator** • **HRCalifornia.com** • **store.calchamber.com**
Child Support Wage Garnishments	• State Department of Social Services, Office of Child Support (866) 249-0773 at **www.childsup.ca.gov** • Franchise Tax Board at **www.ftb.ca.gov/aboutFTB/manuals/arm/cpm/**
Living Wages	• Communities with Living Wage Ordinances at **http://laborcenter.berkeley.edu/livingwage/resources.shtml**

CalChamber also provides many ongoing and comprehensive educational opportunities for small business owners, HR beginners and experienced HR professionals alike. These include online training, and special HR seminars and webinars. For more information, please visit the CalChamber store website at **store.calchamber.com**.

Chapter 6

Ensuring Workplace Safety

You must provide a safe working environment for all your workers. The law requires you to reasonably protect your employees from work-related illness and injuries and workplace violence.

In this chapter, you can find answers to questions about:

- Basic standards

- Injury and Illness Prevention Program (IIPP)

- OSHA inspections

- Heat illness

Basic Standards

Every employer must follow regulations created by the U.S. Occupational Safety and Health Administration (OSHA) and the California Division of Occupational Safety and Health (DOSH), better known as Cal/OSHA (see "Glossary of Terms, Laws and Agencies" on page 331). These regulations set standards for workplace safety.

The Cal/OSHA standards you must comply with vary on the size of your company and whether your company is deemed high- or low-hazard. Six basic standards apply to just about every company:

- IIPP (see page 218)

- Emergency Action Plan (see page 221)

- Fire Prevention Plan (see page 222)

- Work Surfaces, Control Devices and Emergency Equipment (see page 224)

- Hazard Communication Program (HAZCOM) (see page 225)

- Repetitive Motion Injuries (Ergonomics) (see page 227)

Individual standards require more detailed plans, such as the Emergency Action Plan, that describe how you will help your employees stay safe on the job. Knowing which safety standards apply to your company and communicating them clearly to your employees is essential for avoiding inspections and, more importantly, preserving the welfare and safety of your workplace and employees.

If your company is exempt from complying with part or all of a standard, you should consider establishing a plan or program for handling potential situations, especially if the information can be added to your employee handbook or employee manual. You can get copies of the exact standards from Cal/OSHA. See "Where Do I Go for More Information?" on page 255.

California employers face Cal/OSHA inspections, citations and compliance schedules. Cal/OSHA's inspection program targets workplaces where there is a likelihood of health and safety hazards and/or violations of standards. Cal/OSHA must have reasonable cause to conduct an inspection, but court decisions have granted Cal/OSHA broad discretion in determining what is reasonable cause.

Why Do I Need to Follow These Standards?

If you don't follow these standards and don't create appropriate safety plans or programs, Cal/OSHA can cite you for violating the applicable standard. In addition, documenting your plans for compliance can help you prove your intentions of complying if you receive a citation, which can help reduce the citation.

Sharing the information in these standards with your employees also helps you provide them with the knowledge they need to avoid or respond to potential dangers. For example, advise them on the best escape route in case of a fire, where you store the first aid kit, what health dangers they might be exposed to at work and how they can communicate their safety concerns to you.

Should I Perform Self-Inspections Related to These Standards?

It's a good practice to perform your own inspections of your site and equipment, your employees' safety practices and your safety documents:

- Internal inspections present the best defense against and preparation for inspections by outside agencies.

- Many OSHA standards require you to document periodic inspections for compliance.

- During an inspection, you may identify a potential hazard, find a broken safety guard or determine that your employees need refresher safety training.

- Inspections keep you familiarized with your site, processes and operations so you can evaluate your workplace's efficiency and productivity.

Smoking In the Workplace

New legislation changed the rules relating to smoking in the workplace and expanded already-existing smoke-free workplace protections. These rules took effect **June 9, 2016**.

In part, the new legislation:

- Treats the use of e-cigarettes and other nicotine-delivery devices, such as vaporizers, as "smoking" – thus extending existing smoking bans to cover such products.

- Expands smoke-free workplace protections by getting rid of most of the existing exemptions that permitted smoking in certain work environments, such as bars, hotel lobbies, warehouse facilities.

- Eliminates the ability to have employer-designated smoking break rooms.

- Expands the workplace smoking ban to include owner-operated businesses and to eliminate any small business exception for employers with five or fewer employees.

- Raises the legal smoking age from 18 to 21, except for active military personnel.

Proposition 64 and Workplace Policies

In 2016, California joined several other states in legalizing recreational use of marijuana by adults. Proposition 64, also known as the Adult Use of Marijuana Act, legalized the recreational use of marijuana for adults 21 years old and over. The provisions related to the legalization of marijuana and workplace protections took effect November 9, 2016.

However, Proposition 64 maintains the status quo for employers seeking to maintain a drug- and alcohol-free workplace. In other words, employer policies related to drug possession, use and impairment as well as testing are not compromised with the legalization of marijuana use under Proposition 64.

Proposition 64 explicitly states that it is intended to "allow public and private employers to enact and enforce workplace policies pertaining to marijuana." The initiative also provides that it will not be construed or interpreted to amend, repeal, affect, restrict or pre-empt:

> "The rights and obligations of public and private employers to maintain a drug and alcohol free workplace or require an employer to permit or accommodate the use, consumption, possession, transfer, display, transportation, sale or growth of marijuana in the workplace, or affect the ability of employers to have policies prohibiting the use of marijuana by employees and prospective employees, or prevent employers from complying with state or federal law (Section 11362.45 (f))."

Even with the passage of Proposition 64, employers may continue to prohibit use, possession and impairment at work and may continue to test for use when appropriate. Proposition 64 is not intended to interfere with these workplace policies or practices.

Injury and Illness Prevention Program

Every company must create an effective Injury and Illness Prevention Program (IIPP) to keep its workforce free from work-related injuries and illnesses.

The IIPP essentially contains a generalized plan for keeping the workforce free from work-related injuries and illnesses, including workplace violence. The online formspack that comes with this book contains an approved *Injury and Illness Prevention Program for Non-High Hazard Employers*.

No single law governs how all organizations should address the issue of workplace violence. The steps you should take to prevent violence in the workplace depend on the risk factors present in your particular workplace. However, an increasing amount of legislation is enacted to protect against violence in certain highly charged and vulnerable workplaces. California laws might play a role in how your organization prepares for or responds to acts of violence in the workplace.

New
2016
Effective **July 1, 2016**, Cal/OSHA requires specified types of hospitals, including general acute care hospitals or acute psychiatric hospitals, to adopt workplace violence prevention plans as part of the hospitals' injury and illness prevention plans. The intent is to protect health care workers and other facility personnel from aggressive and violent behavior.

Does the Law Require Me to Comply With This Standard?

Yes, every employer must have an IIPP. You may be exempt from some of the written recordkeeping requirements if you are an establishment:

- With fewer than 20 employees during the calendar year and in an industry not on the designated high hazard list and you have a workers' compensation Experience Modification Rate (ExMod) of 1.1 percent or less

- With fewer than 20 employees during the calendar year on a designated list of Low Hazard Industries

If you fall into one of these two categories, you can limit written documentation of the IIPP to the following requirements:

- The identity of the person(s) with authority and responsibility for program implementation as required by Title 8 of the California Code of Regulations, section 3203(a)(1)

- Scheduled periodic "inspections" to identify unsafe conditions and work practices as required by Title 8 of the California Code of Regulations, section 3203(a)(4)

- Training and instruction provided to employees as required by Title 8 of the California Code of Regulations, section 3203(a)(7)

Local government entities are not required to keep records of the steps taken to implement and maintain their IIPPs. These include:

- Counties, cities and districts

- Public or quasi-public corporations

- Public agencies

- Any public entity, other than a state agency, that is a member of, or created by, a joint powers agreement

Does the Law Require Me to Create a Written Program?

Yes. You can use the *Injury and Illness Prevention Program for Non-High Hazard Employers*, described in Table 16 on page 249, to help you get started.

Your plan must specify:

- Management approval of the plan and the person(s) responsible for implementing it

- A company safety policy statement
- A system to identify workplace hazards
- A plan for periodic scheduled inspections
- A plan for investigating injuries
- A plan for safety training
- How you will communicate with employees about safety
- The recordkeeping and posting requirements and any exceptions to these

Does the Law Require Me to Provide Training?

Yes. Training is required when you:

- Implement your IIPP
- Assign a new employee to a position
- Transfer an existing employee to a new position
- Make changes to workplace conditions

Provide refresher training as necessary. You can use the *Individual Safety Training Certificate*, *Initial Safety Training Certificate* and *Training Sign-In Sheet*, described in Table 16 on page 249, to document training sessions.

Does the Law Require Me to Provide Personal Protective Equipment?

Some standards, such as those governing chemical use or certain types of machinery, require you to supply equipment to protect your employees.

PPE, or Personal Protective Equipment, includes items such as gloves, masks and special clothing used to protect against hazardous, toxic or infectious materials.

Does the Law Require Me to Perform Inspections?

Yes. You can choose the frequency, depending on how hazardous your work environment is.

Does the Law Require Me to Record and/or Report Anything?

Yes. Any injury that requires medical treatment beyond first aid and all occupational illnesses must be investigated, recorded and reported. You can use the *Accident, Injury and Illness Investigation* form described in Table 16 on page 249, to help you document the incident.

For more information on knowing what to record and when, see "Reporting and Recording Work-Related Injuries and Illnesses" on page 239.

Emergency Action Plan

The Emergency Action Plan standard requires you to create and follow a plan for handling emergencies, including evacuating employees, providing emergency medical attention and reporting emergencies to employees and community agencies.

Does the Law Require Me to Comply With This Standard?

Yes, every employer must have a program. You are exempt from the written plan requirements if you employ 10 or fewer staff.

Does the Law Require Me to Create a Written Program?

Yes, if you have more than 10 employees. You can use the *Emergency Action Plan*, described in Table 16 on page 249, to help you document your program. Your plan must specify:

- Person(s) responsible for implementing the plan or portions of the plan
- How to communicate emergencies to employees
- Fire and emergency evacuation policies
- Personnel assigned to provide first aid and emergency medical attention

Does the Law Require Me to Provide Training?

Yes. Train employees when you establish or change your plan, and when you hire new employees. Conduct emergency training and drills periodically. You can use the

Individual Safety Training Certificate, Initial Safety Training Certificate and *Training Sign-In Sheet*, described in Table 16 on page 249, to document training sessions.

Does the Law Require Me to Provide Personal Protective Equipment?

Yes. You must comply with blood-borne pathogens exposure regulations and exposure prevention requirements for any employee who provides emergency first aid, and you must provide any other equipment employees need to handle emergencies. See "Where Do I Go for More Information?" on page 255 for links to helpful websites.

Does the Law Require Me to Perform Inspections?

No, but you should cover this as part of your periodic IIPP inspections.

Does the Law Require Me to Record and/or Report Anything?

Not for the Emergency Action Plan, but recordkeeping is required for your IIPP. Follow those requirements in case of an incident.

Fire Prevention Plan

The Fire Prevention Plan standard requires you to know what fire hazards your employees are exposed to and to create and follow a plan for handling fires. For companies with more than 10 employees, the plan must be in writing.

Does the Law Require Me to Comply With This Standard?

Yes, every employer must have a plan.

Does the Law Require Me to Create a Written Program?

Yes, if you employ more than 10 employees. You can use the *Fire Prevention Plan*, described in Table 16 on page 249, to help you document your program.

Your plan must specify:

- Person(s) responsible for implementing the fire prevention program
- Known fire hazards in the area
- Your fire prevention practices
- What fire control measures you put in place (i.e. sprinkler systems)
- The frequency of inspection and maintenance of fire control devices
- Alarm systems
- Special employee responsibilities

Does the Law Require Me to Provide Training?

Yes. Train employees on fire prevention and safe work practices, either as part of your IIPP training or as a separate fire prevention program. You can use the *Individual Safety Training Certificate, Initial Safety Training Certificate* and *Training Sign-In Sheet,* described in Table 16 on page 249, to document training sessions.

Does the Law Require Me to Provide Personal Protective Equipment?

PPE is not required. But standard fire protection equipment, such as fire extinguishers, sprinkler systems and alarms, is required.

Does the Law Require Me to Perform Inspections?

Yes. Use the *Fire Prevention Checklist,* described in Table 16 on page 249, to help you determine what and when you should inspect.

Does the Law Require Me to Record and/or Report Anything?

Yes. Record employee training in fire prevention, and document periodic inspections and fire protection equipment maintenance.

Work Surfaces, Control Devices and Emergency Equipment

The Work Surfaces, Control Devices and Emergency Equipment standards cover employee-occupied areas and set minimum safety limits for lighting, flooring, housekeeping, entrances and exits.

Does the Law Require Me to Comply With This Standard?

Yes, every employer must comply with the standards. Use the *Safety Inspection for Work Spaces and Surfaces Checklist*, described in Table 16 on page 249, to help you comply.

Does the Law Require Me to Create a Written Program?

No. Include general information about potential hazards in your written IIPP.

Does the Law Require Me to Provide Training?

Only if you use engineered controls, such as guard rails. Include the training as part of your IIPP training.

Does the Law Require Me to Provide Personal Protective Equipment?

Not unless another standard also applies, such as working with chemicals, projectiles or machinery.

Does the Law Require Me to Perform Inspections?

Inspections are not required. IIPP inspections cover most situations.

Does the Law Require Me to Record and/or Report Anything?

Yes. Record employee training and document any inspections.

HAZCOM

The Hazard Communication Program (HAZCOM) standard requires all employers to communicate workplace hazards to employees, particularly when employees handle, or may be exposed to, hazardous substances during normal work or foreseeable emergencies.

Cal/OSHA modified the California HAZCOM standard to include:

- Revised criteria for classifying chemical hazards

- Revised labeling provisions that include requirements for use of standardized signal words, pictograms, hazard statements and precautionary statements

- A specified format for safety data sheets (previously referred to as "Material Safety Data Sheets")

- Revisions related to definitions of terms used in the standard

- Requirements for employee training on labels and safety data sheets

Cal/OSHA made the modifications to the state standard because the federal OSHA made revisions to federal hazardous communications rules.

Does the Law Require Me to Comply With This Standard?

All employers must comply, except in a few, limited situations. See "Where Do I Go for More Information?" on page 255 for a link to the federal Standard Industry Code (SIC) website.

Does the Law Require Me to Create a Written Program?

Yes. Use the *Hazard Communication Program* form, described in Table 16 on page 249, to help you document the program.

You must explain how you will meet requirements for labeling hazardous substances and other forms of warning that you will provide to employees.

You must obtain and maintain safety data sheets from manufacturers for all labeled containers and items on your inventory of hazardous substances. Your suppliers must provide the safety data sheets.

Safety data sheets contain information provided by a product's manufacturer that describes the product's chemical properties, potential hazards and instruction in safe handling. Inspections are optional as long as you properly maintain all standard documents, such as safety data sheets, labels and warnings.

All labels will be required to have pictograms, a signal word, hazard and precautionary statements, the product identifier and supplier identification. Labels cannot be removed or defaced. A pictogram "quickcard" is currently available on this OSHA webpage at ***https://www.osha.gov/Publications/ HazComm_QuickCard_Pictogram.html***.

Does the Law Require Me to Provide Training?

Train all new employees and provide refresher training when you receive new information on hazards and standards. New training is required whenever a new chemical hazard is introduced into the employees' work area.

Employers must provide training on new labels and safety data sheets. In addition, provide Proposition 65 warnings in the training. You can use the *Individual Safety Training Certificate* and *Training Sign-In Sheet*, described in Table 16 on page 249, to document training sessions.

Does the Law Require Me to Provide Personal Protective Equipment?

Not unless another standard also applies, such as working with chemicals, projectiles or machinery.

Does the Law Require Me to Perform Inspections?

Inspections are optional as long as you properly maintain all standard documents, such as safety data sheets, labels and warnings.

Does the Law Require Me to Record and/or Report Anything?

Yes. You must develop and maintain an inventory of all hazardous substances, and document employee training and compliance with the standard. Ensure that hazardous substances in the workplace have safety data sheets. You must document employee training and compliance with the standard.

Repetitive Motion Injuries (Ergonomics)

The Repetitive Motion Injuries Standard, commonly referred to as the Ergonomics standard, requires employers to address workplace injuries due to repetitive motion hazards, which are work tasks that require repeated actions with the additional stress of improper ergonomics or work-station design.

 Ergonomics is the scientific study of the relationship between people and their work environments.

Does the Law Require Me to Comply With This Standard?

Yes, all employers must do what they can to prevent repetitive motion injuries (RMIs). The formal requirements of the standard apply only when:

- More than one employee suffers an RMI.
- The RMIs are musculoskeletal injuries diagnosed by a licensed physician.
- The RMIs were predominantly caused by a repetitive job, process or operation.
- The affected employees performed a job, process or operation of identical work activity.
- The reports of the two RMIs occurred within 12 months of each other.

Does the Law Require Me to Create a Written Program?

No. But a written procedure can assist you in properly implementing the standard. You can use the *Office and Commercial Establishment Safety, Including Ergonomics and Office Chemical Safety* form, described in Table 16 on page 249, as a guide. Your written program should describe:

- How the standard applies and step-by-step instructions for compliance
- Any interim actions you will take to prevent RMIs
- How you will verify the diagnosis of an RMI
- How you will conduct worksite evaluations
- How to implement controls of RMI hazards

Does the Law Require Me to Provide Training?

Yes, you must provide initial training. But refresher training is not required. The standard itself specifies training program content and implementation. See the *Office and Commercial Establishment Safety, Including Ergonomics and Office Chemical Safety* form, described in Table 16 on page 249, for an example of the required training elements.

Does the Law Require Me to Provide Personal Protective Equipment?

Only as a supplement to engineering controls (workstation redesign, adjustable fixtures, etc.) and administrative controls (job rotation and work pacing).

Does the Law Require Me to Perform Inspections?

You need to evaluate a representative number of jobs, processes or operations for proper ergonomic design and to determine if they involve certain motions, positions or other bodily movements hazardous to muscles and joints.

Does the Law Require Me to Record and/or Report Anything?

You must keep records of all worksite evaluations conducted, control measures taken, training provided and Cal/OSHA *Log 300* reporting completed.

Heat Illness

Exposure to conditions of extreme heat and high humidity can subject employees to physical conditions that can range from inconvenient to life-threatening.

Cal/OSHA's heat illness regulations apply to all outdoor places of employment. The heat illness prevention measures required by the regulation may be included in an employer's written Injury and Illness Program, or in a separate document.

Employers subject to all provisions of the regulations, including the high-heat procedures, include agriculture, construction, landscaping, oil and gas extraction, and transportation or delivery of agricultural products, construction materials or other heavy materials.

Cal/OSHA revised the state's heat illness prevention standard, and the revised standard took effect May 1, 2015. The revisions detail exactly what needs to be in an employer's heat illness prevention plan and included changes to:

- When employees must be permitted access to shade;

- What is considered "potable water" that must be made available to employees;

- The monitoring of employees taking a "preventative cool-down rest;" and

- High heat procedures.

 The revised heat illness regulations significantly change the obligations of employers with outdoor places of employment. Employers with outdoor workplaces will need to review their compliance obligations.

Cal/OSHA created a chart to provide guidance on the new requirements. The chart can be downloaded free of charge from HRCalifornia at ***www.hrcalifornia.com*** and from Cal/OSHA's heat illness information page at ***www.dir.ca.gov/dosh/ heatillnessinfo.html***. Cal/OSHA also updated its Heat Illness Prevention Enforcement Q&A webpage and plans to revise educational materials on its website.

Employers with outdoor workforces are advised to review the guidance document and consult legal counsel with any questions.

Providing Water

Employees must have access to potable drinking water meeting certain requirements. The water must be "fresh, pure, suitably cool, and provided to employees free of charge."

The water must be fit to drink and free from odors that would discourage workers from drinking the water. Containers provided to employees must be clean and water provided from non-approved, non-tested water sources (e.g. untested wells) is unacceptable, according to the guidance.

Where drinking water is not plumbed or otherwise continuously supplied, it must be provided in sufficient quantity at the beginning of the work shift to provide one quart per employee per hour for drinking for the entire shift.

Access to Shade

Shade is required to be present when the temperature exceeds 80 degrees Fahrenheit. The employer must maintain one or more shaded areas at all times while employees are present. These shaded areas must be open to the air or ventilated or cooled by other safe means.

The amount of shade must be enough to accommodate the number of employees on recovery or rest periods and those taking onsite meal breaks (the prior standard stated that the shade must accommodate at least 25 percent of the employees on the shift at any time).

Employees must be able to sit in a normal posture fully in the shade without physically touching other employees. The shaded area must be located as close as possible to the areas where employees are working.

When the outdoor temperature in the work area does not exceed 80 degrees Fahrenheit, employers must either provide shade as described in the preceding paragraph or provide timely access to shade upon an employee's request. Employees must be allowed and encouraged to take a cooldown rest in the shade when they feel the need to do so to protect themselves from overheating. Such access to shade must be permitted at all times.

Except for employers in the agricultural industry, cooling measures other than shade (e.g., use of misting machines) may be provided in lieu of shade if the employer can demonstrate that these measures are at least as effective as shade in allowing employees to cool.

Recovery Periods Protected

An employer with employees who work outside cannot require an employee to work during any "recovery period" taken to avoid heat-related illness, as required under Cal/OSHA's heat illness standard. A "recovery period" is defined as a "cooldown period afforded an employee to prevent heat illness."

A worker who takes a preventative cooldown rest:

- Must be monitored and asked if he/she is experiencing heat illness symptoms;

- Must be encouraged to remain in the shade; and

- Must not be ordered back to work until any sign or symptoms have abated, **but in no event less than five (5) minutes in addition to the time needed to access the shade**.

If an employee exhibits signs or reports symptoms of heat illness during the rest, the employer is required to provide first aid or emergency response. According to Cal/OSHA's guidance, first aid should be initiated without delay due to the fact that progression to more serious illness can be rapid. If heat illness is suspected, emergency medical personnel should be immediately contacted.

Employers must be aware of other "preventative cooldown rest periods" requirements, which are a separate set of requirements that apply to the high-heat procedures described in "High Heat Procedures."

An employer who does not provide an employee with a rest and recovery period must pay a one-hour-of-pay premium penalty for each day that the recovery period is not provided. This mirrors the meal and rest period requirements. Rest and recovery periods are paid breaks and count as hours worked.

High-Heat Procedures

Under the heat illness prevention standard, employers in the agriculture, construction, landscaping, oil and gas extraction, and certain transportation and delivery industries must implement high-heat procedures when temperatures equal or exceed 95 degrees.

These procedures must include the following, to the extent practicable:

1. Ensuring that effective communication by voice, observation or electronic means is maintained so that employees at the work site can contact a supervisor when necessary. An electronic device, such as a cell phone or text messaging device, may be used for this purpose only if reception in the area is reliable.

2. Observing employees for alertness and signs or symptoms of heat illness. Under the revised standard, employers are required to ensure effective employee observation and monitoring of signs or symptoms of heat illness. According to the guidelines, whichever method is used the employer must be able to ascertain the condition of employees at regular intervals. Under the regulations, the employer must implement one or more of the following:

   - Direct observation of 20 or fewer employees by a supervisor/designee; or

   - Mandatory buddy system; or

   - Regular communication with employees working alone; or

   - Other effective means of observation.

3. Designating one or more employees on each worksite as authorized to call for emergency medical services, and allowing other employees to call for emergency services when no designated employee is available.

4. Reminding employees throughout the work shift to drink plenty of water.

5. Holding pre-shift meetings before work begins to review high heat procedures, encourage employees to drink plenty of water and remind employees of their right to take a cool-down rest when necessary. This is a new obligation for covered employers. According to the guidance, the meetings are meant to briefly remind supervisors and employees of the high-heat procedures and not meant to review every element covered in the training. Topics to be covered include staying hydrated, taking cool-down rests, identifying employees who should call for emergency medical services, and how employees will be observed.

For employees employed in the agriculture industry, when temperatures reach 95 degrees or above, the employer must ensure that the employees take a minimum 10-minute preventative cooldown rest period every two hours.

Acclimatization

Acclimatization is a process by which the body adjusts to increased heat exposure. The body needs to adapt when working in hotter environments.

According to Cal/OSHA, employees are more likely to develop heat illness if they don't take it easy when a heat wave strikes or when starting a job that newly exposes them to heat. Most people are usually acclimated within four to 14 days of regular work involving at least two hours per day in the heat.

The revised heat illness standard sets new acclimatization procedures that apply to **all** outdoor places of employment. All employees must be closely observed by a supervisor during a "heat wave" — defined as any day in which the "predicted" high temperature will be at least 80 degrees and at least 10 degrees higher than the average high daily temperature in the preceding five days.

Employers are also required to be extra vigilant with new employees — close observation by a supervisor or designee is required for the first 14 days of employment.

Emergency Response Procedures

The heat illness standard contains more detailed requirements regarding emergency response procedures. Employers must implement effective emergency response procedures, including:

- Ensuring effective communication so that employees can contact a supervisor or emergency medical services when necessary

- Responding to signs and symptoms of possible heat illness, including first aid measures and how emergency medical services will be provided

- Implementing procedures for contacting emergency responders and, if necessary, transporting employees to a place where they can be reached by a medical provider

- Ensuring that clear and precise directions to the work site are available to be provided to emergency providers, when needed

When signs or symptoms of heat illness appear, additional burdens on the employer apply:

- If a supervisor observes, or an employee reports, signs or symptoms of heat illness, the supervisor must take immediate action commensurate with the severity of the illness

- If the signs and symptoms indicate severe heat illness (such as decreased consciousness, staggering, vomiting, disorientation, irrational behavior or convulsions) the employer must implement emergency response procedures

- Any workers who display or report any signs or symptoms of heat illness must not be left alone or sent home without being offered on-site first aid or emergency medical services

Employers are not required to provide medical personnel on site and supervisors and employees are not expected to have medical expertise.

Training Requirements

Employee training must be provided before an employee or supervisor begins outdoor work. Effective training in the following topics shall be provided to all supervisory and non-supervisory employees:

- The environmental and personal risk factors for heat illness, as well as the added burden of heat load on the body caused by exertion, clothing and personal protective equipment

- The importance of frequently consuming small quantities of water, up to four cups per hour, when the work environment is hot and employees are likely to be sweating more than usual while performing their duties

- The importance of acclimatization

- The different types of heat illness and the common signs and symptoms of heat illness

- The importance to employees of immediately reporting to the employer, directly or through the employee's supervisor, symptoms or signs of heat illness in themselves or in co-workers

- The employer's procedures for contacting emergency medical services, and if necessary, for transporting employees to a point where they can be reached by an emergency medical service provider

Employers must ensure that workers are adequately trained on employer responsibilities and how to recognize and react to heat illness signs or symptoms, including appropriate first aid and/or emergency responses.

Training must be understood by employees and provided in a language the employees understand. Inspectors will look for indicators that the employer has made a good faith effort to communicate all the essential information to employees.

Supervisor Training

Before supervising employees working in the heat, the supervisor(s) must receive training on the following topics:

- The information required to be provided by employee training requirements above

- The procedures the supervisor is to follow to implement the applicable provisions in this section

- The procedures the supervisor is to follow when an employee exhibits symptoms consistent with possible heat illness, including emergency response procedures

- How to monitor weather reports and how to respond to hot weather advisories

Employers must compile and maintain written procedures for:

- Employee training

- Employer procedures for compliance

- Employer procedures for responding to symptoms of possible heat illness

- Procedures for ensuring that, in the event of an emergency, directions to the worksite can be provided

Employers must ensure that supervisors are adequately trained on employer responsibilities and how to recognize and react to heat illness signs or symptoms, including appropriate first aid and/or emergency responses.

Other Standards

If you belong to a designated high-hazard industry, other specific Cal/OSHA standards may apply to your company:

- **Permissible Exposure Limits:** Applies if employees may be exposed to an airborne contaminant.

- **Chemical Protection:** Applies if employees use or are exposed to a certain level or concentration of hazardous chemicals, such as lead, benzene, formaldehyde and other carcinogens.

- **Respiratory Protection:** Applies if employees use any respirator, except for voluntary filtering dust masks.

- **Exposure to Hazardous Substances in Laboratories:** Applies if employees are exposed to hazardous substances in a laboratory operation, except for test kits, and manufacturing and process simulations.

- **Blood Borne Pathogens:** Applies if employees are assigned to provide an emergency medical response, or may potentially be exposed to blood borne pathogens.

- **Permit Required Confined Space Entry:** Applies if employees must work in a facility that contains a confined space, such as a tunnel, underground storage tank or utility vault, that presents or contains a hazard.

- **Lockout/Tagout and Machinery Guarding:** Applies if employees may be exposed to hazardous machinery motion during normal operations or servicing.

- **Forklifts and Material Handling:** Applies if employees operate a forklift or industrial truck, or if onsite materials are handled in volume.

- **Occupational Exposure to Noise:** Applies if employees are exposed to noise averages over 85 dBA during a work shift.

- **Process Safety Management (PSM) of Acutely Hazardous Materials (also known as the "Access Standard"):** Applies if employees are exposed to certain highly dangerous chemicals at or above the specified threshold quantities.

- **Patient Protection and Health Care Worker Back and Musculoskeletal Injury Prevention Plan:** Applies if employees lift/transfer patients in a health care facility. State law requires employers to adopt this plan as part of their IIPP. The plan must include a safe patient handling policy reflected in professional occupational safety guidelines for the protection of patients and health care workers in health care facilities.

For additional information on high-hazard industries, visit the Department of Industrial Relations (DIR) Model IIPP website at ***www.dir.ca.gov/dosh/ dosh_publications/iiphihzemp.html***.

Creating a Written Program

Employers should consider establishing a plan or program for handling potentially dangerous situations. Know which safety standards apply to your organization and communicate these standards to your employees. Understanding the safety standards is essential to avoiding Cal/OSHA fines and preserving the safety of your employees and workplace.

When you create a written program, either for your IIPP or for any other standard, base it on processes and policies you put in place for your company. The following section guides you through the process of developing a written program.

Research and Prepare

Gather any existing documents you have that can help you fill in the information (such as a fire escape plan, local emergency contact information, safety data sheets or workplace violence policies).

Find out if Cal/OSHA considers your company to belong to a high-hazard industry. For general guidelines on high hazard employers, see the Cal/OSHA's Model IIPP website at ***www.dir.ca.gov/dosh/dosh_publications/iiphihzemp.html***.

Find out if Cal/OSHA considers your workplace to be at-risk for workplace violence. For workplace violence guidelines, visit Cal/OSHA's Workplace Security website at ***www.dir.ca.gov/dosh/dosh_publications/worksecurity.html***.

Identify lacking or missing processes or policies, and what else you need to implement. Create two levels of information; general and detailed. The general information will go in your IIPP and your employee handbook. The detailed information will go in the appropriate document for each specific standard.

Compile Information

Use the *Injury and Illness Prevention Program for Non-High Hazard Employers*, described in Table 16 on page 249, to create your IIPP and to determine what information you need to supply.

> Keep in mind that your IIPP doesn't need to cover every detail. The IIPP is only an outline of your entire compliance plan.

Use the detailed information to complete the written programs for all other standards. Consider adding text for standards that don't require written programs to your employee handbook or safety manual.

Maintain the Plan

The easiest way to help your company avoid violations, injuries and lawsuits is to keep your compliance information up-to-date and to communicate changes to your employees.

Safety Training

Most Cal/OSHA standards require training, which is an effective way for you to keep employees informed of your policies and procedures. The regulations don't specify the type of training or the frequency. The following section describes the essentials of developing a training program.

Who Should Provide the Training?

Designate an internal or external resource qualified to provide training, based on the requirements of the standard. Remember that you must also provide training to independent contractors.

What Standards Require Employers to Provide Training?

Determine which standards require you to train your employees. You can also refer to the *Cal/OSHA Training Requirements*, described in Table 16 on page 249, for information on training requirements for all Cal/OSHA standards.

 Keep in mind that even when a particular standard doesn't require training, the IIPP often does.

Compile all the subjects into a list to determine if you can combine subjects to cover multiple standards. You can use this list as a foundation for selecting your method of training.

When Should the Training Happen?

Provide the training:

- To all new employees and existing employees who transfer to new positions
- After an incident or change of process (e.g., when you install new equipment or if you move certain operations to a new site)
- As an annual refresher

What Methods Should Be Used to Provide Training?

The method you use to provide training is up to you, depending on how complex the training needs to be, the number of employees you need to train and your budget. Keep in mind that supervisors may need separate training.

In addition, always document the training employees receive to show your compliance with the IIPP and that you take safety seriously.

Providing Personal Protective Equipment to Employees

Providing PPE (for example, gloves, lead aprons, hard hats and keyboard wrist rests) to your employees, if required, helps prevent injuries and illnesses. Use the following guidelines to help you determine what your employees need to work safely.

1. Evaluate your workplace for the need for PPE. Consider all the jobs, processes and operations (day-to-day and emergency) employees will perform. Some examples of evaluation questions might be:

   - Do your employees handle, or are they exposed to, chemicals or blood borne pathogens?

   - Do your employees perform tasks that require the same bodily motions to be repeated?

   - Do your employees work in areas with falling items, flying projectiles or heavy machinery?

   - Do your employees lift heavy or cumbersome objects, or work in areas that require forceful exertion to perform tasks?

2. Document the situations that require your employees to use PPE, and identify which PPE items you will supply.

3. Provide and maintain PPE for all employees exposed to hazards.

4. Perform periodic inspections:

   - Make sure the PPE is in good working order and is readily accessible.

   - Verify that employees use PPE properly and consistently.

 You can't charge employees for the use and cost of PPE.

Reporting and Recording Work-Related Injuries and Illnesses

Recording and reporting work-related fatalities, injuries and illnesses are two separate processes required by Cal/OSHA's *Log 300* regulation. You don't always have to do both.

 To determine if you must comply with *Log 300* requirements, use CalChamber's Log 300 Wizard at ***https://www.calchamber.com/hrcalifornia/forms-tools/wizards/Pages/log-300-wizard.aspx***.

Reporting includes notifying Cal/OSHA of a serious work-related injury or death. For more information, see "What Qualifies As a "Serious" Injury?" on page 240. All employers must report fatal or serious incidents within eight hours of the incident or fatality. Report fatal or serious incidents to the Cal/OSHA district office nearest to your business. To find the nearest Cal/OSHA district office, go to this DIR website at ***www.dir.ca.gov/DOSH/DistrictOffices.htm***.

Recording involves creating and maintaining records of work-related injuries, both to keep documents as references, and to prepare in case an inspection requires you to present your records. You are exempt from recording if you employ 10 or fewer staff or if your company is classified in a specific low hazard Standard Industry Code (SIC) category. SICs classify businesses by their primary activity, and get used for a variety of statistical purposes.

In 2016, the federal Occupational Safety and Health Administration (federal OSHA) issued a final rule relating to the tracking and reporting of workplace injuries, which requires electronic submission of injury and illness data that employers currently report on written forms.

Although, the federal electronic reporting rule takes effect on **January 1, 2017**, federal OSHA has given states that operate their own safety and health programs, such as California, extra time to implement the new requirements.

Until Cal/OSHA implements the federal changes here in California, it will not enforce the federal rules. Employers should be on the lookout for California's implementation of these federal rules. At the time of this book's publication, additional information from Cal/OSHA was not available.

What Qualifies As a "Serious" Injury?

A serious injury is a work-related incident that results in the:

- Death of an employee

- Hospitalization of an employee for more than 24 hours for treatment other than observation

- Loss or serious disfigurement of any body part

How Do I Know if I Must Report an Incident?

You must submit incident reports in two situations:

- When an employee is seriously or fatally injured

- When you receive an annual survey form from the Bureau of Labor Statistics or a specific request from Cal/OSHA

California law mandates a fine of $5,000 for employers who don't report a serious injury or death. Individual employees serving in supervisory, management or similar roles may be individually liable for up to one year in jail and/or a $15,000 fine. Corporations face fines up to $150,000.

How Long Do I Need to Keep These Records?

You must save the *Log 300* forms for five years after the end of the year the records cover.

During the storage period, you must update the *Log 300* forms to include newly discovered recordable injuries or illnesses and to show changes that occurred in the classification of previously recorded injuries and illnesses.

The *Log 300* forms are available in the online formspack for this product.

Cal/OSHA

California's Division of Occupational Safety and Health (DOSH), better known as Cal/OSHA, oversees the protection of workers from health and safety hazards on the job through its research and its standards, enforcement and consultation programs.

Employers face inspections, citations and compliance schedules. A limited appeals process for employers is in place, but the best way to comply is simply to maintain a safe workplace.

What Should I Know About the Cal/OSHA Inspection Process?

Cal/OSHA inspections follow a process governed by the Labor Code and the Cal/OSHA Policy and Procedure Manual:

1. **Unannounced Inspections**. You receive no advance notice, except:

   - When apparent imminent danger requires prompt correction

   - To ensure availability of essential personnel or access to the site, equipment or specific process

   - When the Cal/OSHA chief or his/her designee decides that giving advance notice would help achieve a thorough inspection

2. **Opening conference**. The Cal/OSHA inspector presents credentials and provides the reason for the inspection to someone with the authority to consent to the inspection.

   You can ask for a postponement of the inspection but only for a good reason, such as:

   - All essential personnel are not available

   - The inspector's credentials or the stated reasons for the inspection lack credibility

   The inspector can obtain a search warrant if you refuse the inspection.

3. **Document request**. The inspector usually asks to review the following documents:

   - Cal/OSHA *Log 300* forms for the current year and for the five previous years

   - Your written IIPP

   - Any written programs required by a standard that your business must follow

   - Codes of safe practice at a construction site

   - A copy of any permit issued by Cal/OSHA

4. **Walk-through**. The inspector conducts a walk-through of the premises subject to the inspection, accompanied by key personnel from your company.

   This can take the form of a wall-to-wall inspection or involve only the limited area defined by the inspector's represented reasons for the inspection (such as an employee complaint about the warehouse). It's good practice to restrict the inspector's access to the areas specifically designated for inspection.

   During a wall-to-wall inspection, the inspector may stop to examine machinery, interview employees and observe working situations. Your personnel accompanying the inspector may be asked to explain an operation or answer questions.

5. **Exit and closing conferences**. When the inspection is over, the inspector:

   - Summarizes the results of the inspection

   - Makes any pertinent observations

   - Discusses findings and conclusions

   - Requests information, documents or further inspections

If the inspector issues no citations, this is considered an exit conference and nothing else follows. If the inspection results in a citation or another action (such as a Special

Order), the exit conference is followed by a formal closing conference, approximately one month after the issuance of any citations.

When Does Cal/OSHA Perform Inspections?

Cal/OSHA's inspection program targets workplaces with a likelihood of health and safety hazards and/or violations of standards. Due to constitutional limitations on government searches and seizures, the agency must have reasonable cause to conduct an inspection. However, court decisions have granted Cal/OSHA broad discretion in determining what is reasonable cause.

Cal/OSHA inspects when:

- An employer reports a fatality or serious injury or illness

- An employee complains

- The issuance of a permit requires a follow-up inspection

- The Cal/OSHA general administrative plan calls for inspections for a certain type of employer (the targeted group shifts periodically based on injury/illness statistics for that industrial classification)

- An industry has been selected as part of the TICP

The **TICP**, or Targeted Inspection and Consultation Program, is a Cal/OSHA program that identifies certain high-hazard employers and requires them to pay a fee to fund a special inspection unit. Cal/OSHA also offers other consultation services to help businesses avoid investigations and costly fines. You can find more information on these programs on this DIR website at ***www.dir.ca.gov/dosh/consultation.html***.

How Can I Prepare for an Inspection?

You should develop policies for handling an inspection, designate key personnel to participate, train them in procedures to follow and advise them on handling potential issues that may emerge as the inspection progresses. Your policy can be formal or informal but should cover the key phases of an inspection. See "What Should I Know About the Cal/OSHA Inspection Process?" on page 241.

To find resources that can help you develop these procedures, check out "Where Do I Go for More Information?" on page 255.

What Happens If the Inspector Finds a Violation?

You could receive a citation with civil penalties based on the violation's severity, extent, likelihood and size of your business. These penalties include:

- Non-serious or minor violations, such as not hanging the required posting included on the *California and Federal Labor Law Poster* (available at *store.calchamber.com*) — up to $7,000 per violation

  - Repeat or willful violations — from $5,000 to $70,000

  - Serious violations — up to $25,000

  - Failure to correct or abate a violation — up to $15,000 for each day the failure continues

  - Substantial fines if you fail to report a fatal or serious incident. For details, see "How Do I Know if I Must Report an Incident?" on page 240.

- A "Special Order" forcing you to remedy any unsafe condition, device or other workplace hazard to employee safety and health not covered by any existing standard. In a sense, this creates a special standard for you.

- A "Notice to Comply" if the violation is a general or regulatory offense and doesn't immediately relate to employee safety and health.

- An "Information Memorandum" to direct your attention to a workplace condition with the potential of becoming a hazard to the safety or health of employees.

- An "Order to Take Special Action" in situations where an unsafe workplace condition, covered by an existing standard, requires specific instruction.

- Cal/OSHA issuing an "Order Prohibiting Use" ("yellow tagging") when any condition, equipment or practice poses an imminent hazard to employees that could cause death or serious physical harm immediately or before you can eliminate the hazard.

Whatever the result of your violation, you must:

- Post the citation, order or notice of violation in a place where employees working nearby can easily read it.

- Correct the problem within a specified amount of time and notify Cal/OSHA of the correction.

Cal/OSHA can require an employer to abate (fix) serious workplace safety violations and can also issue civil penalties. An employer can appeal the citation.

The state Occupational Safety and Health Appeals Board (OSHAB) is prohibited from modifying civil penalties for abatement or credit for abatement unless the employer:

- Fixed the violation at an initial inspection or a subsequent inspection prior to issuance of the citation; or

- Submitted a signed statement and supporting evidence within 10 working days after the date fixed for abatement showing that the violation has been fixed.

In cases of serious, repeat serious or willful serious violations, California law generally prohibits a stay or suspension of an abatement requirement while an appeal or petition for reconsideration is pending, unless the employer can demonstrate that a stay or suspension will not adversely affect the health and safety of employees.

Make sure to review the content of the citation or order for accuracy in terms of its statement of the violated standard's requirements, your observations of the inspection and your understanding of the inspector's findings.

If you object to the citation and can produce enough evidence, you can appeal. For more information, see "What Should I Know About Appealing a Citation or Order?" on page 245.

What Should I Know About Appealing a Citation or Order?

You can appeal to the OSHAB within 15 business days of receiving a citation or order.

How the Appeals Process Works

1. Because the time allotted to appeal is so short (15 business days), you should start the decision-making process immediately upon receiving an order or citation. You should identify issues that you can appeal, and consider:

   - The size of the penalty

   - The cost and time allowed for correction, as compared to an appeal

   - The potential for a repeat citation

   - Your likelihood of success, given the strength of your defenses

2. Communicate your desire to appeal to the OSHAB by hand delivery, mail, fax or telephone.

The OSHAB provides you with information on the appeal process and an appeal form. If you return the form within 10 business days, the appeal form is considered complete.

After the appeal process begins, OSHAB's assignment of a docket number may take up to six months. When the docket number is issued, the OSHAB sends a copy of the form to you with a docket number and OSHAB stamp affixed.

You must post a copy of the docketed appeal form at or near the site of the already posted citation. The posting must remain in place until the appeal hearing begins or you receive an order disposing of the appeal.

3. Since notification of docketing can be a lengthy process, begin preparing your defense for the hearing while the incident/inspection/facts are current and fresh.

Hearings typically happen no more than six months from the docketing of the appeal. You can investigate Cal/OSHA's information by filing a discovery letter on the agency, with copies sent to the OSHAB and any other interested party. You can subpoena witnesses or physical evidence.

You can't communicate with the OSHAB unless all parties to the appeal receive notification. You may serve a document on another party by personal delivery, first-class mail, overnight delivery or fax. You can do this by a declaration, a written statement or by a letter of transmittal.

4. You can request an informal conference.

This meeting between you, your representatives, Cal/OSHA's district manager and the inspector responsible for the citation allows you to discuss any evidence in an attempt to resolve any disputes and avoid the need to continue with the appeal.

District managers must hold the conference no more than 10 business days after issuing citations. If you already filed an appeal, the conference can occur any time up to the date of the hearing.

You must notify employees of the conference, its date and location. The usual way to do this is to post this information near the already posted citation and a copy of the conference confirmation issued by Cal/OSHA.

At this stage, the district manager, based on new evidence or a new interpretation, can withdraw or amend citations, including the existence of the violations, proposed penalties and correction methods and schedules.

5. If you don't reach a settlement, you will make your defense in an official hearing before an Administrative Law Judge (ALJ).

At least 30 days prior to the hearing, the OSHAB will send the parties a notice of hearing, advising them of the location, date and time. A hearing is postponed only if an emergency arises, or if a party or witness has a pre-existing scheduling conflict. If either party fails to appear at the hearing, the OSHAB will send a notice of intent to dismiss. To reinstate the matter, the absent party must establish just cause within 10 business days for the failure to appear.

 You must notify employees of the pending hearing, usually by posting this information near the already posted citation.

6. At the close of the hearing, all the proceedings are considered submitted for decision. The ALJ summarizes the evidence received, makes findings and files a proposed decision along with his/her reasons for the decision within 30 business days of the hearing's close.

   The OSHAB may confirm, adopt, modify or set aside the proposed decision. The OSHAB then sends copies of its decision to each party. If no one files a petition for reconsideration, the decision is final and can't be reviewed by any court or agency.

7. Either party can take up to 30 business days to file a petition for reconsideration. The petition must set forth, specifically and in full detail, every issue to be considered by the OSHAB. Anything not raised in the petition is waived and can't be re-examined. If the OSHAB does not act upon a petition within 45 business days, the petition is considered denied.

   Upon reconsideration, the OSHAB can make another decision or let the original one stand. If no one requests a judicial review, the decision is final.

8. Any party that disagrees with a decision after reconsideration or the denial of a petition must apply to the Superior Court for a writ of mandate within 30 business days of the OSHAB's decision or denial.

Minimum Compliance Elements

1. Hang your *2017 California and Federal Labor Law Poster* (available from *store.calchamber.com*), which includes mandatory postings and Cal/OSHA postings that all employees and applicants must be able to see, in a prominent place (such as a break room). It includes the Healthy Workplaces, Healthy Families Act of 2014 Paid Sick Leave poster.

   If you have employees working in a city or county with a local minimum wage and/or paid sick leave ordinance, you may also need to post required local notices and provide additional notices to employees at the time of hire.

2. Create and follow an Injury and Illness Prevention Program (IIPP) (see "Injury and Illness Prevention Program" on page 218), and make sure your employees know about the workplace safety practices it covers (see "Basic Standards" on page 215).

Forms and Checklists

The following table describes forms and checklists associated with workplace safety.

 TIP You can find these forms in your online formspack, described in detail in "Online Forms" on page 12.

Table 16. Forms And Checklists

Notice Or Form	What Do I Use It For?	When Do I Use It?	Who Fills It Out?	Where Does It Go?
Accident, Injury and Illness Investigation	To help you document information about a workplace incident that involves an accident, injury or both.	As soon as possible after an incident occurs.	The employer.	If you don't have to report the incident, keep the document for at least one year (longer if you are documenting compliance). If you must record the incident on the *Log 300* form, keep the document for five years.
Cal/OSHA Training Requirements	To determine which standards require you to provide safety training for your employees.	Use the form for reference when planning your safety training program.	No filling out needed.	Incorporate the information in the document into your training program.

Table 16. Forms And Checklists *(continued)*

Notice Or Form	What Do I Use It For?	When Do I Use It?	Who Fills It Out?	Where Does It Go?
Emergency Action Plan	To help you create a written plan for handling emergency situations, and to satisfy Cal/OSHA compliance.	Before your business opens, or as soon after as possible.	The employer.	Make the information in your plan available to your employees through training and in your employee handbook or safety manual. Keep and maintain the document as long as the company operates.
Ergonomics Checklist - Computer and Keyboard Issues	As an inspection tool to help you identify potential ergonomic problems related to computers and keyboards.	Annually and as needed.	The employer.	N/A
Ergonomics Checklist - Hand Tool Use	As an inspection tool to help you identify potential ergonomic problems related to hand tool use.	Annually and as needed.	The employer.	N/A
Ergonomics Checklist - Manual Handling	As an inspection tool to help you identify potential ergonomic problems related to manual handling.	Annually and as needed.	The employer.	N/A
Ergonomics Checklist - Task-Work Methods	As an inspection tool to help you identify potential ergonomic problems related to task/work methods.	Annually and as needed.	The employer.	N/A

Table 16. Forms And Checklists *(continued)*

Notice Or Form	What Do I Use It For?	When Do I Use It?	Who Fills It Out?	Where Does It Go?
Ergonomics Checklist - Workstation Layout	As an inspection tool to help you identify potential ergonomic problems related to workstation layout.	Annually and as needed.	The employer.	N/A
Fire Prevention Checklist	To determine which fire hazards are present in your workplace so you can create and maintain a written plan for preventing and handling workplace fires.	Before your business opens, or as soon after as possible.	The employer.	Use the checklist as an inspection tool. Keep and maintain the document as long as the company operates.
Fire Prevention Plan	To help you create a written plan for preventing and handling workplace fires and to satisfy Cal/OSHA standard compliance.	Before your business opens, or as soon after as possible.	The employer.	Make the information in your plan available to your employees through training and in your employee handbook or safety manual. Keep and maintain the document as long as the company operates.
Hazard Assessment and Correction Record	To document hazard identification and correction, and to assure compliance with applicable Cal/OSHA standards.	When an unsafe working condition is brought to your attention.	The employer.	In your files.

Table 16. Forms And Checklists *(continued)*

Notice Or Form	What Do I Use It For?	When Do I Use It?	Who Fills It Out?	Where Does It Go?
Hazard Communication Program	To document training provided to an employee and to satisfy Cal/OSHA standard compliance.	Before your business opens, or as soon after as possible.	The employer.	Make the information in your plan available to your employees through training and in your employee handbook or safety manual. Keep and maintain the document as long as the company operates.
Heat Illness Prevention Plan - Outdoor Employees	To develop your company's plan and procedures for complying with Cal/OSHA regulations on heat illness prevention for outdoor workers.	Before your business opens, or as soon after as possible.	The employer.	Make the information in your plan available to your employees through training and in your employee handbook or safety manual. Keep and maintain the document as long as the company operates.
Initial Safety Training Certificate	To document the first training provided to an employee.	When you hire someone, reassign someone or identify a previously unknown hazard.	The employer.	Keep this document in the employee's personnel file. Provide a copy of this document to the employee if requested.

Table 16. Forms And Checklists *(continued)*

Notice Or Form	What Do I Use It For?	When Do I Use It?	Who Fills It Out?	Where Does It Go?
Individual Safety Training Certificate	To document training provided to an employee and to satisfy Cal/OSHA standard compliance.	When the employee successfully completes the training.	The employee does.	Keep the certificate in the employee's personnel file. Provide a copy of the certificate to the employee if requested.
Injury and Illness Prevention Program for Non-High Hazard Employers	To outline your plan for compliance with all OSHA standards, including a detailed plan for: • Handling emergency situations; • Preventing and handling workplace fires; • Addressing ergonomic issues; and • Documenting information about workplace hazards.	Before your business opens, or as soon after as possible.	The employer.	Make the information in your plan available to your employees through training and in your employee handbook or safety manual. Keep and maintain the document as long as the company operates.
Office and Commercial Establishment Safety, Including Ergonomics and Office Chemical Safety	To identify and address office hazards.	Before your business opens, or as soon after as possible.	The employer.	Keep and maintain the document as long as the company operates.

Table 16. Forms And Checklists *(continued)*

Notice Or Form	What Do I Use It For?	When Do I Use It?	Who Fills It Out?	Where Does It Go?
Safe Practices for Construction Workplaces - Sample Code	The sample code in this form was developed by the California Department of Occupational Safety and Health. It is a suggested code, general in nature and is intended as a basis for preparing a code that fits the specific contractor's operations more exactly.	Use this form to assist you in preparing a code of safe practices.	N/A	N/A
Safety Inspection for Work Spaces and Surfaces Checklist	To help you identify and prevent work space and surface hazards in your workplace and to satisfy Cal/OSHA standard compliance.	During periodic inspections, and after incidents or a change in process.	The employer.	Keep the checklist as a record of periodic inspections for five years after you fill it out.
Safety Program Self Audit Checklist	To help ensure that your workplace safety program complies with state requirements and is well tailored to reducing risks and claims in your workplace.	Before your business opens, or as soon after as possible.	The employer.	Keep and maintain the document as long as the company operates.

Table 16. Forms And Checklists (*continued*)

Notice Or Form	What Do I Use It For?	When Do I Use It?	Who Fills It Out?	Where Does It Go?
Training Sign-In Sheet	To record and track employee attendance at training courses.	Before or after completing a training course.	You prepare the form and employees sign it.	Keep the documents as proof that an employee attended mandatory training for five years after the training.
Training Sign-In Sheet - Spanish	To record and track employee attendance at training courses.	Before or after completing a training course.	You prepare the form and employees sign it.	Keep the documents as proof that an employee attended mandatory training for five years after the training.
Worker Training and Instruction Record	To document and track all training provided to an employee.	Whenever an employee attends or completes training.	The employer.	Maintain in your training files and a copy in the employee's personnel file.

Where Do I Go for More Information?

CalChamber and federal and state government agencies offer a variety of resources to help you ensure safety in your workplace.

Table 17. Additional Resources

For Information On	Check Out These Resources
General	From CalChamber: • **store.calchamber.com** • **HRCalifornia.com**
Workers' Compensation	From CalChamber: • **2017 California Labor Law Digest**

Table 17. Additional Resources *(continued)*

For Information On	Check Out These Resources
State Government	• California Department of Industrial Relations at ***www.dir.ca.gov*** • California Division of Occupational Safety and Health at ***www.dir.ca.gov/DOSH/dosh1.html*** • California's Occupational Safety and Health Standards Board at ***www.dir.ca.gov/oshsb/oshsb.html*** • Model Injury and Illness Prevention Program for High Hazard Employers at ***www.dir.ca.gov/dosh/dosh_publications/iiphihzemp.html*** • Cal/OSHA Guidelines for Workplace Security at ***www.dir.ca.gov/dosh/dosh_publications/worksecurity.html*** • User's Guide to Cal/OSHA at ***www.dir.ca.gov/dosh/dosh_-publications/osha_userguide.pdf*** • For contact information for various Cal/OSHA offices, see the *Cal/OSHA Poster* (located in the ***2017 California and Federal Labor Law Poster*** and the ***Required Notices Kit with Poster***) • HAZCOM regulations; ***www.dir.ca.gov/title8/5194.html*** • Repetitive motion (ergonomics); ***www.dir.ca.gov/title8/5110.html*** • Log 300/300A at ***www.dir.ca.gov/dosh/dosh_publications/RecKeepOverview.pdf***
Federal Government	OSHA's SIC manual at ***www.osha.gov/pls/imis/sic_manual.html***

TIP CalChamber also provides many ongoing and comprehensive educational opportunities for small business owners, HR beginners and experienced HR professionals alike. These include safety posters and special HR seminars and webinars. For more information, please visit the CalChamber website at ***store.calchamber.com***.

Chapter 7

Discrimination

Employment discrimination happens in many ways, some of which may not be intentional. For example, a supervisor does not usually decide to overlook a person for promotion because of the person's race or gender.

Certain acts can constitute unlawful discrimination because of their effect, regardless of the motivation for these acts. You can begin to protect yourself by understanding discrimination, taking steps to avoid situations that would inspire lawsuits and by knowing how to handle complaints when they do arise.

In this chapter, you can find answers to questions about:

- Protected classes
- The Americans with Disabilities Act (ADA)
- California's Fair Employment and Housing Act (FEHA)

Discrimination

The word "discrimination" is often used as a synonym for anything an employee may personally believe is unfair. In employment law, however, the word "discrimination" is more narrowly defined.

Discrimination, legally speaking, covers only actions taken against people because they belong to certain protected classes as outlined in applicable state and federal laws. See "Protected Characteristics and Activities" on page 259.

Discrimination means treating those people differently, and disadvantageously, compared with other people not in the same class. Remember, almost everyone is part of a protected class because everyone belongs to a race; has a marital status; is perceived as one gender or another; and associates with people in protected classes.

Discrimination can occur in two ways:

- **Disparate (unequal) treatment** — when an employee or applicant is treated differently, specifically because of his/her protected class status

- **Disparate (unequal) impact** — an employment practice that appears neutral on its face but discriminates against protected classes in practice (for example, height and weight requirements may unequally impact women)

Discrimination and Employment Practices

You commit a discriminatory employment practice if you, among other things:

- Base any employment decision regarding hiring, benefits, promotion or discipline in whole or in part on an individual's protected class status

- Rely on stereotypes about the competence, appearance, health, interest or qualifications of individuals in protected classes

- Engage in any employment practice that adversely impacts the hiring, training, classification, promotion or retention opportunities of individuals in a protected class

- Engage in, or permit your employees to engage in, harassment of any member of any protected class

- Act on the perception or assumption of a disability without evaluating the individual's fitness for the job

- Retaliate against an employee, applicant or independent contractor for opposing sexual harassment or other unlawful discrimination, or for filing a complaint, testifying, assisting or participating in an investigation, proceeding or hearing, etc.

- Refuse to honor an otherwise eligible employee's request for pregnancy disability leave or for leave under CFRA or FMLA (see "Glossary of Terms, Laws and Agencies" on page 331 for more details)

- Refuse to reasonably accommodate disabilities, religious requirements, etc.

- Inquire on a written job application (except in limited circumstances) whether a job applicant has ever been arrested

Retaliation

Both federal and state laws protect employees and applicants from employer retaliation for engaging in activity that is protected by anti-discrimination laws.

California employers should be aware that retaliation claims consistently show up at the top of the list of workplace discrimination charges filed against employers.

At the federal level, the Equal Employment Opportunity Commission (EEOC) released detailed breakdowns in early 2016 of the 89,385 charges of workplace discrimination that the agency received in fiscal year 2015.

Retaliation claims were the number one charge, and increased by nearly 5 percent from fiscal year 2014. Retaliation claims accounted for nearly 45 percent of all charges filed with the EEOC.

California law defines retaliation as any adverse employment action taken against an individual who opposed a legally prohibited practice or who filed a complaint, testified, assisted or participated in an investigation or proceeding conducted by California's Department of Fair Employment and Housing or by the federal EEOC.

Courts will look for a causal link between the protected activity and the adverse action. Timing is everything. If retaliation is established, you will have to show the legitimate, nondiscriminatory business reason for the adverse action.

California law protects applicants, employees and unpaid interns, although federal law does not protect unpaid interns.

Protected Characteristics and Activities

You may not discriminate against a person because he/she belongs to certain protected classes. In addition, California's Fair Employment and Housing Act (FEHA) protects not only actual membership in the classes that FEHA specifies, but also perceived membership in one or more of those classes.

For example, an individual could file a sexual orientation discrimination charge, claiming that he was discriminated against because he was perceived as homosexual even if he is not, in fact, homosexual.

Age

If you employ five or more employees, you may not:

- Use age as a consideration for employment decisions, unless it is a bona fide occupational qualification (BFOQ)

- Discriminate against someone who opposed, filed a charge against, testified or participated in an investigation of unlawful employment practice under the Age Discrimination in Employment Act (ADEA) (see "Glossary of Terms, Laws and Agencies" on page 331 for more information on the ADEA)

- Place an employment notice or advertisement indicating a preference, limitation or specification based on age, unless it is a BFOQ

- Terminate employees based on salary if the terminations create a disproportionate impact on older workers

- Force an employee to retire because he/she reached a certain age

- Discriminate on the basis of age with regard to the terms, conditions or privileges of employment; for example, denying an employee aged 40 or over the educational opportunities that you give to younger employees

AIDS/HIV+ Status

These conditions are considered protected disabilities. If you employ five or more employees, you may not:

- Use blood tests as a condition of employment or to determine insurability

- Terminate, deny insurance coverage or refuse to hire individuals exposed to the AIDS virus

 There may be limited exceptions in the medical field.

Disability

You can't discriminate against a disabled person or someone you perceive to be disabled. You may face serious consequences if you discriminate against persons with disabilities in your employment decisions, or if you fail to make reasonable accommodation for an applicant's or employee's disability.

Federal and state laws create significant protections for people with disabilities. The federal Americans with Disabilities Act (ADA) covers employers with 15 or more employees, and California's FEHA covers employers with five or more employees.

For more information about the ADA, FEHA and how disabilities are defined, see "Disability Discrimination" on page 272.

 In California, a **disability** is a physical or mental impairment that limits one or more of the major life activities.

Domestic Partner Status

State law prohibits discrimination and/or harassment based on a person's status as a registered domestic partner. State law gives domestic partners the same rights as spouses. Conversely, you can't discriminate against someone based on marital status in favor of another person who is in a registered domestic partner relationship.

Gender

If you employ five or more employees, you can't discriminate or allow harassment on the basis of gender. Gender is defined as an employee's or applicant's actual sex or as the employer's perception of the employee's/applicant's sex.

This includes your perception of the employee's/applicant's identity, appearance or behavior, regardless of whether that identity, appearance or behavior is different from that traditionally associated with the employee's/applicant's sex at birth.

"Gender" includes both "gender identity" and "gender expression," and discrimination on either basis is prohibited:

- Gender identity means a person's identification as male, female or a gender different from the person's sex at birth; it specifically includes transgender persons.

- Gender expression is defined as "a person's gender-related appearance or behavior, whether or not stereotypically associated with the person's assigned sex at birth."

Laws relating to gender-based discrimination do not affect the employer's ability to require an employee to adhere to reasonable workplace appearance, grooming and dress standards. But, employers must allow an employee to appear or dress consistently with the employee's gender identity or gender expression.

California law prohibits the state from entering into contracts for goods or services of $100,000 or more with a contractor that discriminates between employees on the basis of gender identity, such as being transgender, when providing benefits.

Transgender Employees in the Workplace

Some employers may encounter workplace issues related to transgender employees. In 2014, the Equal Employment Opportunity Commission (EEOC) filed its first lawsuits on behalf of transgender workers, marking a significant step in the agency's strategy to interpret Title VII to cover gender identity discrimination.

FEHA regulations specifically define transgender as a "general term that refers to a person whose gender identity differs from the person's sex at birth. A transgender person may or may not have a gender expression (meaning a person's gender related appearance or behavior regardless of person's sex at birth) that is different from the social expectations of the sex assigned at birth."

The EEOC and California's DFEH have increased awareness by publishing guidelines and filing lawsuits against companies on behalf of transgender employees.

These developments highlight that transgender employees should be permitted to use the restroom that corresponds with their gender presentations. To provide options for workers, employers can consider creating single user or unisex restroom facilities, but should not force a transgender employee to exclusively use that facility.

 New 2017

AB 1732 sets a new requirement that, beginning **March 1, 2017**, all single-user toilet facilities in any business establishment, place of public accommodation or government agency must be identified as "all-gender" toilet facilities.

For additional guidance on how to address this sensitive workplace topic, employers can refer to the Occupational Safety and Health Administration's *A Guide to Restroom Access for Transgender Workers* at ***https://www.osha.gov/Publications/ OSHA3795.pdf***, which the agency developed in alliance with the National Center for Transgender Equality. In addition, the DFEH has prepared *Transgender Rights in the Workplace* which can be found at ***http://www.dfeh.ca.gov/res/docs/Publications/ Brochures/2016/DFEH163TGR.pdf***.

Pay and Gender

California's Fair Pay Act, which was effective January 1, 2016, revises and expands previous state relating to gender pay inequality or disparity and provides greater protections than federal law.

Under prior state law, you could not pay an employee less than the rate paid to an opposite-sex employee in the same establishment for equal work on jobs that required equal skill, effort and responsibility. This standard was removed from California law.

Under the new California Fair Pay Act, employers are prohibited from paying any of their employees less than employees of the opposite sex for "substantially similar work." The term "substantially similar work" replaced the "equal work" for "equal skill, effort and responsibility" standard contained in the prior law.

 SB 1063 expands the Fair Pay Act beyond gender wage inequality to address racial/ethnic wage disparity. The legislation prohibits an employer from paying any of its employees wage rates that are less than the rates paid to employees of another race or ethnicity for substantially similar work.

 In addition, AB 1676 specifies that, under the Fair Pay Act, prior salary cannot, by itself, justify any disparity in compensation. The legislative findings state that the law is intended to "help ensure that both employers and workers are able to negotiate and set salaries based on the requirements, expectations, and qualifications of the person and the job in question, rather than on an individual's prior earnings, which may reflect widespread, long-standing, gender-based wage disparities in the labor market."

Genetic Information/Genetic Characteristics

State and federal law create different levels of protection for a person's genetic information/genetic characteristics.

State Law (Genetic Information)

Under California's FEHA, employers are prohibited from discriminating against employees on the basis of genetic characteristics and genetic information. This means information about any of the following:

- The individual's genetic tests

- The genetic tests of family members of the individual

- The manifestation of a disease or disorder in family members of the individual

Genetic information includes any request for, or receipt of, genetic services, or participation in clinical research that includes genetic services, by an individual or any family member of the individual. Genetic information does not include information about the sex or age of any individual.

Federal Law (Genetic Characteristics)

Genetic characteristics means any inherited characteristic or scientifically or medically identifiable gene or chromosome or combination or alteration thereof known to be a cause or increase the risk of a disease or disorder in a person or his/her offspring.

The Genetic Information Nondiscrimination Act (GINA) prohibits use of genetic information to make decisions about health insurance and employment, and restricts the acquisition and disclosure of genetic information.

GINA applies to private employers with 15 or more employees and generally prohibits employers from requesting, requiring, or purchasing an applicant's or employee's genetic information, even if the employer never uses that information.

According to the EEOC, "genetic information" includes:

- Information about an individual's genetic tests

- Information about the genetic tests of a family member

- Family medical history

- Requests for, and receipt of, genetic services by an individual or a family member

- Genetic information about a fetus carried by an individual or family member, or about an embryo legally held by the individual or family member using assisted reproductive technology

The EEOC published detailed information on GINA and its final regulations on its website at *www.eeoc.gov/laws/types/genetic.cfm*.

Height/Weight

You can't establish height and weight standards unless you can show that such restrictions relate directly to, and are an essential function of, the job.

Immigrant Status

Many state laws affect immigrants. State law includes protections that address retaliation against immigrant workers who complain about unfair wages or working conditions. All California workers, regardless of whether they are authorized to work in the United States, are protected by California's labor and employment laws.

California law clarifies that these protections extend to child workers. California law pre-empts federal immigration laws protecting immigrant workers and guarantees their access to the same California employment laws as legally authorized workers.

Retaliation and Unfair Immigration Practices

Employers are prohibited from engaging in "unfair immigration-related practices" when an employee asserts protected rights under the Labor Code.

Employers cannot use immigration law to retaliate against employees who exercise their employee rights. An "unfair immigration related practice" includes the following actions when taken for retaliatory purposes:

- Requesting more or different documents than are required under federal immigration law, or refusing to honor documents tendered pursuant to federal law that, on their face, reasonably appear to be genuine

- Using the federal E-Verify system to check the employment authorization status of a person at a time or in a manner not required under federal law or not authorized under any memorandum of understanding governing the use of the federal E-Verify system

- Threatening to file or the filing of a false police report

- Threatening to contact or contacting immigration authorities because an employee complained that he/she was paid less than the minimum wage

The definition of an unfair immigration-related practice is expanded to include threatening to file or filing a false report or complaint with any state or federal agency.

In addition, an employer cannot discriminate, retaliate or take adverse action against an employee who updates his/her personal information "based on a lawful change of name, [S]ocial [S]ecurity number, or federal employment authorization document."

Employers who engage in unfair immigration-related practices will face various penalties, including an employee's right to bring a civil action and potential suspension of certain business licenses.

 Workers in California are entitled to the protections of the state Labor Code regardless of whether they are legally authorized to work in the United States. If you hire unauthorized employees, you must pay them and follow the state labor laws.

License Revocation for Threatening to Report Immigration Status

The state may suspend or revoke an employer's business license where that employer reports, or threatens to report, the immigration status of any employee because the employee makes a complaint about employment issues. It also allows for disbarment of attorneys for similar conduct against witnesses or parties in a lawsuit.

This covers reports, or threats to report, employees, former employees, prospective employees or family members, as defined, to immigration authorities. Employers are not subject to the suspension or revocation of a business license for requiring a worker to verify eligibility for employment under the *Form I-9*. For more information on the *Form I-9*, see "Completing the *Form I-9*" in Chapter 2, page 43.

Criminal Extortion for Threatening to Report Immigration Status

A person may be guilty of criminal extortion if the person threatens to report the immigration status or suspected immigration status of an individual, or his/her relative or a member of his/her family.

Language

You can't deny someone an employment opportunity because that person's accent makes him/her unable to communicate well in English, unless you can show that the ability to communicate effectively in English is necessary to the job. If you employ five or more employees, you can't enact an English-only policy unless the language restriction is justified by a business necessity and you notify your employees of the circumstances when the language restriction must be observed.

Lawful, Off-Duty Conduct

If you employ even one person, you can't discriminate against applicants and employees for lawful conduct they engage in during nonworking hours away from the company premises, including:

- Exercising free speech rights

- Engaging in political activity

- Reporting information to the government

- Moonlighting (working a second job for a different employer)

- Engaging in conduct you feel to be morally in conflict with your business

Marital Status

This is an individual's state of marriage, non-marriage, divorce or dissolution, separation, widowhood, annulment or other marital status.

California recognizes same-sex marriages as lawful. In addition, the United States Supreme Court has ruled that it is unlawful to exclude same-sex spouses from the definition of "spouse" under federal law. Employers may not discriminate against an employee in a same-sex marriage.

If you employ even one person, you can't condition benefits or employment decisions on whether the employee is considered a "principal wage earner" or "head of household." You also can't use job responsibilities, such as travel or customer entertainment, as justification for discrimination. You can't impose a "no employment of spouses" rule, but you can establish a policy that outlines how you situate spouses within the company.

Medical Condition

This includes any health impairment related to or associated with a diagnosis of a health impairment such as cancer, or a record or history of any health impairment, as well as an individual's genetic characteristics. See "Genetic Information/Genetic Characteristics" on page 263.

If you employ even one employee, you can't base employment decisions on an employee's or applicant's medical condition or request any sort of medical examination until after you make an offer of employment.

National Origin/Ancestry

The broad definition of national origin/ancestry means the country the applicant or employee, or his/her ancestors, came from. If you employ even one person, you can't base employment decisions on an employee's or applicant's national origin.

California's Vehicle Code and Government Code provide that it is a violation of the FEHA for an employer to discriminate against an individual because he/she holds or presents an AB 60 driver's license. The FEHA specifies that "national origin" discrimination includes discrimination on the basis of possessing a driver's license granted under section 12801.9 of the Vehicle Code.

For more information, see "California Driver's License" in Chapter 2, page 48.

Pregnancy

If you employ even one person, you can't discriminate in any way against an employee due to that employee's pregnancy, perceived pregnancy, or potential to become pregnant.

The federal Pregnancy Discrimination Act requires that you treat a pregnant employee the same as any other employee. When a female employee becomes unable to work due to pregnancy, childbirth or related medical conditions, you must treat her disability the same as any other disability.

California's FEHA prohibits employment discrimination on the basis of pregnancy, childbirth, breastfeeding or related medical condition, and requires employers to grant up to four months of pregnancy leave when an employee is unable to work due to pregnancy disability leave.

 Pregnancy leave does not need to be taken in one continuous period of time. Employees are eligible for up to four months of leave per pregnancy, not per year. For more information, see "Pregnancy Disability Leave" in Chapter 3, page 87.

California law also requires employers with five or more full-time employees to provide Pregnancy Disability Leave (PDL) to a woman who is "disabled by pregnancy." A woman is "disabled by pregnancy" if her health care provider deems that she is unable, because of pregnancy, to perform any one or more of the essential job functions of her job, or to perform any of these functions without undue risk to herself, the successful completion of her pregnancy or to other people.

Race/Color

If you employ even one person, you can't base employment decisions on an employee's or applicant's race.

Religion

California's FEHA protects employees against religious discrimination. The FEHA also sets forth religious accommodation requirements for employers. All aspects of religion, religious belief, observance and practice, including dress and grooming practices, are protected:

- "Religious dress practice" is construed broadly to include the wearing or carrying of religious clothing, head or face coverings, jewelry, artifacts, and any other item that is part of the observance by an individual of his or her religious creed.

- "Religious grooming practice" includes all forms of head, facial and body hair that are part of the observance by an individual of his/her religious creed.

You must also accommodate the known religious creed (such as allowing the person time off for religious observance) of an applicant or employee unless you can demonstrate that such accommodation imposes undue hardship. You can't discriminate against or retaliate against an employee for requesting an accommodation, regardless of whether you provide the accommodation.

Religious corporations and associations are generally exempt from laws governing this protected class. The absence of a religion (atheism and agnosticism) is also a protected class.

Sex

If you employ even one person, you can't base employment decisions on an employee's or applicant's sex or gender. "Sex" also includes pregnancy, childbirth and medical conditions related to pregnancy and childbirth.

The definition of "sex" under the FEHA was changed to specifically include "breastfeeding and medical conditions related to breastfeeding." Employers are clearly prohibited from discriminating against employees or job applicants because of breastfeeding and related medical conditions.

Both state and federal law prohibit discriminatory compensation decisions based on sex. For more information about California law and pay discrimination, see "Wages and Salaries" in Chapter 5, page 164.

Sexual Orientation

Employees in California are protected from employment discrimination based on their actual or perceived sexual orientation. "Sexual orientation" is defined as "heterosexuality, homosexuality and bisexuality."

Employers of four or fewer employees and religious nonprofit organizations are exempt from state sexual orientation anti-discrimination laws.

Federal Title VII bars sex and gender discrimination in employment but does not explicitly prohibit workplace discrimination based on sexual orientation. However, the federal Equal Employment Opportunity Commission (EEOC) has stated its position that discrimination against an individual because of that person's sexual orientation is a violation of Title VII's prohibition of sex discrimination in employment.

Union Membership

Employees enjoy the right to organize and form unions. You must bargain with unions.

Unpaid Interns and Volunteers

California's FEHA prohibits harassment of unpaid interns and volunteers. Protections against discrimination were also extended to unpaid internships or other programs that provide unpaid work experience.

Additionally, religious belief protections and religious accommodation requirements are now extended to anyone in an apprenticeship training program, an unpaid internship or any other program to provide unpaid experience for a person in the workplace or industry.

Veteran Status

You can't base employment decisions on an employee's or applicant's status as a veteran. Military personnel also enjoy limited protection from termination for a period of time after returning to work.

"Military and veteran status" has been added to the list of categories protected from employment discrimination under the Fair Employment and Housing Act. The law provides an exemption for an inquiry by an employer regarding military or veteran status for the purpose of awarding a veteran's preference as permitted by law. Legislation from prior years required veteran preference on civil service employment lists.

Whistleblowers

If you employ even one person, you can't:

- Retaliate against an employee who discloses information to a government or law enforcement agency if your employee has reasonable cause to believe that the information discloses a violation of state or federal statute; or a violation of or noncompliance with a state or federal rule or regulation

- Retaliate against an employee who refuses to participate in an activity that would result in a violation of law

- Retaliate against an employee if the employee's action occurred when he/she worked for a former employer

Whistleblower protections:

- Include reports alleging a violation of a local rule or regulation

- Protect an employee who discloses, or may disclose, information regarding alleged violations internally "to a person with authority over the employee or another employee who has authority to investigate, discover or correct the violation"

- Prohibit retaliation when the employer simply believes that the employee may disclose information even if the employee has not actually done so

These protections also apply to an employee who is a family member of a person who engaged in, or was perceived to engage in, the protected conduct or made a complaint protected by these provisions.

Fines for retaliation are up to $10,000 for each violation. The Attorney General of California maintains a whistleblower hotline to receive calls from individuals with knowledge about possible violations of state or federal statutes.

You must display a posting that details employees' rights and responsibilities under the whistleblower laws and includes the telephone number of the whistleblower hotline. The posting is included on the *2017 California and Federal Labor Law Poster* available from *store.calchamber.com*.

Workers' Compensation Claims

If you employ even one person, you can't discharge, threaten or discriminate in any way against an employee because he/she received an award from, filed or even intends to file a workers' compensation claim.

Disability Discrimination

Disability discrimination laws protect qualified individuals with disabilities from disparate treatment by employers. A qualified individual with a disability is a person who meets legitimate skill, experience, education or other requirements, and can perform the essential functions of the position with or without reasonable accommodation. An individual is not unqualified simply because he or she can't perform marginal or incidental job functions.

"Disabilities" Defined Under Federal and California Laws

The federal Americans with Disabilities Act (ADA) prohibits employers of 15 or more employees from discriminating against qualified individuals with disabilities. The ADA also requires an employer to provide reasonable accommodation for a qualified applicant's or employee's known disability, unless it would impose undue hardship on the employer's business, or unless the applicant or employee would cause a direct safety threat to others.

A person is considered disabled under federal law if he/she:

- Has a physical or mental impairment that substantially limits one or more of the "major life activities," which include:

  – Working, caring for oneself, sleeping, learning, walking, interacting with others, working, and other physical, mental and social activities

- Has a record of such an impairment

- Is regarded as having such an impairment

- Is regarded by the employer as having some condition that has no present disabling effect but may become a physical disability

- Has any health impairment that requires special education or related services

California's FEHA provides greater protection from disability discrimination than the ADA. Under the FEHA, a person is considered disabled if he/she is "limited" in one or more of the major life activities, rather than "substantially limited" in those activities as required under the ADA. The FEHA covers employers of five or more employees and requires employers to reasonably accommodate people with disabilities.

You can't ask questions during a job interview that would be likely to lead to information about a disability unless the questions are job-related and consistent with business necessity. You can't request a medical examination until after you make an offer of employment.

Employers also have an additional duty to comply with FEHA under CFRA to engage in the interactive process and determine whether additional leave is an appropriate reasonable accommodation after CFRA leave is exhausted.

Drug or Alcohol Abuse as a Disability

The federal ADA and California's FEHA do not protect individuals who currently use drugs. You can terminate, discipline or refuse to hire any individual who currently uses controlled substances or who is addicted to them.

There are exceptions. The ADA and FEHA protect people who:

- Formerly abused alcohol or illegal drugs;

- Successfully rehabilitated themselves, either through a supervised rehabilitation program or through their own program; and

- No longer use illegal drugs.

This protection extends to individuals participating in a drug or alcohol rehabilitation program. Although individuals with a record of drug use who successfully completed a rehabilitation program and no longer use illegal drugs may be protected, addiction-related misconduct that violates company policy or performance standards is not protected under the ADA or FEHA.

What Is a Reasonable Accommodation?

A "reasonable accommodation" is any modification or adjustment in a job, an employment practice or the work environment that allows a qualified individual with a disability to enjoy an equal employment opportunity.

Examples of reasonable accommodations include:

- Modifying a work schedule

- Providing an interpreter

- Making facilities accessible

- Acquiring accessibility equipment

- Providing an extended leave of absence

The reasonable accommodation obligation is an ongoing duty, and may arise any time a person's disability or job changes. You must engage in a timely, good faith interactive process to determine and provide effective, reasonable accommodations. You should document this process.

 You can't retaliate against an employee for requesting reasonable accommodation.

What Should I Know About Essential Functions?

Essential functions are fundamental job duties of the position or the reason the job exists. You don't have to alter the essential functions of a job — that's not considered a reasonable accommodation.

You need to establish the essential functions of a job to determine whether an individual with a disability is able to perform the job with or without reasonable accommodation, and as a defense against any subsequent claim of discrimination.

When determining essential functions; document all important job functions, be accurate and realistic, stay current, be flexible and review job descriptions with the employee in that job.

The law doesn't require you to reasonably accommodate a qualified individual with a disability if you can prove that the accommodation would cause undue hardship. The EEOC and the California Department of Fair Employment and Housing (DFEH) determine undue hardship on a case-by-case basis, taking into consideration the size of your business and the availability of tax incentives and assistance from the government.

 The concept of **undue hardship** includes any accommodation that is unduly costly, extensive or substantial, or an accommodation that would fundamentally alter the nature of the operation of your business. This is a difficult standard to meet. Consult legal counsel before making any determination.

You don't need to hire or retain a person who poses a direct threat to the health and safety of co-workers. The risk must be current, not speculative, not remote, not lessened by accommodation and based on reasonable medical judgment or other objective evidence.

Responding to a Discrimination Complaint

Because of the serious nature of discrimination claims, you need to know what to do ahead of time. If an employee files a discrimination complaint, properly handling the complaint could prevent the situation from escalating into a lawsuit.

You should take all discrimination complaints very seriously. When an employee makes a complaint, you must be prepared to conduct an investigation. Follow this basic process:

1. Interview the complainant and document the complaint.

2. Determine if a formal investigation is necessary.

3. Decide on interim actions.

4. Conduct a formal investigation.

5. Take quick corrective action.

For a complete discussion of these steps and conducting a thorough investigation, see "Responding to a Complaint" in Chapter 8, page 292.

Penalties Related to Discrimination

The penalties for engaging in unlawful employment discrimination differ based on the law that was violated and the agency or court that assesses the penalty. All discrimination cases can have a substantial financial impact and lay the groundwork for similar claims by other employees. Under California law, liability for a discrimination claim belongs solely to you, the employer.

Remedies Under California's FEHA

If you are found to have engaged in an employment practice that is unlawful under the FEHA, you can be required to:

- Pay actual damages for injuries or losses that the complainant suffered, including loss of back pay and front pay for lost future wages where reinstatement is inappropriate

- Pay compensatory damages — for pain, suffering, humiliation and embarrassment

- Pay punitive damages

- Pay attorneys' fees

- Pay costs

- Conduct training for all employees, supervisors and management on FEHA and your internal grievance procedures

- Pay expert witness fees to the prevailing party

- Pay fines of up to $25,000 for perpetrators of hate crime violence

The California DFEH may bring a civil action directly to court if the agency determines an employer has failed to eliminate an unlawful employment practice.

Remedies Under Title VII

The federal Civil Rights Act of 1991 expanded the right of plaintiffs to compensatory and punitive damages. It allows those who claim intentional discrimination or harassment based on sex, race, religion, national origin or color under Title VII, or disability under the ADA or Rehabilitation Act, to obtain compensatory and punitive damages.

The compensatory and punitive damages are measured by the size of the employer's workforce, up to a maximum of $300,000:

- 1 - 14 employees: no damages recoverable (employers with fewer than 15 employees are not covered by these federal acts, but are covered by FEHA)

- 15 - 100 employees: $50,000

- 101 - 200 employees: $100,000

- 201 - 500 employees: $200,000

- 500+: $300,000

Front Pay and Title VII

The $300,000 cap on damages awarded under Title VII does not apply to "front pay" (money that an employee would have continued to earn if he/she was not illegally fired). In federal courts hearing employment discrimination lawsuits, employers face the possibility of employees being awarded unlimited amounts of front pay.

Minimum Compliance Elements

1. Hang your *2017 California and Federal Labor Law Poster* (available from *store.calchamber.com*), which includes mandatory postings that all employees and applicants must be able to see, in a prominent place (such as a break room). It includes the Healthy Workplaces, Healthy Families Act of 2014 Paid Sick Leave poster.

   If you have employees working in a city or county with a local minimum wage and/or paid sick leave ordinance, you may also need to post required local ordinances and provide additional notices to employees at the time of hire.

2. Create and follow a written policy forbidding harassment, discrimination and retaliation in your workplace, and enforce it consistently for all employees (see "Establish a Policy" on page 286).

3. Take every discrimination complaint seriously — establish a complaint procedure, tell your employees about it and follow it faithfully if you learn of suspicious behavior (see "Responding to a Discrimination Complaint" on page 275).

4. Hold a mandatory training session so all your employees and managers can learn about discrimination (see "Provide Training" on page 288).

5. Accommodate employees with disabilities so they can work equally with their non-disabled colleagues (see "What Is a Reasonable Accommodation?" on page 273).

Forms and Checklists

The following table describes forms and checklists associated with discrimination and harassment.

TIP You can find these forms in your online formspack, described in detail in "Online Forms" on page 12.

Table 18. Forms And Checklists

Notice Or Form	What Do I Use It For?	When Do I Use It?	Who Fills It Out?	Where Does It Go?
Harassment Complaint Procedure	To explain your company's harassment complaint procedure.	Distribute the procedure along with your non-harassment policy to new employees and perhaps annually to all employees.	N/A	Give a copy to all employees or incorporate in your employee handbook that's distributed to all employees.
Harassment Complaint Procedure - Spanish	To explain your company's harassment complaint procedure.	Distribute the procedure along with your non-harassment policy to new employees and perhaps annually to all employees.	N/A	Give a copy to all employees or incorporate in your employee handbook that's distributed to all employees.
Harassment Discipline Checklist	Not required. This form will help you decide how to discipline a harasser.	Before and after an investigation.	N/A	N/A
Harassment Investigation Credibility Assessment Guidelines	Not required. This form will help you evaluate the people involved in your investigation.	Before and after an investigation interview.	N/A	N/A

Table 18. Forms And Checklists *(continued)*

Notice Or Form	What Do I Use It For?	When Do I Use It?	Who Fills It Out?	Where Does It Go?
Harassment Investigation Interview Guidelines	Not required. This form will help you conduct a legal, useful investigation interview.	When preparing for an investigation interview.	N/A	N/A
Manager's Checklist to Avoid Discrimination	Not required. This form will help your managers and supervisors avoid discriminatory behavior.	In any situation where a discrimination complaint could be filed.	N/A/	Just read it as a guideline and give it to your managers.
Sexual Harassment Investigation Checklist	Not required. This form will help you run your investigation smoothly and legally.	When considering an investigation interview.	N/A	N/A
Sexual Harassment Hurts Everyone pamphlet (available in the **2017 Required Notices Kit**)	Required. This pamphlet describes the problem and the penalties of sexual harassment, and what an employee with a complaint should do.	Whenever you hire a new employee, or engage an independent contractor, etc.	N/A	Give it to your workers and make sure they understand its contents.

Where Do I Go for More Information?

CalChamber and federal and state government agencies offer a variety of resources to help you prevent discrimination and harassment.

Table 19. Additional Resources

For Information On	Check Out These Resources
General	From CalChamber: • The **2017 California Labor Law Digest**, the most comprehensive, California-specific resource to help employers comply with complex federal and state labor laws and regulations • **Sexual Harassment Hurts Everyone** pamphlets, sold separately or as part of CalChamber's **Required Notices Kit** • **store.calchamber.com** • **HRCalifornia.com**
EEOC	• Equal Employment Opportunity Commission 350 The Embarcadero, Suite 500 San Francisco, CA 94105-1260 (415) 625-5600 or (800) 669-4000 • Compliance Manual "Threshold Issues" section at **www.eeoc.gov/policy/docs/threshold.html** • The EEOC's enforcement guidance on employer liability for unlawful harassment by supervisors at **www.eeoc.gov/policy/docs/harassment.html**
DFEH	Department of Fair Employment and Housing 2218 Kausen Drive, Suite 100 Elk Grove, CA 95758 (916) 478-7251 or (800) 884-1684 **www.dfeh.ca.gov**

TIP

CalChamber also provides many ongoing and comprehensive educational opportunities for small business owners, HR beginners and experienced HR professionals alike. These include online sexual harassment prevention training, special HR seminars and webinars. For more information, please visit our website at **store.calchamber.com**.

Chapter 8

Preventing Harassment

Sexual harassment remains a serious area of concern for employers. Sexual harassment lawsuits spur record settlements and damage awards to victims. Employers bear liability for harassing acts that supervisors and employees commit.

Sexual harassment is not the only type of unlawful harassment prohibited in the workplace. It is illegal to harass an employee based on the employee's race, national origin, religion or any other protected characteristic.

You can begin to protect yourself by understanding harassment, taking steps to avoid situations that would inspire lawsuits and by knowing how to handle complaints when they do arise.

In this chapter, you can find answers to questions about:

- The definition of harassment
- Liability
- Effective harassment-prevention policies
- Harassment-prevention training
- Investigations

Harassment Defined

Sexual harassment is the most common type of workplace harassment and gets the most attention, but the law shields all workers in any size company from any type of harassment.

It's your duty as an employer to create a work environment free from harassment for all your workers, whatever their gender, age, race or other protected class status might be.

Types of Harassment

Harassment is a pattern of unwelcome behavior. If an individual indicates that advances, attentions, remarks or visual displays are unwanted and should stop but the behavior continues, that constitutes harassment.

 Though most harassment is a pattern of conduct, a single incident may constitute harassment under California law if the conduct is sufficiently severe.

Harassment can include several behaviors:

- Sexual harassment. Courts and government enforcement agencies define two broad categories of sexual harassment:

  - *Quid pro quo*: this conditions job continuance, benefits, promotions, etc., on receiving sexual favors

  - *Hostile environment*: a pattern of unwelcome sexual comments, touching or visual displays of a supervisor or co-worker creates an offensive working environment that inhibits the employee's ability to work

- Verbal harassment — epithets, continued requests for dates, derogatory comments, slurs, obscenities, sexually explicit or racial jokes, graphic commentary about someone's body, verbal abuse, questions about personal practices, use of patronizing terms or remarks or threats and demands to submit to sexual advances

- Physical harassment — assault, unwanted touching, grabbing, brushing against or interfering with a person's movement

- Visual harassment — offensive cartoons, posters, drawings, gestures or staring

- Retaliation — this can include threats of demotion or termination and is usually directed at a person for reporting or threatening to report harassment

Federal and State Law

Sexual harassment is prohibited under federal and state law. The differences between federal and state law may be important if your business is faced with a lawsuit because there are some important differences in terms of liability.

Sexual harassment can include behaviors such as asking for sexual favors, sexual touching or offensive language. Not all sexual conduct in the workplace rises to the level of unlawful "sexual harassment." Generally, the conduct must be so frequent or severe that it creates a hostile or offensive work environment or results in an adverse employment decision (such as a firing).

The Equal Employment Opportunity Commission (EEOC) enforces federal prohibitions against sexual harassment. The EEOC defines "sexual harassment" as "unwelcome sexual advances, requests for sexual favors and other verbal or physical conduct of a sexual nature.

Conduct may constitute sexual harassment when:

- It's an employment condition (submitting to harassing conduct is made a term of employment).

- It's an employment consequence (submitting to or rejecting harassing conduct is used as the basis for employment decisions).

- It's an offensive job interference (harassing conduct unreasonably interferes with an employee's work performance or creates an intimidating, hostile or offensive work environment).

The Department of Fair Employment and Housing (DFEH) enforces California prohibitions against sexual harassment. In addition to federal law, under California law, the definition of harassment states that sexually harassing conduct does not need to be motivated by sexual desire. Hostility based on someone's gender can amount to unlawful sexual harassment regardless of whether the treatment was motivated by any sexual desire.

California courts use a "reasonable victim" standard as a means to determine if a particular situation constitutes harassment. Though any person of any gender can be subject to unlawful harassment, courts ask whether a reasonable person in the position of the victim would consider the conduct sufficiently severe or pervasive to create a hostile or abusive working environment.

Characteristics/Activities Protected From Harassment

Certain characteristics and activities are protected against harassment, regardless of company size. These characteristics and activities include an employee's:

- Sex

- National origin/ancestry

- Membership in a union

For a complete list of these characteristics, see "Protected Characteristics and Activities" in Chapter 7, page 259.

Liability for Sexual Harassment

In most cases, the employer will be held responsible for harassment that occurs in the workplace or in connection with the employment relationship. The degree to which the employer will be held liable depends, in part, on the source of the unlawful conduct.

An employee who believes he/she is being harassed can file a claim against your company and against any supervisors engaging in harassing behavior. If you fail to take action to stop harassment, you and any supervisors involved may be liable for damages if an employee files a complaint.

Harassment By Supervisors

Under California law, employers are strictly liable for sexual harassment of a subordinate by a supervisor. Strict liability means that the employer has absolute legal responsibility for any harm — the employer does not have to be found careless or negligent.

Because employers can be strictly liable for the harassing acts of their supervisors, the question of who actually is a "supervisor" under federal and state law matters. For harassment lawsuits filed under federal law, a "supervisor" is defined as a person who has the power to hire and fire or to cause another significant change in employment status.

California's FEHA provides a broader definition of who is a "supervisor" under state law:

- "Supervisor" means any individual having the authority, in the interest of the employer, to hire, transfer, suspend, layoff, recall, promote, discharge, assign, reward, or discipline other employees, or the responsibility to direct them, or to adjust their grievances, or effectively to recommend that action, if, in connection with the foregoing, the exercise of that authority is not of a merely routine or clerical nature, but requires the use of independent judgment.

Although the company can be held partially legally responsible for the conduct, in some circumstances the supervisor's personal assets are also at risk.

Harassment By Co-Workers

You are liable for harassment between co-workers only if you knew (or should have known) about the conduct and fail to take immediate and appropriate corrective action.

> **Example:** An employee informed a supervisor about harassing behavior, but the supervisor's response was to tell the employee to "relax and not be so sensitive."

> **Example:** An HR representative's friend told the HR person "off the record" that he felt he was being harassed, but the HR representative did nothing.

If you did not know about the conduct but should have known it was going on, you must show that you took reasonable steps to prevent harassment from occurring. These steps include distributing sexual harassment pamphlets, creating a harassment-prevention policy and providing effective sexual harassment training.

Harassment By Third Parties

You may be responsible for the acts of people who are not your employees who harass employees, applicants or independent contractors in your workplace. You are liable for such conduct if you, your agents or supervisors knew or should have known of the conduct and failed to take immediate and appropriate action.

These third parties could include customers, vendors or employees of service companies called to your workplace.

 Any workplace relationship is subject to a harassment complaint: employee/ independent contractor, vendor/employee, employee/employee or supervisor/ employee, among others.

Harassment-Prevention Policies

It is very important to implement harassment-prevention policies. Employers in California have an obligation to inform employees about their protections against harassment in the workplace. This is part of your duty to ensure a workplace free from harassment.

Harassment-prevention policies can also protect you. In one case, a court found that an employer's stated "zero tolerance" policy requiring investigation and documentation of every report of sexual harassment, posting anti-harassment posters in the workplace, requiring all employees to review training videos and consistent implementation of these requirements was sufficient to avoid liability.

Your policies should also outline the discipline plan, point out that retaliation will not be tolerated and explain that harassers may be held personally liable in a lawsuit.

Establish a Policy

You must maintain written policies that explain your commitment to protecting your employees from harassment. Your employee handbook should include your harassment, discrimination and retaliation prevention policy. Use the appropriate *Harassment, Discrimination and Retaliation Prevention Policy* (described in Table 20 on page 303).

Your policy should:

- Include a list of all protected categories under FEHA.

- State that the law prohibits supervisors, co-workers and third parties from engaging in discriminatory, harassing or retaliatory behavior prohibited by FEHA.

- Clearly describe the types of conduct that constitute harassment under state and federal laws.

- Instruct supervisors to report any and all complaints to a designated company representative so you can attempt to resolve the claim internally.

- Prohibit conduct that is disrespectful or unprofessional.

- Include an enforceable statement that the company's rules prohibit this conduct, regardless of whether the conduct amounts to a legal violation.

- Include a statement about an employee's right to complain about harassment or participate in an investigation without fear of retaliation.

- Explain that the employee does not need to complain to his/her supervisor or directly to the harasser.

- Explain your process for promptly, thoroughly and objectively investigating all complaints — harassment as well as other prohibited conduct.

- Include a statement that, in response to any allegation of misconduct, the company will conduct a fair, timely and thorough investigation that provides all parties with appropriate due process and reaches a reasonable conclusion.

- A statement that you will take appropriate and immediate measures to discipline offenders consistent with your policy.

 FEHA's amended regulations, effective April 1, 2016, specify that the policy may be disseminated to employees in one or more of the following ways:

- Printing and providing a copy of the policy to all employees with a form for the employee to sign and return acknowledging receipt.

- Sending the policy via e-mail with an acknowledgment return form.

- Posting current version of your policy on a company intranet with a tracking system documenting that all employees have read and acknowledged receipt of the policy.

- Discussing policies upon hire and/or during new hire orientation; and/or

- Any other way that ensures employees receive and understand the policy.

Policy Limitations

Simply maintaining an harassment-prevention policy and creating internal complaint procedures does not completely insulate you from liability for sexual harassment. You must consistently follow those policies and procedures to better protect yourself against liability.

If your harassment-prevention policy does not specifically prohibit sexual harassment or if your investigation procedure requires employees to first report an incident to a supervisor (who might actually be the harasser), your policies and procedures are not effective.

Update your policies and procedures as often as needed. For details, see "Responding to a Complaint" on page 292.

Policies In a Multilingual Workforce

The purpose of policies, beyond complying with the law, is to ensure employees have notice of their rights and responsibilities. A multilingual workforce can make it more difficult for an employer to communicate harassment-prevention policies to employees.

An employer with a multilingual workforce should take additional steps to make sure that policies are clearly communicated and effective to employees.

FEHA's amended regulations, effective April 1, 2016, require employers to translate their harassment, discrimination and retaliation prevention policy into any language that is spoken by at least 10 percent of the workforce. It is a good practice to translate all policies and communicate them in the language(s) spoken by your workforce.

If possible, provide a complaint mechanism that identifies an official who speaks the language(s) of your workforce, or explain that an interpreter will be provided, if necessary.

Harassment-Prevention Training

Putting a training program in place can save you time, money and stress. If training can prevent one angry employee from filing a lawsuit, it's worth it.

Provide Training

Training is the best way for you to communicate your expectations to your employees, including those relating to harassment in the workplace. In addition to the supervisor training required by California law, you may want to consider providing harassment training to all your employees.

For harassment training other than the mandatory supervisor training, you can hire a professional trainer or lead the training sessions yourself. You can take advantage of online training, worksheets and many other teaching materials.

 Mandatory supervisor training is different; it must meet specified requirements set by law. For more information, see "Mandatory Supervisor Training" on page 288.

Farm labor contractors must certify to the Labor Commissioner that their employees received required sexual harassment prevention training before they may receive a farm labor contractor's license. This training is separate and apart from the mandatory supervisor training discussed in "Mandatory Supervisor Training" on page 288.

Mandatory Supervisor Training

California employers with 50 or more employees must give supervisors in California two hours of sexual harassment training within six months of hire or promotion, and every two years thereafter.

The minimum employee count of 50 includes temporary employees (including those hired through temporary staffing agencies) and independent contractors.

The employer is covered if there are 50 or more employees or contractors employed each working day in any consecutive weeks in the current or preceding calendar year. Because the law does not specify that the 50 employees must be within the state, it would apply to California employers with 50 total employees, including employees outside the state.

Training must be provided to all employees with "supervisory authority," a broadly defined term in California that generally includes anyone possessing the authority to exercise independent judgment to:

- Hire, transfer, suspend, lay off, recall, promote, discharge, assign, reward or discipline other employees

- Direct the work of other employees or adjust their grievances

- Effectively recommend any of these actions

Employees who make recommendations to managers about such matters must receive training if those recommendations are likely to result in managers taking employment actions. The training must include information and practical guidance regarding federal and state sexual harassment laws, including harassment prevention and correction and remedies available to victims.

The training must be "interactive," meaning that video training is not sufficient without discussion, role-playing, a question-and-answer session or other similar techniques led by a qualified trainer. Web-based training provided by qualified organizations, such as CalChamber, that includes interactive components will meet the law's requirements.

Training on the prevention of "abusive conduct" must now be a part of mandatory sexual harassment prevention training for supervisors and be covered in a meaningful manner. The training should explain the negative effects abusive conduct has on the victim and the workplace, including a reduction in productivity and morale.

Abusive conduct is specifically defined as "conduct of an employer or employee in the workplace, with malice, that a reasonable person would find hostile, offensive and unrelated to an employer's legitimate business interests."

Abusive conduct, as defined, may include:

- Repeated infliction of verbal abuse, such as the use of derogatory remarks, insults and epithets;

- Verbal or physical conduct that a reasonable person would find threatening, intimidating or humiliating; or

- The gratuitous sabotage or undermining of a person's work performance.

A single act does not constitute abusive conduct, unless especially severe and egregious.

An employer with a multi-lingual workforce should take additional steps to make sure that the training is clearly and effectively communicated to employees who speak a language other than English. An employer should make sure to translate policies and communicate them in the language(s) spoken by its workforce.

 FEHA's amended regulations, effective April 1, 2016, require employers to translate their harassment, discrimination and retaliation prevention policy into any language that is spoken by at least 10 percent of the workforce.

Keep in mind that meeting these requirements does not necessarily provide a defense against sexual harassment or a sexual harassment lawsuit, and that failing to meet the requirements does not necessarily establish employer liability for harassing behavior under the FEHA.

Tracking Training

The regulations permit employers to use one or a combination of the following tracking methods to track compliance.

Individual Tracking: An employer may track its training requirement for each supervisory employee on an individual calendaring basis by measuring the "every two years" requirement from the date of completion of the last training of the individual supervisor.

Training Year Tracking: An employer may designate a "training year" in which it trains its supervisory employees. If this method is adopted, employers still must retrain all supervisors every two years by the end of the designated training year, even those newly hired or promoted supervisors that received training in the prior year.

 Employers may use either individual tracking, training year tracking or a combination of both.

Duplicate Training

Employers may not need to re-train new hires if the new hire received the required training from the previous employer. Newly hired supervisors who received harassment-prevention training from their previous employer prior to their new employment may fall under "duplicate training."

The regulations allow employers to accept the employee's previous training as valid and schedule the individual training based on the prior training date. However, the new employer bears the responsibility of proving that the prior training was sufficient and meets the legal requirements of AB 1825.

Additionally, the supervisor must read and acknowledge receiving the new employer's harassment-prevention policy within six months of being hired or promoted.

Documentation and Recordkeeping Requirements

The regulations also state that compliant training completion documentation must include:

- The name of the person trained

- The date of training

- The type of training

- The name of the training provider

- The sign in sheet (new requirement under the amended FEHA regulations, effective April 1, 2016)

- A copy of all certificates of attendance or completion issued (new requirement under the amended FEHA regulations, effective April 1, 2016)

- A copy of all written or recorded materials that comprise the training (new requirement under the amended FEHA regulations, effective April 1, 2016)

Employers must retain these records for a minimum of two years and be able to provide copies upon request.

Types of Training

California law specifically defines the credentials a qualified trainer must possess. Ensure whatever type of training you choose for your employees is provided by a qualified trainer.

Classroom training: Also referred to as "in-person" training, classroom training is instruction featuring content created by a trainer and provided to supervisors by a trainer in a setting removed from the supervisor's daily duties.

E-Learning: Individualized, interactive and computer-based training created by a trainer and an instructional designer. Supervisors must have the opportunity to ask a trainer questions and get a response within two business days after asking the question.

If you use e-learning to comply with the training requirements, the amended FEHA regulations effective April 1, 2016, require the trainer **you use** to maintain all written questions received and all written responses or guidance provided for two years after the date of the responses.

Webinar: An Internet-based seminar with content created and taught by a trainer and transmitted over the Internet or an intranet in real time. Employers using a webinar for training must document that each supervisor not physically present in the same room as the trainer actually attended the training and actively participated in the training's interactive content, discussion questions, hypothetical scenarios, quizzes or tests and activities. Webinars must provide supervisors with the opportunity to ask questions, get answers to those questions or otherwise seek guidance and assistance.

 Amended FEHA regulations effective April 1, 2016, require employers, for two years after the date of the webinar, to maintain a copy of the webinar; all written materials used by the trainer; all written questions submitted during the webinar; and must document all written responses or guidance the trainer provided during the webinar.

Other: The regulations authorize other effective, interactive training including audio, video or other computer technology only in conjunction with classroom, webinar or e-learning training. These tools can supplement the required training — on their own, these tools will not fulfill the training requirements.

Responding to a Complaint

Sexual harassment in the workplace is a serious area of concern. Sexual harassment lawsuits can spur record settlements and damage awards to victims. You must take sexual harassment allegations very seriously, and you must prepare the appropriate staff to correctly respond to these allegations.

When an employee makes a sexual harassment complaint, you must conduct a thorough, impartial investigation. If performed properly, the investigation:

- Reassures employees that complaints will be heard and resolved within the company

- Explains to all parties that company policy prohibits any retaliatory behavior

- Minimizes the chance of disciplining or terminating an employee for something he/she did not do

- Makes it less likely that an outside agency and/or attorney will become involved

You may find that the allegations can be resolved after only an informal investigation, or you may discover that a full, formal investigation is warranted. It's always important to document the process you followed, take corrective action as necessary — such as disciplining employees, rewriting policies or providing additional training — and follow up with the appropriate parties to ensure the issue was adequately resolved.

Time Limits for Filing Sexual Harassment Claims

Employees have a couple of options when it comes to pursuing a sexual harassment lawsuit, but time limits do apply. In general, an employee who wants to file a sexual harassment lawsuit against an employer must file a claim with California's DFEH within one year of the alleged act(s) of harassment or file a claim with the federal Equal Employment Opportunity Commission (EEOC) within 180 days of the alleged violation.

The time limit for filing claims is generally measured from when the harassment occurred. If the harassment occurred over a long period of time, the time limit is generally measured from the last unlawful act.

If an employee first files a charge with the DFEH, the employee can then file a charge with the EEOC within 300 days of the alleged violation or within 30 days of receiving notice that the DFEH terminated its proceedings, whichever is earlier.

 An employee is not required by law to share his/her complaints with a manager or other employer representative first before filing a claim with the DFEH.

Plan Your Investigation

When an employee files a complaint or you become aware that your policies may have been violated, follow this basic process:

1. Interview the complainant and document the complaint (see page 294).

2. Determine if a formal investigation is necessary (see page 295).

3. Decide on interim actions (see page 295).

4. Conduct a formal investigation (see page 296).

5. Take quick corrective action (see page 300).

Interview the Complainant and Document the Complaint

After finding out the general nature of the complaint, make sure the employee feels comfortable that you can objectively address the complaint or that you will identify an investigator who can. Then:

- Arrange for a private, comfortable setting.

- Provide ample time and opportunity to gather the facts. Make sure the employee knows he/she can take as much time as needed, and can come back if he/she recalls other facts later.

- Encourage him/her to speak freely and make all complaints known.

- Re-state your policies against both harassment and retaliation for having filed a complaint, and ask him/her to report any retaliation to you immediately.

- Tell him/her your procedure for resolving complaints.

- Instruct him/her to keep information about the complaint as confidential as possible, given the particular circumstances.

- Tell him/her that you will only disclose information on a need-to-know basis.

- Ask for any suggestions for a resolution to the problem. Stress that you may not be able to follow these suggestions, but you will take them into consideration.

- Ask if he/she would like to recommend anyone else you could speak with to back up the allegations.

- Review the interview notes and prepare a formal statement. Although the complainant is not required to, request that he or she sign the statement.

Taking Notes

When you take notes on the interview(s):

- Document the date, beginning and ending time of the interview.

- Record only the facts and descriptions of what occurred during the interview, not your interpretations of the interview, the employee or the situation.

- Keep these notes in a separate place from notes regarding other business issues, and don't record them in a bound notebook or format that might contain information outside of the particular complaint.

- Keep notes about different employees on separate pieces of paper.

 Accurate, consistent note-taking plays a critical role in your investigation.

Determine If a Formal Investigation Is Necessary

Certain situations automatically trigger your duty to investigate:

- A formal complaint, written or oral

- A subtle verbal or written complaint that a co-worker makes the concerned employee feel uncomfortable

- A charge from the EEOC or DFEH

- A civil lawsuit

- An observation of harassment

- An anonymous note stating that prohibited or questionable behavior is occurring

In other situations, you may need to determine if you need additional information to resolve an employee's concerns. Consider whether:

- The problem has a simple, straightforward solution or if the problem is more complex

- It involves more people than just this complainant

- It stems from a single incident or a pattern of conduct

- You need more facts than the employee can provide

- You need the help of other experts (legal counsel, security personnel or risk management professionals)

If you need more information, conduct a formal investigation.

Decide on Interim Actions

You may need to take action during the investigation to protect the health and safety of employees and the integrity of your company's policies or guidelines.

Leave of Absence

If you suspect an employee of ongoing harmful behavior, you may place the individual on leave pending the completion of an investigation. Give the employee a leave of absence notice that states:

- His/her name
- The estimated time required for the investigation
- Who to contact if he/she has any questions or concerns
- Any expectations of yours, such as:
  - Full cooperation and complete honesty during the investigation
  - All information and documentation relevant to the investigation
  - Confidentiality
  - How the employee's return to work will be handled

Conduct a Formal Investigation

Carefully plan how to conduct the formal investigation. A poorly planned investigation may expose both the company and the investigator to liability.

Select the Investigator

Select someone who employees view as:

- Fair
- Objective
- Reasonable
- Able to make difficult decisions

If the complaint progresses to legal action, the investigator may be called as a witness. If you want your attorney to defend you during litigation, don't use him/her to conduct the investigation. Find a third party instead.

Make sure that the complainant feels comfortable with the investigator. If you choose a third-party investigator, he/she must be a private investigator or attorney licensed to practice in California.

California law prevents outside third parties from performing harassment investigations unless they are licensed attorneys or licensed private investigators. If you intend to hire an outside third party to perform investigations, make sure that person holds the proper license. An HR consultant who is not a licensed attorney or private investigator can't legally perform these investigations. Using an outside HR consultant, as opposed to in-house HR staff, could negatively affect the validity of any investigation results if a lawsuit should occur.

Gather Supporting Documents

Identify all documents relevant to an investigation. They may:

- Provide background information to help verify facts

- Identify people to interview

- Identify which questions to ask

Throughout the investigation, ask repeatedly for any documentation that might be helpful.

Interview Appropriate People

Interview the following people in this order:

1. The complainant — for guidance on conducting this interview, see "Interview the Complainant and Document the Complaint" on page 294.

2. The person who is named by the complainant — keep in mind that everyone is innocent until proven guilty.

 The law requires that you conduct an objective, thorough investigation. If you make assumptions before talking to the person who's being accused of misconduct, you aren't being objective.

- State that you're investigating a complaint of workplace misconduct.

- Review the allegations in their entirety, and give him/her the opportunity to respond generally. This allows you to get his/her emotional response to the allegations.

- Give him/her an opportunity to tell his/her side of the story.

- Ask questions that provide chronological answers. You can use the *Harassment Investigation Interview Guidelines*, described in Table 20 on page 303, to help you form questions.

- Remind him/her of the company policy against retaliation, and make sure he/she understands that this applies to retaliation against him/her as well as retaliation against the complainant.

- Tell him/her that he/she should not do anything to impede or interfere with the investigation.

- Review the interview notes and prepare a formal statement. Although the alleged harasser is not required to, request that he/she sign the statement.

3. Any witnesses — since being interviewed as part of an investigation can be quite stressful for an interviewee, make an effort to put him/her at ease.

- Emphasize that you haven't reached a conclusion.

- Tell him/her that you will only share the information he/she provides with people who have a need to know, and stress to the witness that he/she should not do anything to impede or interfere with the investigation.

- Reiterate the company policy against retaliation against him/her as well as the alleged harasser or the complainant.

- Use the *Harassment Investigation Interview Guidelines*, described in Table 20 on page 303, to structure your interview. Go through events chronologically, and ask for any information he/she has to confirm or refute what you were told.

- Ask if he/she is aware of any other workplace misconduct.

- Ask if he/she knows whether the complainant harbors any bias against the alleged harasser, and vice-versa.

 Divulge only enough information necessary to learn what information this witness has to offer.

Examine Facts and Assess Credibility

You must determine whether the information you gathered is credible before relying on it to reach a conclusion. You need to make credibility assessments while conducting interviews. Ask yourself:

- Did the person raise the complaint in a timely manner? If not, why? Why did he/she raise the complaint now?

- Did similar things happen in the past that did not result in a complaint? If so, why?

- Did any person you interviewed say something that you found later to be untrue?

- Did anyone change his/her story or withdraw an allegation?

- Is the complainant's story consistent and plausible? Does it make sense? Does it correspond with the information learned from other witnesses?

- Does any evidence exist to corroborate the complaint?

- What would motivate the complainant to fabricate facts?

- Did you observe any indications of bias, hostility or self-interest? Part of this involves observing:

  - Body language

  - Tone of voice

  - Eye contact

  - Reactions to questions

  - Word selection (for example, "girl" vs. "woman")

Don't fear making decisions on credibility, but make sure you can back them up with a reasonable explanation. For additional questions to consider, see the *Harassment Investigation Credibility Assessment Guidelines*, described in Table 20 on page 303.

Reach a Conclusion

After analyzing the facts and assessing credibility, you should determine only whether company policy was or was not violated.

 You should not attempt to make a determination as to whether the law was violated. Only legal counsel should make legal conclusions.

Document the Findings and Conclusions

Write an investigation summary that includes:

- The sequence and process followed for the investigation

- The key facts relied on to make the final decision, such as interviews and any relevant support documentation

- The criteria used to assess credibility

- The bottom-line, factual conclusions: for example, "The alleged harasser did touch [name of complainant], and this touch was unwanted and offensive"

- Any complaints that were not resolved in the investigation, and why

Keep this summary and other relevant documentation, interview notes, etc., in a file labeled as "Need-to-Know, Confidential." Limit access to this file to only those with a legitimate business reason to know the information. Even the complainant and the alleged harasser do not need access to this file in the normal course of business.

Communicate Results

1. Notify the complainant of the results. Discuss:

- The conclusion you reached

- How you reached the conclusion

- What actions you will take that affect him/her

- What he/she should do if he/she experiences any retaliation

- That you expect him/her to keep all aspects of the investigation confidential

 Though you shouldn't divulge the nature of the disciplinary action against the person being accused, you may want to indicate that you will take action consistent with your company policy.

2. Notify the alleged harasser of the results. Discuss:

- The complaint(s) raised

- The steps you took to investigate

- How you reached the conclusion

- Any complaints that weren't resolved and why

- The actions you will take as a result of the investigation

- Whom to contact if he/she wants to ask questions or wants information in the future

Take Quick, Corrective Action

You need to move quickly in determining what action to take. Consider the following:

- Do any federal, state or local laws require you to take certain actions?

- What did the company do in the past for similar violations of policy?

- How serious was the policy violation?

- Did the employee violate any other policies in the past?

- How long has the employee been employed with your company? What is his/her performance history?

After weighing these factors, determine the amount of discipline this situation warrants. Some of your options include:

- No action

- Verbal discussion/counseling

- Written warning

- Training

- Transfer

- Suspension

- Termination

You can use the *Harassment Discipline Checklist*, described in Table 20 on page 303, to help make sure you cover all the issues. Terminating a harasser is acceptable when, after an investigation, you have reasonable grounds for believing that the employee engaged in sexual harassment.

 Be careful not to give information about allegations, investigations or resulting discipline to anyone but those with a legitimate business need to know.

Penalties Related to Harassment

The important thing for employers to remember about sexual harassment is that employees or supervisors can be held personally liable for harassing behaviors — in addition to any liability imposed on your company.

The amount of liability you may face varies on the type and severity of the claim, repeat offenses and whether you can provide a relevant defense. The penalties include reinstatement, payment of back wages and payment of damages and attorneys' fees. Damages can total enormous sums of money. Courts have levied damages large enough to destroy small businesses. Typically, courts base fines on a business's assets.

For more information, see "Penalties Related to Discrimination" in Chapter 7, page 275.

Minimum Compliance Elements

1. Hang your *2017 California and Federal Labor Law Poster* (available from *store.calchamber.com*), which includes mandatory postings that all employees and applicants must be able to see, in a prominent place (such as a break room). It includes the Healthy Workplaces, Healthy Families Act of 2014 Paid Sick Leave poster.

   If you have employees working in a city or county with a local minimum wage and/or paid sick leave ordinance, you may also need to post required local ordinances and provide additional notices to employees at the time of hire.

2. Pass out the mandatory *Sexual Harassment* pamphlets (located in the *Required Notices Kit* available from *store.calchamber.com*), forbidding unlawful harassment at your company.

3. Create and follow a written harassment, discrimination and retaliation prevention policy in your workplace, and enforce it consistently for all employees (see "Establish a Policy" on page 286).

4. Take every harassment complaint seriously — establish a complaint procedure, tell your employees about it and follow it faithfully if you learn of suspicious behavior (see "Responding to a Complaint" on page 292).

5. Require all employees to attend harassment-prevention training (see "Provide Training" on page 288).

6. Make sure that supervisors and managers receive harassment-prevention training every two years, as specified by law (see "Mandatory Supervisor Training" on page 288).

Forms and Checklists

The following table describes forms and checklists associated with discrimination and harassment.

 TIP You can find these forms in your online formspack, described in detail in "Online Forms" on page 12.

Table 20. Forms And Checklists

Notice Or Form	What Do I Use It For?	When Do I Use It?	Who Fills It Out?	Where Does It Go?
Harassment Complaint Procedure	To explain your company's harassment complaint procedure.	Distribute the procedure along with your harassment, discrimination and retaliation prevention policy to new employees and perhaps annually to all employees.	N/A	Give a copy to all employees or incorporate in your employee handbook that's distributed to all employees.
Harassment Complaint Procedure - Spanish	To explain your company's harassment complaint procedure.	Distribute the procedure along with your harassment, discrimination and retaliation prevention policy to new employees and perhaps annually to all employees.	N/A	Give a copy to all employees or incorporate in your employee handbook that's distributed to all employees.
Harassment Discipline Checklist	Not required. This form will help you decide how to discipline a harasser.	Before and after an investigation.	N/A	N/A

Table 20. Forms And Checklists *(continued)*

Notice Or Form	What Do I Use It For?	When Do I Use It?	Who Fills It Out?	Where Does It Go?
Harassment Discrimination and Retaliation Prevention Policy - Five or More Employees	To tell your employees that your company prohibits harass-ment, discrimina-tion and retaliation in the workplace.	You must distribute the policy to all employees.	You and the employee.	Give a copy to all employees and incorporate in your employee handbook that's distributed to all employees.
Harassment Discrimination and Retaliation Prevention Policy - Five or More Employees - Instructions	To understand your obligations related to the *Harassment, Discrimination and Retaliation Prevention Policy - Five or More Employees.*	Download and read these instructions prior to using the *Harassment, Discrimination and Retaliation Prevention Policy - Five or More Employees.*	N/A	N/A
Harassment Discrimination and Retaliation Prevention Policy - Less Than Five Employees	To tell your employees that your company prohibits harass-ment, discrimina-tion and retaliation in the workplace.	You must distribute the policy to all employees.	You and the employee.	Give a copy to all employees and incorporate in your employee handbook that's distributed to all employees.
Harassment Discrimination and Retaliation Prevention Policy - Less Than Five Employees - Instructions	To understand your obligations related to the *Harassment, Discrimination and Retaliation Prevention Policy - Less Than Five Employees.*	Download and read these instructions prior to using the *Harassment, Discrimination and Retaliation Prevention Policy - Less Than Five Employees.*	N/A	N/A

Table 20. Forms And Checklists *(continued)*

Notice Or Form	What Do I Use It For?	When Do I Use It?	Who Fills It Out?	Where Does It Go?
Harassment Discrimination and Retaliation Prevention Policy - Spanish - Five or More Employees	To tell your Spanish-speaking employees that your company prohibits harassment, discrimination and retaliation in the workplace.	You must distribute the policy to all employees.	You and the employee.	Give a copy to all employees and incorporate in your employee handbook that's distributed to all employees.
Harassment Discrimination and Retaliation Prevention Policy - Spanish - Less Than Five Employees	To tell your Spanish-speaking employees that your company prohibits harassment, discrimination and retaliation in the workplace.	You must distribute the policy to all employees.	You and the employee.	Give a copy to all employees and incorporate in your employee handbook that's distributed to all employees.
Harassment Investigation Credibility Assessment Guidelines	Not required. This form will help you evaluate the people involved in your investigation.	Before and after an investigation interview.	N/A	N/A
Harassment Investigation Interview Guidelines	Not required. This form will help you conduct a legal, useful investigation interview.	When preparing for an investigation interview.	N/A	N/A
Manager's Checklist to Avoid Discrimination	Not required. This form will help your managers and supervisors avoid discriminatory behavior.	In any situation where a discrimination complaint could be filed.	N/A/	Just read it as a guideline and give it to your managers.

Table 20. Forms And Checklists *(continued)*

Notice Or Form	What Do I Use It For?	When Do I Use It?	Who Fills It Out?	Where Does It Go?
Sexual Harassment Investigation Checklist	Not required. This form will help you run your investigation smoothly and legally.	When considering an investigation interview.	N/A	N/A
Sexual Harassment Hurts Everyone pamphlet (available in the **2017 Required Notices Kit**)	Required. This pamphlet describes the problem and the penalties of sexual harassment, and what an employee with a complaint should do.	Whenever you hire a new employee, or engage an independent contractor, etc.	N/A	Give it to your workers and make sure they understand its contents.

Where Do I Go for More Information?

CalChamber and federal and state government agencies offer a variety of resources to help you prevent discrimination and harassment.

Table 21. Additional Resources

For Information On	Check Out These Resources
General	From CalChamber: • The *2017 California Labor Law Digest*, the most comprehensive, California-specific resource to help employers comply with complex federal and state labor laws and regulations • *Sexual Harassment Hurts Everyone* pamphlets, sold separately or as part of CalChamber's *Required Notices Kit* • *store.calchamber.com* • *HRCalifornia.com*
EEOC	• Equal Employment Opportunity Commission 350 The Embarcadero, Suite 500 San Francisco, CA 94105-1260 (415) 625-5600 or (800) 669-4000 • Compliance Manual "Threshold Issues" section at *www.eeoc.gov/policy/docs/threshold.html* • The EEOC's enforcement guidance on employer liability for unlawful harassment by supervisors at *www.eeoc.gov/policy/docs/harassment.html*
DFEH	Department of Fair Employment and Housing 2218 Kausen Drive, Suite 100 Elk Grove, CA 95758 (916) 478-7251 or (800) 884-1684 *www.dfeh.ca.gov*

TIP CalChamber also provides many ongoing and comprehensive educational opportunities for small business owners, HR beginners and experienced HR professionals alike. These include online sexual harassment prevention training, special HR seminars and webinars. For more information, please visit our website at *store.calchamber.com*.

Chapter 9

Terminating Employment

Ending an employment relationship, often called "termination" or "separation," involves more than just an employee leaving your business. You must:

- Manage the termination process to avoid liability;

- Make sure the relevant paperwork is completed;

- Provide the appropriate forms and notices to the employee; and

- Properly calculate and deliver the employee's final paycheck.

Protect yourself from an overly complicated separation or even lawsuits with good preparation and by using a consistent approach in the separation process.

In this chapter, you can find answers to questions about:

- Types of separation

- Ending the employment relationship

- Calculating a final paycheck

- Wrongful termination

Types of Separation

Several distinct types of separation exist, and different laws and guidelines apply to each. This section provides required processes and best practices to guide you through each of these separation events.

Voluntary Quit

When an employee quits, either with or without notice, the separation is called a "voluntary quit."

You may wish to confirm the voluntary quit by asking for a letter of resignation. Or you may use the *Notice to Employee as to Change in Relationship*, described in Table 22 on page 323, because it contains all the important information.

Be sure to provide the final paycheck:

- Within 72 hours of the employee's final employment date (if you received less than 72 hours' notice)

- On the employee's last day of work (if you received 72 hours' notice or more)

Discharge (Involuntary Termination)

California is an at-will employment state. Employers may discharge employees at any time if the employees are not working under contract and if the discharge isn't based on a discriminatory reason. Follow the parameters of your company policy or union agreement to avoid possible wrongful termination lawsuits.

A termination should never be a surprise to an employee. Document all attempts at addressing workplace performance and other issues. When necessary, consult legal counsel regarding steps to take prior to terminating an employee.

Review the questions in the *Termination Decision Checklist*, described in Table 22 on page 323. You must provide written notice for involuntary termination. Use the *Notice to Employee as to Change in Relationship*, described in Table 22 on page 323.

Layoff

A layoff occurs when available work ends either temporarily or permanently and through no fault of the employee.

Your policy will dictate whether employees who are laid off have preferential return rights or other rights that terminated employees do not have. Part of your layoff procedure should include a discussion with legal counsel as to whether these employees have additional benefits or rights and how this information will be communicated to the employees.

Document the layoff with a *Notice to Employee as to Change in Relationship*, described in Table 22 on page 323. Provide the employee with any information about severance packages that you offer. Follow the basic process described in "Ending the Employment Relationship" on page 312.

Mass Layoff

Under *federal* law, a mass layoff is:

- For a period of 30 days

- Of 50 or more full-time employees (provided it affects at least 33 percent of the workforce)

- If 500 or more employees will be affected, then the 33 percent requirement does not apply

Under *state* law, a mass layoff is:

- For a period of 30 days

- Of 50 or more full- or part-time employees who have been employed by an employer for at least six of the 12 months preceding the date on which the notice is required for lack of funds or lack of work.

  The California law defines "mass layoff" more broadly than the federal law. The California act does not specify "full-time" employees, and its definition of "employee" does not exclude part-time employees. Consequently, a layoff of any 50 or more employees (full-time or part-time) can trigger the state notice requirements.

You must provide advance notice of the layoff. Consult legal counsel before taking any action. If you need to lay off an employee on a certain statutory leave (pregnancy disability leave, family and medical leave, workers' compensation related leave or disability leave), the employee has no greater rights than if he/she had been at work.

You may want to consider alternatives to layoffs, including job sharing. See "Where Do I Go for More Information?" on page 330 for helpful agencies and websites.

 Under the state and federal Worker Adjustment and Retraining Notification acts (WARN), if you employ 75 or more staff and the layoff will affect 50 or more of them, you must provide advance notice of the layoff.

Job Abandonment

"Job abandonment" means that the employee doesn't show up to work. You can set a policy that limits the number of days an employee can fail to show up for work without contacting you before you consider the job abandoned and terminate the employment relationship.

If you maintain an established and objective job-abandonment policy and you deviate from it, you could be challenged in cases where you apply it.

 Specify in your policy that job abandonment amounts to a "voluntary quit" under company policy. This gives you 72 hours to prepare the final paycheck.

Prepare the final paycheck immediately upon determining that the job was abandoned, unless your policy specifies that job abandonment is a voluntary quit (see "Voluntary Quit" on page 309).

Refusal to Accept Available Work

"Refusal to accept available work" means that the employee refused to perform work that's:

- Appropriate to the individual's health, safety, morals and physical condition

- Consistent with the individual's prior experience and earnings

- A reasonable distance from the individual's residence

This type of separation is likely to occur when something about the work changes; for example, your management changes, you reassign an employee to a new work unit or you begin a new project.

When the employee refuses appropriate, available work, you can exercise your option to terminate the employee. You can choose to offer other work or to put the employee on a temporary leave of absence. If you maintain an established and objective policy and you deviate from it, you could be challenged in cases where you apply it.

Ending the Employment Relationship

There are many different ways to end an employee-employer relationship, but all types require you to perform essentially the same group of tasks. This section will provide guidelines to help you make a sound termination decision.

 See "Protecting Against Wrongful Termination Lawsuits" on page 319 for information on how to protect your company against potential lawsuits.

Consider the questions in the *Termination Decision Checklist*, described in Table 22 on page 323. It will alert you to possible negative repercussions that could follow a termination.

Finally, if the former employee makes a unemployment insurance (UI) claim, use the *Unemployment Insurance - Responding to a Claim Checklist*, described in Table 22 on page 323.

Making the Termination Decision

The decision to terminate an employee is one of the most difficult tasks supervisors or managers face.

1. For a list of the important legal issues to consider when terminating an employee, review the *Termination Decision Checklist*, described in Table 22 on page 323.

2. Maintain an established termination procedure and follow it consistently.

3. For a list of the forms you must fill out or provide to the departing employee, review the *Termination Checklist*, described in Table 22 on page 323.

 If you terminate an employee by phone or letter, the final paycheck rules apply. For information, see "Calculating a Final Paycheck" on page 314.

Preparing for the Termination

1. Gather the relevant documentation, including the employee's personnel file, disciplinary notices and forms required at separation.

2. Provide the Employment Development Department's *For Your Benefit, California's Program for the Unemployed* pamphlet, described in Table 22 on page 323 and located in CalChamber's **Required Notices Kit** available from **store.calchamber.com**.

3. If the employee receives health benefits, fill out and provide the appropriate health insurance and COBRA forms, described in Table 22 on page 323. See COBRA and Cal-COBRA in the "Glossary of Terms, Laws and Agencies" on page 331, for more details.

California employers also need to provide information relating to extension of benefits under Cal-COBRA. California employers should use the modified California versions of the federal COBRA notices which contain information about Cal-COBRA for California employees. The federal model versions do **not** contain information specific for California employers.

4. Prepare the employee's final paycheck, including all wages and accrued, unpaid vacation. You can use the *Final Paycheck Worksheet*, described in Table 22 on page 323 to help you prepare the paycheck.

5. Provide the final paycheck to the employee in the appropriate manner within the required time period, based on the type of separation. In most circumstances, you must provide the final paycheck on the employee's last day of work. For more details, see "Calculating a Final Paycheck" on page 314.

6. **Optional:** Ask the employee to sign the *Final Paycheck Acknowledgment*, described in Table 22 on page 323, to document that you met the last paycheck deadline, as required. It also gives you an opportunity to clarify with the employee that proper payment was received.

7. **Optional:** Conduct an exit interview on the employee's final day of employment or allow him/her to take the *Exit Interview* form (described in Table 22 on page 323) home and return it by mail. The exit interview gives you a chance to learn the employee's thoughts about employment with your company, and to document any employee claims.

Calculating a Final Paycheck

When preparing a final paycheck, gather all time cards and documentation regarding the employee's unpaid work period or outstanding advances or expenses. Calculate the paycheck through the final day of work, based on the employee's:

- Regular rate of pay (see Chapter 5, "Paying Employees")

- Hours worked

- Earned bonuses or commissions

- Accrued vacation

If you can't determine commission wages owed at the time of termination, you must pay the commission owed as soon as the amount is determined — follow your policy and the employee's commission agreement regarding the payout of commissions, even after employees leave your employment.

You can use the *Final Paycheck Worksheet*, described in Table 22 on page 323 to help you. After determining the amount due to the employee, make proper calculations for any deductions, following the guidelines in "Deductions From Employee Pay" in Chapter 5, page 197.

 You can't make deductions from an employee's final paycheck if the employee doesn't return property to you. You face fines if you do so.

To document that the last paycheck deadline was met as required, ask the employee to sign an acknowledgment that he/she received the final paycheck. Use this opportunity to verify that the employee received proper payment. You can use the *Final Paycheck Acknowledgment*, described in Table 22 on page 323.

Final Paycheck Time Requirement

Failing to provide a terminating employee with his/her final paycheck in a timely manner can subject you to waiting time penalties.

 If the employee requests to receive his/her final paycheck by mail, consult legal counsel. This is a complicated issue, and a mistake could lead to penalties.

The time requirement to pay the employee depends on a number of factors, such as whether the employee quit without notice, quit with less than 72 hours' notice, quit with 72 hours' notice or more, or was terminated or laid off.

- Termination: the employee must be paid immediately. **You may not** require the employee to wait until the next regular payday. **You may not** withhold a final paycheck.

- Voluntary quit (less than 72 clock hours' notice): the employee must be paid no later than 72 hours after he/she gave notice.

- Voluntary quit (72 clock hours' notice or more): the employee must be paid on his/her last day of work.

- Obtain written authorization from the employee in advance if you wish to use direct deposit for final pay purposes, even if the employee already authorized direct deposit for regular paydays.

Claims for Unemployment Insurance Benefits

The terminated employee may be eligible for UI benefits, but he/she must file a claim to the EDD to seek the benefits:

1. The employee contacts the EDD to apply for benefits.

2. The EDD mails a notice to you, advising you whether the claimant is eligible and whether your account will be charged for benefits paid to the former employee. Respond to correspondence from the EDD promptly. The agency is serious about its deadlines.

3. You can use the *Unemployment Insurance - Responding to a Claim Checklist*, described in Table 22 on page 323, to determine how to respond to the EDD notice that a claim was filed.

4. To appeal a claim, see "Unemployment Insurance" in Chapter 4, page 137.

References and Former Employees

The law makes it clear that you can communicate information on the job performance or qualifications of a current or former employee upon the request of a prospective employer.

A communication indicating if you would rehire a current or former employee is protected under California law. The law specifically provides protection from claims of libel or slander when you respond to an inquiry as to whether you would rehire a current or former employee. In all cases, to avoid liability, make sure to communicate in a non-malicious way and provide only credible information.

Some companies set a policy of not providing references at all. This may not be a wise decision because it could lead to liability if, for example, a former employee was terminated for violence or is known to be violent. If that employee is hired by another company and commits a violent act on the job, your company could be liable for failing to provide information that could have prevented the incident.

Policy Guidelines

Develop a company policy for handling employee references and follow it consistently. Consider these guidelines when developing your policy on reference checks:

- Determine who in your company will respond to reference requests

- Be consistent when providing employee references

- Create a waiver for former employees to sign at the time employment ends if they want you to release information to potential future employers

- Do not provide standardized letters of reference to former employees

- Determine what information will be provided

- Determine if you will allow oral references or if you will require all references to be in writing

- State that references will be provided only to those with a need to know the information

- Provide only truthful job-related information, rather than personal data

- Document each request for a reference

It may be helpful to create a form for terminating employees that shows the type of information commonly requested in reference checks, such as dates of employment, positions held, rates of pay and eligibility for rehire. This will help ensure that the information provided was truthful, relevant and based on proper documentation.

Wrongful Termination

The increase of wrongful termination lawsuits in the past few decades makes the idea of terminating an employee a frightening one. When faced with an unexpected lawsuit, there's not much you can do. If you protect yourself against the possibility of a wrongful termination lawsuit, you'll have much less to worry about.

Common Types of Wrongful Termination Lawsuits

In every employment relationship, an implied covenant of "good faith and fair dealing" exists. If an ex-employee feels he/she received unfair treatment, he/she may file a wrongful termination suit against you.

 Good faith and fair dealing means that you should make decisions on a fair basis, and you should treat similarly situated employees in the same manner.

Ex-employees may file several types of wrongful-termination lawsuits against you.

Discrimination

The employee claims the separation was based on his/her possession of certain characteristics rather than for legitimate reasons. For examples of these characteristics, see "Discrimination" in Chapter 7, page 257.

Wrongful Termination In Violation Of Public Policy

The employee must show that the public policy involved is derived from an administrative regulation or state or federal statute and is fundamental and of benefit to the general public, rather than just to the employee or employer.

You, in turn, must show that you based your decision to terminate the employee on legitimate business reasons. A well-documented separation process can help you defend against this type of lawsuit. See "Protecting Against Wrongful Termination Lawsuits" on page 319.

Retaliation

You can't terminate an employee as a retaliatory action because the employee exercised a right granted by a federal or state law or by federal or state regulations.

Employees may allege that they were wrongfully terminated because they:

- Refused to violate the law on the employer's behalf (for example, by disposing of hazardous waste improperly)

- "Blew the whistle" to a government agency about employer actions that the employees believed violated the law; or their employer believed that they would do so; or one of the employee's family members blew the whistle

- Participated in an investigation against the employer (for example, a sexual harassment investigation or an investigation of wage-and-hour violations)

Breach Of Contract

The employee claims that you did not fulfill an understood employment contract. This includes written, oral and implied contracts. The employee must prove that the contract exists and that he/she was terminated in violation of that contract.

Your best defense against this type of suit is to not create a contract in the first place. Confirmation of employment at will status in an offer letter and an employment at-will statement signed by the employee upon hire can defeat his/her claim that an implied/oral contract existed.

 A clause in a written contract that allows for termination at-will can protect you from breach-of-contract lawsuits.

Constructive Discharge

In this type of suit, the employee claims that you made working conditions so intolerable that a reasonable person would be compelled to resign, effectively terminating him/her and breaching your implied covenant of good faith and fair dealing. This most often happens when the employee claims that he or she was harassed at work, and that you did nothing to stop it.

An "open door policy" may present your best protection against constructive discharge claims. An open door policy encourages employees to bring employment issues to the attention of the employer, rather than going outside the company. Make sure you document and address employee concerns in an appropriate manner.

Protecting Against Wrongful Termination Lawsuits

Avoiding a wrongful termination lawsuit begins long before you actually terminate an employee. An error or miscommunication in any part of the employment process, from job applications to interviews to employee handbooks to performance reviews, can open you up to a wrongful termination lawsuit. You must take early action to protect yourself against legal action.

Document the Disciplinary Process

Nothing creates a stronger defense against an angry ex-employee than a personnel file documenting that you:

- Consistently followed your established disciplinary process
- Gave the employee honest performance evaluations
- Tracked any behavior/work problems
- Attempted to accommodate the employee's needs/complaints
- Precisely followed your termination policy and process

It is a good idea to keep copies of:

- Any documentation showing that employment was "at will"

- A signed *Notice to Employee as to Change in Relationship*, described in Table 22 on page 323

- Job description(s)

- Performance reviews

- Records of pay changes and promotions/demotions

- Records of disciplinary actions/warnings

- Written complaints, both by and about the employee (for example, harassment or discrimination charges) and records of each complaint's investigation and resolution

Establish Company Policies Ahead of Time

An employee handbook sets forth your rules regarding conduct in the workplace, your performance expectations and creates a fair and simple way to resolve disputes. Once you set forth policies, you need to follow those policies until you discontinue or change them.

If you need to discontinue a policy or implement a new or updated policy, make sure you communicate the new information to employees and document the distribution of the updated handbook. Be careful when you write your policies that you don't limit your ability to take disciplinary actions when needed.

> **Example:** You may follow a disciplinary process that allows for a verbal warning, written warning and suspension before terminating an employee. If you terminate an employee without following your own policy, you may face a claim for a breach of contract.

To avoid this situation, you should describe the disciplinary process in your handbook, but reserve the right to follow whatever course of discipline is warranted in a particular situation.

Watch Your Language

In all communication with employees, be careful to avoid language that could limit your right to terminate an individual employee. California is an at-will state, but certain language or conduct may create a written, oral or implied employment contract that may override the legal presumption that employment is at-will. For details, see "Employment Contracts" in Chapter 2, page 58.

Train Supervisors and Managers

No matter how much care you take to avoid a wrongful termination lawsuit, if your managers and supervisors don't follow your guidelines, you will be the one to pay the price.

Ensure that your managers and supervisors know how to:

- Avoid creating oral or implied employment contracts
- Prevent and deal with harassment or discrimination in the workplace
- Handle problem employees
- Implement the company's discipline policy

Be Aware of Public Policies

State and federal laws include many exceptions to the doctrine of at-will employment, primarily to create protections from discrimination against people who belong to protected classes. For more information, see "Discrimination" in Chapter 7, page 257. When faced with the prospect of terminating an employee in a protected class, be sure you gather all the documentation you will need to show that the termination happened for legitimate, non-discriminatory reasons.

Be Aware of Protected Activities

In addition to protecting certain characteristics, state law also protects certain activities. You can't terminate someone for:

- Performing service — including serving jury duty, performing military service or acting as a volunteer firefighter
- Asserting legal rights — including refusing to commit an illegal act, "whistle-blowing" if he/she believes the company is violating the law or exercising a statutory obligation to report apparent victims of abuse or neglect
- Protecting privacy — including keeping private any arrest records that don't lead to convictions, refusing to authorize disclosure of medical information or disclosing or refusing to disclose wages
- Engaging in lawful behavior — including participating in political activity, enrolling in an adult literacy program, taking time off for a child's school or day care activities or refusing to patronize the employer

Follow a Standardized Method of Separation

To make sure that all employees get treated the same way upon separation, create a standard separation process and don't deviate from the established methods in that process. No specific law requires you to terminate an employee in person, so if you terminate someone by phone or letter, create a standard "script" or form letter that the terminating manager can use.

The sample *Termination Decision Checklist*, described in Table 22 on page 323, can help you decide whether to go forward with the termination and how to proceed. The sample *Termination Checklist*, described in Table 22 on page 323, can help you make sure you've done everything you need to during the separation event. For specific guidelines for different types of separation, see "Types of Separation" on page 309.

Minimum Compliance Elements

1. Hang your **2017 California and Federal Labor Law Poster** (available from **store.calchamber.com**), which includes mandatory postings that all employees and applicants must be able to see, in a prominent place (such as a break room). It includes the Healthy Workplaces, Healthy Families Act of 2014 Paid Sick Leave poster.

   If you have employees working in a city or county with a local minimum wage and/or paid sick leave ordinance, you may also need to post required local ordinances and provide additional notices to employees at the time of hire.

2. Use the *Termination Checklist* to make sure you fill out all the required paperwork for every employee who leaves your company (for a description of this form, see Table 22 on page 323).

3. Use the *Termination Decision Checklist* to alert you to possible negative repercussions that could follow a termination decision (for a description of this form, see Table 22 on page 323).

4. Provide the employee's final paycheck in the correct amount and within the required time period (see "Final Paycheck Time Requirement" on page 315).

Forms and Checklists

The following tables describe required and recommended forms and checklists associated with the termination process.

TIP You can find these forms in your online formspack, described in detail in "Online Forms" on page 12

Table 22. Forms And Checklists

Notice Or Form	What Do I Use It For?	When Do I Use It?	Who Fills It Out?	Where Does It Go?
Authorization to Release Personnel Records	To authorize your company to release various information regarding an employee or former employee's employment.	Upon termination.	An employee or former employee should sign this form.	Maintain in employee's personnel file.
Cal-COBRA – Notice to Carrier	Required for **all** types of separation if your insurance plan covers between two and 19 participants.	Within 31 days of the time of the qualifying events of either separation or reduction in hours.	The employer.	Send the original form to your insurance carrier within 31 days of the qualifying event. Keep a copy of the form in your personnel records.

Table 22. Forms And Checklists *(continued)*

Notice Or Form	What Do I Use It For?	When Do I Use It?	Who Fills It Out?	Where Does It Go?
Cal-COBRA – Notice to Employee	Required if you change health plans and Cal-COBRA protects former employees.	At least 30 days before a change in group plans.	The employer.	Send the original form to each individual who chose Cal-COBRA coverage. Also, send information about the new group benefit plan(s), premiums, enrollment forms, instructions and anything else necessary to allow the individuals to continue coverage. Keep a copy of the form in your personnel records.
COBRA Continuation Coverage Election Notice - California Employees	Required for **all** types of separation for employers with 20 or more employees, provide an employee health plan and self-administer COBRA.	Within 44 days of a qualifying event if you administer COBRA.	Employee fills it out.	Send via certified mail to the California employee and the employee's spouse.

Table 22. Forms And Checklists *(continued)*

Notice Or Form	What Do I Use It For?	When Do I Use It?	Who Fills It Out?	Where Does It Go?
COBRA Continuation Coverage Election Notice - Outside California	Required for **all** types of separation for employers with 20 or more employees and some of whom are outside California, provide an employee health plan and self-administer COBRA.	Within 44 days of a qualifying event if you administer COBRA.	Employee fills it out.	Send via certified mail to the employee and the employee's spouse.
COBRA Notice to Plan Administrator	Required for **all** California employers with 20 or more employees and that outsource COBRA administration.	Within 30 days of a qualifying event if you do not administer COBRA.	The employer.	Send to the plan administrator.
COBRA Rights - Acknowledgment of Receipt of Notification	Required for **all** types of separation if your insurance plan covers 20 or more participants.	Within 14 days of the time you receive notification of a qualifying event.	Employee signs the notice.	Send via certified mail to the employee and the employee's spouse.

Table 22. Forms And Checklists *(continued)*

Notice Or Form	What Do I Use It For?	When Do I Use It?	Who Fills It Out?	Where Does It Go?
Deceased Employee Compensation Collection Form	Provide this form to the surviving spouse, registered domestic partner, guardian or a conservator of an estate (affiant) to allow collection of the decedent's salary or other compensation. The maximum amount may not exceed $5,000.00 net.	After the death of an employee.	The surviving spouse, registered domestic partner, guardian or conservator of an estate.	Maintain in deceased employee's personnel file.
Employer Proof of Identity and Disbursement of Final Pay—Deceased Employee	Complete this form upon receipt of the *"Deceased Employee Compensation Collection Form."*	After the death of an employee when their survivor(s) request the employee's final pay.	The employer fills it out; the affiant signs it.	Place a copy of this completed form in the decedent's file and provide a copy to the affiant.
Exit Interview	Recommended for **all** types of separation.	On the final day of the employment, or ask the employee to return a paper form by mail.	Employee fills it out unless the interview is conducted orally; in that case, you may fill in the employee's answers.	Keep the exit interview in your personnel records.
Final Paycheck Acknowledgment	To ask an employee to certify receiving his/her final paycheck.	Upon termination of employment. Recommended for **all** types of separation.	The employer fills it out and the employee signs it.	In the employee's personnel file.

Table 22. Forms And Checklists *(continued)*

Notice Or Form	What Do I Use It For?	When Do I Use It?	Who Fills It Out?	Where Does It Go?
Final Paycheck Acknowledgment - Spanish	To ask an employee to certify receiving his/her final paycheck.	Upon termination of employment. Recommended for **all** types of separation.	The employer fills it out and the employee signs it.	In the employee's personnel file.
Final Paycheck Worksheet	Recommended for ALL types of separation.	When preparing the employee's final paycheck. (For more information about how to calculate an employee's final paycheck, see "Calculating a Final Paycheck" on page 314.)	The employer.	Keep the worksheet in your personnel records.
For Your Benefit, California's Program for the Unemployed pamphlet (available in the **2017 Required Notices Kit**)	Required for **all** types of separation.	Upon termination.	N/A	Give a copy to the employee. Use the *Termination Checklist* to document his/her receipt.
HIPP Notice	Required for **all** types of separation.	Upon termination.	N/A	Give a copy to the employee. Use the *Termination Checklist* to document his/her receipt.

Table 22. Forms And Checklists *(continued)*

Notice Or Form	What Do I Use It For?	When Do I Use It?	Who Fills It Out?	Where Does It Go?
HIPP Notice - Spanish	Required for **all** types of separation.	Upon termination.	N/A	Give a copy to the employee. Use the *Termination Checklist* to document his/her receipt.
Notice to Employee as to Change in Relationship	Required for: • Discharge • Layoff • Leave of absence Recommended for **all** types of separation. Written notice must be provided by: • Letter • Employer's own form • The form in your online formspack	In your preparations to terminate an employee.	The employer. You should request the employee's signature, but the law doesn't require you to do so. The notice must include: • Employer name • Employee name • Employee Social Security number • Indication that the action was a discharge, layoff, leave of absence or a change in status • The date of the action	Give a copy to the employee. Keep a copy in the employee's personnel records.

Table 23. Recommended Forms and Checklists

Notification/ Form	What do I use it for?	When do I use it?	Who fills it out?	Where does it go?
Termination Checklist	Recommended for **all** types of separation.	During the separation.	The employer.	Keep the checklist in your personnel records.
Termination Decision Checklist	Recommended for **all** types of separation.	Before deciding to terminate an employee.	N/A	N/A
Unemployment Insurance - Responding to a Claim Checklist	Recommended for **all** types of separation.	After the separation process.	The employer.	Keep the checklist in your personnel records.
Unemployment Insurance Claim - Appealing to an Administrative Law Judge (ALJ) Checklist	To help you prepare an appeal to an ALJ for a UI claim you want to protest.	During the appeal process.	The employer.	Keep a copy in the employee's personnel file.
Unemployment Insurance Claim - Appealing to the Appeals Board Checklist	To help you present your final case to the UI Appeals Board.	At the final stage of the appeal process, after an ALJ rejected your appeal.	The employer.	Keep a copy in the employee's personnel file.
Unemployment Insurance pamphlet (available in the **2017 Required Notices Kit**)	Provide this pamphlet to any employee being terminated, laid off or given a leave of absence.	You must provide this pamphlet whenever you hire a new employee.	N/A	Give a copy to your workers and make sure they understand its contents.

Where Do I Go for More Information?

CalChamber and federal and state government agencies offer a variety of resources to help prepare you for the separation process.

Table 24. Additional Resources

For Information On	Check Out These Resources
General	From CalChamber: • The **2017 California Labor Law Digest**, the most comprehensive, California-specific resource to help employers comply with complex federal and state labor laws and regulations • **Required Notices Kit**, available at **store.calchamber.com** • **HRCalifornia.com**
State Government	California's Employment Development Department at **www.edd.ca.gov**

CalChamber also provides many ongoing and comprehensive educational opportunities for small business owners, HR beginners and experienced HR professionals alike. These include online sexual harassment prevention training, special HR seminars and webinars. For more information, please visit our website at **store.calchamber.com**.

Glossary of Terms, Laws and Agencies

4/10 Workweek

A weekly schedule that allows the employee to work four 10-hour days each week; for exemption from overtime requirements, the schedule must be under an approved alternative workweek.

9/80 Workweek

A two-week schedule that allows an employee to work nine days and 80 hours — five days in one calendar week and four days the following week; for exemption from overtime requirements, the schedule must be under an approved alternative workweek.

Accrue

To accumulate or have due after a period of time.

ADA

Americans with Disabilities Act of 1990. Prohibits employers of 15 or more employees in the private sector, and state and local governments from discriminating against qualified individuals with disabilities. It requires employers to provide reasonable accommodation for individuals with disabilities, unless the accommodating measures would cause undue hardship. *See also* Reasonable Accommodation.

ADEA

Age Discrimination in Employment Act of 1967. Prohibits employers with 20 or more employees from discriminating against individuals 40 years of age and older.

Adverse Action

An employment decision that has a negative impact on hiring, promotion, termination, benefits or compensation.

Affirmative Action

An active effort to improve the employment or educational opportunities of members of protected classes.

ALJ

Administrative Law Judge. A judge appointed by an administrative agency for the purpose of conducting hearings and rendering decisions under the agency's unique jurisdiction. Typically, an ALJ's decisions are reviewed by the agency and by the courts.

Alternative Workweek

An alternative scheduling method that allows employees to work a standard workweek over less than a five-day period in one week or a 10-day period in two weeks without incurring overtime.

At-Will Employment

A legal concept, mandated by California law, assuring both employer and employee that either party can terminate the relationship at any time and for any reason or no reason.

Back Pay

A type of damages awarded in an employment lawsuit that represents the amount of money the employee would have earned if the employee was not fired or denied a promotion illegally.

Bereavement Leave

Time off for a funeral or for mourning when an employee's family member dies.

BFOQ

Bona fide occupational qualification. Qualifications and characteristics reasonably necessary to perform duties, tasks or processes required to conduct normal business operations.

California Labor Commissioner

Sets and enforces regulations for employee wages, paycheck deductions, breaks, vacation, jury/witness duty, or temporary military leave, the workweek, minors, employee access to personnel files, "lawful conduct" discrimination, exempt status, and independent contractor status. The commissioner also assesses fines and files charges with the District Attorney on behalf of underpaid employees, and investigates, holds hearings, takes action to recover wages, assesses penalties, and makes demands for compensation.

Cal-COBRA

California Continuation of Benefits Replacement Act. Requires insurance carriers and HMOs to provide COBRA-like coverage for employees of smaller employers (2–19 employees) not subject to COBRA.

Cal/OSHA

California Occupational Safety and Health Administration. Enforces California laws and regulations pertaining to workplace safety and health and provides assistance to employers and workers about workplace safety and health issues.

CFRA

California Family Rights Act. Provides employees 12 weeks of leave for bonding with a newborn or adopted child, caring for a family member with a serious health condition, and/or caring for the employee's own serious health condition. This law applies to companies with 50 or more employees.

Civil Rights Act of 1991

Amended Title VII, creating, among other things, the right to jury trials, and allowing those claiming intentional discrimination or harassment based on sex, race, religion, national origin or color under Title VII, or disability under the ADA or Rehabilitation Act, to obtain compensatory and punitive damages measured by the size of the employer's workforce, up to a maximum of $300,000.

Claimant

Individual making a claim for Unemployment Insurance, Workers' Compensation or other benefit.

COBRA

Consolidated Omnibus Budget Reconciliation Act of 1985. Requires employers with 20 or more employees to offer all employees covered by health care the option of continuing to be covered by the company's group health insurance plan at the worker's own expense for a specific period (often 18 months) after employment ends.

Collective Bargaining Agreement

An agreement resulting from "collective bargaining," or the negotiations between representatives of a union and employers. A collective bargaining agreement establishes employees' terms and conditions of employment, such as wages, hours of work, working conditions and grievance procedures.

Commission

Compensation paid to an employee based on a proportional amount of sales of the employer's property or services.

Compensation

Any monetary payment related to work, including wages, commissions and bonuses.

Compensatory Time Off (CTO)

Gives a nonexempt employee time off for extra hours worked instead of paying overtime; commonly referred to as "comp time" and almost always illegal for private sector employers.

Concurrent Leave

Two different types of leave (for example PDL and FMLA) that are used up simultaneously. Table 6 in Chapter 3, page 107 provides an overview of the ways PDL, FMLA/CFRA, Workers' Compensation and disability leaves interact concurrently.

Conflict of Interest

A conflict between the private interests and the official responsibilities of a person in a position of trust.

Constructive Discharge

A wrongful termination claim that the working conditions were so intolerable that a reasonable person would be forced to resign.

CTD

Cumulative trauma disorder. *See also* RMI.

Deduction

An amount of money withheld from an employee's gross earnings for legally required or permitted purposes, such as taxes, garnishments, contributions to retirement plans or health plan premiums.

DFEH

California Department of Fair Employment and Housing. Enforces California's non-discrimination laws. DFEH has jurisdiction over private and public employment, housing, public accommodations, and public services. DFEH receives and investigates discrimination complaints, and provides technical assistance to employers regarding their responsibilities under the law.

DIR

California Department of Industrial Relations. Seeks to improve working conditions for California's wage earners and to advance opportunities for profitable employment in California. DIR has these major areas of responsibility: labor law, workplace safety and health, apprenticeship training, Workers' Compensation, statistics and research, mediation, and conciliation.

Disability

In California, a physical or mental impairment that limits one or more of the major life activities.

Disability Insurance

A voluntary plan, for employers who do not want to participate in SDI, that provides short-term benefits for employees who are disabled by a non-work-related illness or injury.

Disparate (Unequal) Impact

Disparate impact refers to an employment practice that appears neutral but discriminates against a protected class in practice.

Disparate (Unequal) Treatment

Disparate treatment refers to an applicant or employee that belongs to a protected class receiving different treatment because of his or her membership in a protected class.

DLSE

California Division of Labor Standards Enforcement. Investigates wage claims and discrimination complaints and enforces California's labor laws and Wage Orders.

DOL

U.S. Department of Labor. Administers a variety of federal labor laws including those that guarantee workers' rights to safe and healthful working conditions, a minimum hourly wage and overtime pay, freedom from employment discrimination, Unemployment Insurance, and other income support.

DOSH

California Division of Occupational Safety and Health. Enforces the state's occupational and public safety laws and provides information and consultative assistance to employers, workers and the public about workplace and public safety matters.

Double-Time

Two times an employee's regular rate of pay. *See also* **Overtime**.

EAP

Employee assistance program. A workplace program provided by the employer to assist employees in recovering from or dealing with personal issues or problems.

EDD

California Employment Development Department. Helps California employers meet their labor needs, job seekers obtain employment, and the disadvantaged and welfare-to-work recipients to become self-sufficient. It supports state activities and benefit programs by collecting and administering employment-related taxes (UI, SDI, employment training tax and personal income tax).

EEOC

Equal Employment Opportunity Commission. A federal agency that interprets discrimination law, collects employment data and handles employee complaints.

Employee

Any person rendering actual service in any business for an employer.

Employee Benefit Plans

Welfare and pension plans voluntarily established and maintained by an employer, an employee organization, or jointly by one or more such employers and an employee organization. Governed by ERISA.

Employer

Any person engaged in any business or enterprise in California with one or more persons in service. An employer can be an individual, association, organization, partnership, business trust, limited liability corporation or corporation.

Engineered Controls

Protective devices designed to reduce or eliminate the risk of workplace injury. Examples include machine guards, adjustable fixtures and tool redesign.

English-only policy

Prohibits the use of other languages in the workplace. It is illegal in California unless certain conditions are met, including business necessity and employee notice.

Equal Pay Act

Part of the federal Fair Labor Standards Act, which requires "equal pay for equal work." Employers are required to pay employees of the opposite sex in the same establishment equal wages for equal work without regard to an employee's gender.

Ergonomics

The scientific study of the relationship between people and their work environments. The goal of the field is to minimize workplace injuries and illnesses through improved workplace design.

ERISA

Employee Retirement Income Security Act. Regulates employee benefit plans and the numerous persons (for example, employers and unions) involved in establishing and maintaining these plans. ERISA sets uniform minimum standards to assure that employee benefit plans are established and maintained in a fair and financially sound manner. In addition, employers have an obligation to provide promised benefits and satisfy ERISA's requirements for managing and administering private pension and welfare plans.

Essential Functions

Fundamental job requirements of the position, or the reason the job exists.

Exempt

An employee who is not subject to any of the laws pertaining to overtime, meal periods, and rest periods.

Fair Pay Act

The Fair Pay Act prohibits California employers from paying any employees less than employees of the opposite sex for substantially similar work.

Family Leave

Family and medical leave, typically called "family leave," is time off available to employees for specific reasons, as defined in federal and state statutes.

Family leave covers time off for bonding with a newborn or adopted child; caring for a family member with a serious health condition; caring for the employee's own serious health condition; and under federal law, caring for an ill or injured servicemember; and qualifying exigency related to a close family member's military service.

FCRA

Fair Credit Reporting Act. Requires specific disclosures in a specific format, in addition to any waiver that might be on an application, before checking the applicant's credit, and restricts an employer's ability to use credit reports for employment purposes.

FEHA

California's Fair Employment and Housing Act. Prohibits discrimination/ harassment on the basis of race/color, religious creed, national origin/ancestry, physical disability, mental disability, medical condition (including no genetic testing), marital status, sex, age, and sexual orientation. This law provides more protection than the ADA.

Fitness for Duty

A medical practitioner's certification releasing an individual under his/her care to assume or resume full or modified duties before hire or following a leave of absence due to illness or injury.

Flat Rate

Pay based on a job completed, not the number of hours spent completing it.

Flexible Schedule

An eight-hour work schedule where some employees begin the shift early in the day and others begin their work later in the day.

FLSA

The federal Fair Labor Standards Act. Regulates minimum wages, overtime, and working conditions for all employees of businesses that engage in interstate commerce and have an annual gross volume of sales of not less than $500,000, or an individual employee who is involved in interstate commerce, contracts to do work for a firm engaged in interstate commerce, or travels across state lines in the course of employment.

FMLA

Family and Medical Leave Act. Provides up to 12 weeks of job-protected, unpaid leave during a pre-defined 12-month period for employees who work for a public agency, a local education agency, or an employer in the private sector who has 50 or more employees each working day during at least 20 calendar weeks in the current or preceding calendar year.

Front Pay

A type of damages awarded in an employment lawsuit that represents the amount of money the employee would have earned if he or she was reinstated or hired into the higher-paying position from which he or she was illegally rejected.

Full Time

An employee who works the number of hours designated by the employer as "full time."

Garnishments

Money withheld by court order from an employee's check to pay for debt, back taxes or child support.

Good Faith and Fair Dealing

Employment decisions that are made fairly, treating similarly situated employees in the same manner.

Harassment

Behavior toward a person that a reasonable person would find unwelcome or hostile.

HAZCOM

Hazard Communication Program. Requires all employers to communicate workplace hazards to employees, particularly when employees handle or may be exposed to hazardous substances during normal work or foreseeable emergencies.

HIPAA

Health Insurance Portability and Accountability Act. Limits the extent to which a new employer's health plan can establish barriers, such as pre-existing conditions, that will delay or prevent new employees from becoming fully covered under a new plan.

HIPP

Health Insurance Premium Payment program. A California program that requires all employers to provide departing employees with notice of a state program that pays COBRA payments under certain circumstances.

HMO

Health maintenance organization. An organization that provides comprehensive health care to voluntarily enrolled individuals and families in a particular geographic area by member physicians with limited referral to outside specialists, and that is financed by fixed periodic payments determined in advance.

Hostile Work Environment

An unproductive work environment caused by unwelcome sexual comments, touches, or visual displays.

IIPP

Injury and Illness Prevention Program. A company's general plan for keeping its workforce free from work-related injuries and illness, mandated by California law.

Independent Contractor

A person or company that supplies goods or services to an individual or business. The independent contractor should not have any of the characteristics of an employee.

INS

U.S. Immigration and Naturalization Service. The INS has been renamed to the U.S. Citizenship and Immigration Services (USCIS). See USCIS.

Intern

Students who perform work in the course of their studies, as part of the curriculum.

IRCA

Immigration Reform and Control Act. A federal law requiring employers to verify all employees' legal eligibility to live and work in the United States.

IRS

Internal Revenue Service. The nation's tax collection agency, which administers the Internal Revenue Code enacted by Congress.

IWC

Industrial Welfare Commission. A defunct California agency that monitored the hours and conditions of employment; was responsible for the content of the Wage Orders.

Just Cause

A fair and honest cause or reason, acted on in good faith by the employer.

Kin Care

Care of a sick child, spouse, parent, parent-in-law, sibling, registered domestic partner, child of a registered domestic partner, grandparent or grandchild, using up to half of an employee's annual accrual of paid sick leave.

Labor Commissioner

See California Labor Commissioner.

Lay Off

To cease to employ a worker, often temporarily, because of economic reasons.

Living Wage

A wage sufficient to provide the necessities and comforts essential to an acceptable standard of living. Generally mandated by local ordinances.

Log 300

A series of recordkeeping forms for recording workplace injuries and illnesses. Part of a Cal/OSHA record-keeping requirement.

Major Life Activities

Caring for oneself, sleeping, learning, walking, interacting with others, working, and other physical, mental, and social activities. Used to determine whether a worker is disabled.

Makeup Time

Allows nonexempt employees to request time off for a personal obligation and make up the time within the same workweek without receiving overtime pay.

Mass Layoff

The laying off of 50 or more employees, under WARN.

Meal Period

An unpaid, 30-minute block of time for nonexempt employees for every period of work that lasts for more than five hours; must begin no later than four hours and 59 minutes into the employee's work period.

Medical Certification

A statement from an employee's health care provider as to the necessity of time off from work. Usually required by an employer when an employee is off for a reason protected by law.

Minimum Salary

The smallest amount a salaried exempt employee can make, in order to be considered exempt.

Minimum Wage

The smallest hourly wage a nonexempt employee can make. *See also* Regular Rate of Pay.

Minor

Any person under the age of 18 who is required to attend school, or any person under the age of six.

Misdemeanor

A criminal offense that is more serious than an infraction, but less serious than a felony. A misdemeanor is punishable by fine, incarceration in county jail, or a combination of both.

MSD

Musculoskeletal disorder. See RMI.

NLRA

Federal National Labor Relations Act. Prohibits employers from basing any employment action on employee participation in labor organization (union) activities. Such activities include attending union meetings, speaking with union representatives, and discussing union activities with other employees.

Negligence

A lack of prudent care (neglect).

Noncompete Agreements

An agreement between an employer and an employee which says that when an employee leaves the company, the employee will not work for a competitor for a certain amount of time. With few exceptions, noncompete agreements are illegal in California under most circumstances.

Nonexempt

An employee who is subject to the laws pertaining to overtime, minimum wage, meal periods and rest breaks.

Occupational Wage Order

Same as a Wage Order. Contains the instructions for payment of wages to nonexempt employees as well as specific rights and responsibilities of the employee and the employer. *See Wage Orders*.

Open-Door Policy

A policy encouraging employees to bring employment issues to the attention of the employer, rather than going outside the company.

Open Enrollment

A period of time during which employees can sign up for an employer's group health plan or benefit plan, such as a retirement fund.

OSHA

Occupational Safety and Health Administration. The federal agency that ensures safe and healthful workplaces by issuing standards, performing inspections, and levying penalties for violations.

Overtime

Hours worked beyond a "normal" amount of hours for a day or week. For nonexempt employees with a regular workweek, normal is eight hours per day.

For employees with an alternative workweek, normal could be nine or 10 hours. For more information on alternative workweeks, see Chapter 5, "Paying Employees." *See also* Pyramiding of Overtime.

Part Time

An employee who works less than the number of hours that qualify him/her as a full-time employee, according to your policy.

PDA

Pregnancy Discrimination Act of 1978. An amendment to Title VII, requires that employers treat a pregnant employee the same as any other employee, and that when a female employee becomes unable to work due to pregnancy, childbirth, or related medical conditions, the employer treat her disability the same as any other disability.

PDL

Pregnancy Disability Leave. California employers with five or more employees must provide as much as four months of leave for employees disabled by pregnancy and pregnancy-related conditions.

PFL

Paid Family Leave. A wage replacement program funded through employee contributions and administered by the Employment Development Department for employees unable to work when they are needed to care for a family member.

PPE

Personal protective equipment. Items such as gloves, masks, and special clothing used to protect against hazardous, toxic, or infectious material.

PTO

Paid time off. An informal term referring to an employer-defined combination of sick pay, holiday pay, and/or vacation.

Pension Plan

Provides retirement income or defers income until termination of covered employment or beyond. Governed by ERISA.

Personal Days

Time off associated with a particular event, such as an employee's birthday.

Piece Rate

An amount paid for completing a particular task or making a particular piece of goods.

Plant Closing

The shutting down of a facility or laying off 50 or more employees. *See also* WARN, *Mass Layoff.*

Proposition 65

Requires that employers with 10 or more employees warn any person (employees and others who may enter a laboratory) prior to their exposure to a chemical known to the state of California to cause cancer, birth defects, or other reproductive harm.

Proposition 209

Bars California's state and local governments from granting preferential treatment to any individual or group on the basis of race, sex, ethnicity, or national origin in the operation of government hiring contracting, and education. This state measure does not affect the affirmative action programs required by the federal government.

Protected Class

Different classes of individuals who receive specific legal protection against discrimination and harassment based on the individuals belonging to a protected class, including individuals over the age of 40.

Pyramiding of Overtime

Not required by California law, exists when an employee earns overtime on top of overtime already paid.

Qualifying Event

For benefits purposes, one of several defined events that permits a change of benefits enrollment status outside of open enrollment periods or that entitles an eligible beneficiary to COBRA or Cal-COBRA benefits.

Qualified Beneficiary

An employee covered under an employer's group health plan.

Quid Pro Quo

Latin, meaning "this for that." A type of sexual harassment that conditions job continuance, promotions, benefits, etc. in exchange for sexual favors.

Rate of Pay

A fixed amount of payment based on a unit of time or a piece of work performed.

Reasonable Accommodation

Any change in the work environment or in the way a job is performed that enables a person with a disability to enjoy equal employment opportunities. *See also* Disability.

Registered Domestic Partner

Either one of an unmarried heterosexual couple over the age of 62 or a same-sex couple registered with the California Secretary of State.

Regular Rate of Pay

The calculated amount of an employee's actual earnings, which may include an hourly rate, commission, bonuses, piece work, and the value of meals and lodging.

Religious Holidays

A day specified for religious observance. Employers must make reasonable accommodations for employee requests for time off for religious holidays.

Reporting Time Pay

Payment to a nonexempt employee who reports to work at his/her normal time and is not put to work, or is given less than half the hours for which he/she was scheduled.

Rest Period

A 10-minute, paid block of time for nonexempt employees for each four hours worked; should be scheduled near the middle of the work period.

Retaliation

California regards retaliation as any adverse employment action that results because an individual has opposed practices prohibited by the Fair Employment and Housing Act, or has filed a complaint, testified, assisted or participated in any manner in an investigation, proceeding or hearing conducted by the Department of Fair Employment and Housing or its staff.

Retirement Plan

A fund that provides individuals with income after retirement. Employees and employers contribute money to a fund during an employee's term of employment, and employees receive a defined income from the fund upon retirement.

RMI

Repetitive motion injury. A problematic injury that builds over time, caused by overuse or overexertion of some part of the musculoskeletal system. Often referred to as cumulative trauma disorders (CMDs) or musculoskeletal disorders (MSDs).

Safety Data Sheets

An information sheet provided by the manufacturer of a product that describes the product's chemical properties, potential hazards, and instruction in safe handling (formerly called "material safety data sheets").

Salary

A fixed amount of money for each payroll period, whether weekly, bi-weekly, semi-monthly or monthly.

SDI

California State Disability Insurance. Provides temporary disability benefits for employees who are disabled by a non-work-related illness or injury. Benefits are paid by the Employment Development Department from employee contributions in the form of a tax.

Seventh-Day Rule

Nonexempt employees who work on each day of your established seven-day workweek are entitled to overtime at the rate of time and one-half for the first eight hours worked and double time for any hours worked beyond that on that seventh day.

Severance Pay

Money paid to an employee at the time of termination or layoff, to compensate in part for the sudden job loss. Not required by law.

Sexual Harassment

Unwelcome verbal, visual or physical conduct of a sexual nature that is severe or pervasive and affects working conditions or creates a hostile work environment.

SIC

Standard Industry Code. System that classifies businesses by their primary activity. The SIC is used for a variety of statistical purposes.

Split Shift

Any two distinct work periods separated by more than a one-hour meal period.

Standby

Time the employee spends on call that cannot be used for his/her benefit. Depending on the limitations on the employee during this time, the standby time may be paid or unpaid.

Statute

A law enacted by the legislative branch of a government.

Telecommute

To work at home by the use of an electronic linkup with a central office. Employees may use an electronic linkup with a central office or other technology to work from a location away from their office.

TICP

Targeted Inspection and Consultation Program. A Cal/OSHA program that identifies certain high-hazard employers, and requires a fee paid to fund a special inspection unit.

Time-And-One-Half

The regular hourly rate for the job an employee is doing, plus one-half the regular rate of pay. *See also* **Double-Time**, *Overtime*.

Title VII, Civil Rights Act of 1964

Prohibits employers of 15 or more employees from discriminating on the basis of race, color, religion, sex, or national origin.

UI

Unemployment Insurance. An employer-paid tax, which is held in reserve for employees in case they become unemployed.

USCIS

U.S. Citizenship and Immigration Services. The USCIS enforces the laws regulating the admission of foreign-born persons to the United States, and administers various immigration benefits, including work visas and the naturalization of qualified applicants for U.S. citizenship.

USERRA

Uniformed Services Employment and Reemployment Rights Act. This act prohibits discrimination or reprisals against past and present members of the uniformed service. No employer may deny a person initial employment, retention in employment, promotion or any benefit of employment based on a person's membership, application for membership, performance of service, application to perform service or obligation for service in the uniformed services.

VETS

Veterans' Employment and Training Service. Federal agency that enforces the Uniformed Services Employment and Reemployment Rights Act.

Volunteer

A person who intends to give his/her time for public service, religious or humanitarian objectives without wanting pay.

Wage Orders

Contain the instructions for paying nonexempt employees their wages. There are currently 17 Wage Orders, organized according to industry, plus a Minimum Wage Order. The purpose of your business determines which Wage Order applies to you.

Wages

Money received by an employee for labor performed of every description, whether the amount is fixed or determined by the standard of time, task, piece, commission or other methods of calculation.

WARN

Worker Adjustment and Retraining Notification Act. A federal law requiring employers to give employees advance notice of a plant closing or a mass layoff if the action involves a requisite number of employees. California has a similar law that provides more protection than that of federal law, therefore more employees are covered by state law.

Welfare Plan

Provides health benefits, disability benefits, death benefits, prepaid legal services, vacation benefits, day care centers, scholarship funds, apprenticeship and training benefits, or other similar benefits. Governed by ERISA.

Whistleblowing

Any report made by an employee or an employee's family member of suspected illegal activity on the part of an employer.

Workday

Any consecutive 24-hour period starting at the same time each calendar day. If an employer doesn't define the workday, the California Labor Commission will presume a workday of 12:01 a.m. to midnight.

Workweek

Any seven consecutive 24-hour periods, starting on the same calendar day and at the same time each week. If an employer doesn't define the workweek, the California Labor Commissioner will presume a workweek of Sunday through Saturday.

Work Permit

A document establishing the maximum number of days and hours a minor may legally work during the workweek. The permit may also impose other limitations on the scope of the minor's work.

Workers' Compensation

A mandatory "no-fault" insurance program, paid for by employers, to cover medical treatment and wage replacement for an employee who suffers a work-related illness or injury.

Index

model IIPP 236

Department of Labor (DOL) 205
  children of employees, defined 81
  interns 21

DFEH. *See* Department of Fair Employment and Housing (DFEH)

DHS. *See* Department of Homeland Security (DHS)

DIR. *See* Department of Industrial Relations (DIR)

Direct Deposit Authorization 63

Direct deposit of wages 194

Disabilities 261, 272–274
  alcohol abuse as 273
  discrimination 272–274
  drug abuse as 273
  reasonable accommodation 273–274
  subminimum wage 172

Disability Insurance Provisions pamphlet 31, 136

Disability leave 104–106
  Civil Air Patrol leave 122
  reasonable accommodation 104
  termination and 106

Discharge. *See* Termination

Discrimination 257–274
  age 260
  AIDS status 260
  ancestry 267
  claims
    investigating 275
    witnesses 298
  color 268
  compliance 277
  consumer reports 40
  disabilities 261, 272–274
  domestic partner status 261
  employee handbook 286–288
  English-only policies 266
  forms 278–279, 303–306
  gender 23, 261
  genetic characteristics and information 263–264
  height 264
  hiring process 60

HIV status 260
immigration status 264–266
jury/witness duty 116
language 266
lawful conduct 266
liability 275–276
marital status 267
medical conditions 267
national origin 267
penalties 275–276
poster requirements 277, 302
pregnancy 268
protected classes and activities 259–271
race 268
religion 268–269
school activities leave 119
sex 269
sexual orientation 269–270
unequal (disparate) impact 258
unequal (disparate) treatment 258
union membership 270
veteran status 270
wage garnishments 199
wages 164
weight 264
whistleblowers 271
workers' compensation claims 271

Discrimination and Harassment in Employment are Prohibited by Law poster 6

Disparate impact 258

Disparate treatment 258

Disposable earnings 198

Division of Occupational Safety and Health (DOSH) 215, 241
  See also California Occupational Safety and Health Administration (Cal/OSHA)

Doctors. *See* Physicians

Document abuse 47–48

DOL. *See* Department of Labor (DOL)

Domestic employees, paying 191

Domestic partners of employees 145–146
  Cal-COBRA 149
  CFRA 83
  COBRA 148

OSHA. *See* California Occupational Safety and Health Administration (Cal/OSHA)

OSHAB. *See* Occupational Safety and Health Appeals Board (OSHAB)

Overtime 162, 183–189
    calculating pay 185–187
    exempt employees 22
    failure to pay 204
    independent contractors 53
    nonexempt employees 22
    on-call time 181
    paying 190
    reporting time 179
    required 187
    split shifts 179
    standby time 181
    training 182

Overtime Request 213

P

PAGA. *See* Private Attorneys General Act of 2004 (PAGA)

Paid Family Leave (PFL) 132–134
    employers subject to requirements of 3
    Unemployment Insurance 138

Paid Family Leave pamphlet 70, 133
    providing 31

Paid Family Leave tax 198

Paid non-working time 179–182

Paid sick leave 94–102
    accrual methods 95–96
    domestic violence victim leave 115
    notice 195
    wages 98
    See also Healthy Workplaces, Healthy Families Act (2014)

Paid time off (PTO) 102
    crime victims' leave 111
    deductions 203
    disability leave 104, 106
    domestic violence leave 115
    family and medical leaves 81

    jury/witness duty leave 116
    military spouse leave 119
    organ/bone marrow donor leave 109
    Paid Family Leave 134
    Pregnancy Disability Leave 89
    school activities leave 120
    sick leave 101
    State Disability Insurance 136
    workers' compensation 145

Parents of employees 111, 133
    paid sick leave 97

Part-time employees 19

Patient Protection and Affordable Care Act 149–150

Patient Protection and Health Care Worker Back and Musculoskeletal Injury Prevention Plan 236

Pay Day Notice poster 8

Paychecks
    final 314–315
        failure to provide 208, 315
        unused vacation 94
        voluntary quit 310
    form 193
    itemized statement 194
    refused for insufficient funds 207
    See also Wages

Paydays 192–193

PDL. *See* Pregnancy Disability Leave (PDL)

Pension plans 151–152
    See also Retirement plans

Per diem workers. *See* Casual employees

Permissible Exposure Limits standard 235

Permit Required Confined Space Entry standard 235

Permit to Employ and Work - Form B1-4 57, 70

Personal Chiropractor or Acupuncturist Designation Form 156

Personal holidays 94

Personal leave 124

Personal Physician Designation Form 155

Personal protective equipment (PPE) 238–239